FRUIT _TO_ HARVEST

ENDORSEMENTS

This compendium will become a classic reference book for those seriously engaged in work among Muslims.

—**Victor Hashweh**
United Family International
London, United Kingdom

God's Spirit is moving across the Muslim world in unprecedented ways. It is truly astounding. *Fruit to Harvest* is not only encouraging, but it documents best practices of highly effective Christians reaching all corners of the Muslim world. You see the fingerprints of God all over the pages of this book.

—**Dan Hitzhusen**
global church-planting strategist

Fruit to Harvest is an important current resource for anyone working in Muslim ministries or praying for Muslims. Inside you'll find latest trends in Muslim ministry, stories and ideas emanating from the global south and guidance to help identify and reach vast communities still unengaged with the Gospel.

—**Ken**
Nomadic Peoples Network

I found *Fruit to Harvest* to be a collection of captivating stories of mustard seeds of God's kingdom planted in what seemed for generations to be desert places, but now these seeds are becoming large trees before our very eyes. The stories are so significant not only because they are told by the people who have experienced those stories, but also describe how Jesus is building His Church all over the world.

—**Dr. Bekele Shanko**
vice president for Cru & president for GACX

This book is the latest broad update of what God is doing in the Muslim World today. It is based on a large consultation in Chiang May, Thailand, in 2017 with a significant percentage of converts from Islam. Within the turmoil of the news, the church is growing as never before, with implications for nationals and expatriates alike.

—**J. Dudley Woodberry**
dean emeritus and senior professor of Islamic Studies
School of Intercultural Studies, Fuller Theological Seminary

FRUIT TO HARVEST

Witness of God's Great Work Among Muslims

Gene Daniels ▪ Pam Arlund ▪ Jim Haney ▪ EDITORS

WILLIAM CAREY.com PRESS

Fruit to Harvest: Witness of God's Great Work Among Muslims

Published by William Carey Press (an imprint of William Carey Publishing)
10 W. Dry Creek Cir
Littleton, CO 80120 | www.missionbooks.org

William Carey Publishing is a ministry of Frontier Ventures
Pasadena, CA 91104 | www.frontierventures.org

Melissa Hicks, managing editor
Andrew Sloan, copyeditor
Mike Riester, cover and interior design

ISBN's: 978-1-64508-162-3 (paperback),
        978-1-64508-164-7 (mobi),
        978-1-64508-165-4 (epub)

Printed Worldwide

23 22 21 20 19   1 2 3 4 5   IN

Library of Congress Control Number: 2019909603

CONTENTS

133545

ACKNOWLEDGMENTS

We would like to first and foremost recognize the Lord's hand in this project. It would have been impossible to pull together contributors from over twenty-five countries and from more than forty different mission organizations, if the Lord of the harvest had not himself led and guided the team. Anything good that comes from this book is to his glory alone.

However, it is also good and right to acknowledge all those whom the Lord used to bring this book from a raw, unformed idea to the polished page you now hold in your hand. Besides the many authors listed, the following people deserve mention.

The editorial and administrative team: Samuel Answaar (pseudonym), John Becker, Susan Bergman DeVries, Lisa Smart, Catherine Franck, David Greenlee, Luke and Jenny Herin (pseudonyms), K. B. Hauman, Stefan Henger, Mary James (pseudonym), Joshua and Meredith Johnson, Patrick Nabwera, Jeff and Tamara Neely, Jairo de Oliveria, Mandy Reid, Nate and Kimarie Scholz, Keith Swartely, L. D. Waterman (pseudonym), and Ruth Wetsell. And lest we forget, we wish to recognize our "elders" who were present at the Abide, Bear Fruit consultation and whose lives inspire us to fight the good fight and to finish the race marked out for us: Victor and Maha Hashweh, Greg Livingstone, Don McCurry, Safia Miraz, Stuart Robinson, Farida Saidi, David Shenk, and Dudley and Roberta Woodberry.

FOREWORD

This book is a story of God at work in the Muslim world. But it is not the whole story—it is part of a continuum that reaches back in history. In many ways, it was Anglican Henry Martyn, the man who translated the New Testament into Urdu for Muslims in India, who led the way for the many who shared this passion for reaching the Muslim world.

These early Protestant mission stalwarts began to engage Muslims in the 1800s. Carl Pfander went to the Transcaucasus, Turkey, and then to India. The French bishop Thomas Valpy traveled widely, learning Urdu, Punjabi, Persian, Pushto, and Arabic—dying while starting a new work in Muscat, Oman, in 1891. Then, of course, there is Samuel Zwemer, "The Apostle of Islam," whose ministry stretched from Lebanon to the Gulf and then back to Cairo. Besides his personal ministry, his contribution to the Muslim ministry cause was furthered through editing journals, recruiting student missionary volunteers, and widely teaching on reaching Muslims for Christ.

One of Zwemer's most impactful ideas was the historic Muslim ministry conference in Cairo in 1906. The same spirit was alive seventy years later at the North American Lausanne Consultation on Muslim Evangelization, which was held at Glen Eyrie in Colorado Springs, Colorado, in October of 1978.

This meeting was a seminal moment that in many ways prefigured the Abide, Bear Fruit consultation that produced this book. Mission executives, missionaries, overseas nationals, women from various fields, communication experts, Christian cultural anthropologists, theologians, and Christian scholars of Islam gathered at the Glen Eyrie consultation. All of us thought it was a time for new beginnings. Colonialism was over. Talk of contextualization was in the air. Task forces were formed to cooperate in the different areas of expertise represented.

Not only that, but as result of this consultation new missions to Muslims were founded, and some older missions retrained their field workers for Muslim work. The period that followed the Glen Eyrie consultation led to the training of hundreds of mission candidates who then went out to the multicultural world of Islam. It was a period of experimentation.

Many new approaches flowed out of that consultation. Some failed; others proved effective. Always these words of the veteran missionary anthropologist, Paul Hiebert, rang in our ears, and still ring true to this day: "Innovate, then evaluate. Innovate, then evaluate." For those who listened, it led to fruitful practices; and for those who didn't, it led to failure, or even worse—heresy.

Almost thirty years later, it was time to take stock. So in 2007, at Pattaya, Thailand, workers were called together from many parts of the Muslim world. The burning question was "What has proved effective in your experience in terms of evangelism and planting living communities of faith among Muslims?" The data coming in was almost overwhelming. What emerged was a list of sixty-eight fruitful practices that fell into eight different categories. The conference grew out of a multiyear, multiagency effort. Testimonies were from taken from hundreds of missionaries from thirty different agencies working across the Muslim world. Two-thirds of the organizations involved reported at least one living faith community among Muslims. Those who distilled the findings pointed out that these practices were not prescriptive, but descriptive. And all of the practices listed were not universally applicable in every situation. These findings of the Fruitful Practices Task Force have influenced the mission advance in Muslim work ever since.

Sensing the need to follow up on Pattaya 2007, two outstanding leaders blended their teams to call almost one thousand of us together in Chiang Mai, Thailand, from October 12 to 17 in what was the Abide, Bear Fruit Global Consultation on Muslim Ministry. Both of the men in charge have been through many testing fires to leadership.

Allan Matamoros was only eighteen years old when I discovered him in my class on Introduction to Islam and Muslim Evangelism in San Jose, Costa Rica. Later he and others went into the jungles of Costa Rica to live with unreached Indians. Following this, Allan rose to become a key leader in an association of over twenty Costa Rican churches and mission societies dedicated to training missionaries for missions at home and abroad. Eventually he and his wife served with Muslim Peoples International (Pueblos Musulmanes Internacional, or PMI) in Morocco. From there Allan went on to become part of the Vision 5:9 movement, in due time becoming the president. Vision 5:9 refers to Revelation 5:9, the Bible verse that visualizes people from every tribe and language and people and nation gathered around the throne of God at the great ingathering of all believers.

The cochair for the Abide, Bear Fruit consultation was Dick Brogden, who, along with his wife, spent ten years in that boiling cauldron of trouble in Khartoum, Sudan. God molded him through suffering for the next ten years. Then God called him to train young missionaries for his agency, not home in the States, but in the Muslim fields themselves—something they now call "Live Dead": completely alive to the glory of God and dead to self. In preparation, Dick earned his PhD by doing a brilliant study of the way workers in various Muslim countries are applying the teaching of Jesus from John 15:1–17.

The passion of these two servants of the Lord was the driving dynamo behind the gathering in Chiang Mai, Thailand; and the fruit of that gathering is the publication of the book that is now in your hand.

As I was writing this foreword, two images, two metaphors, came to mind. The first of these was the image of the vine, the living vine, which is Jesus—down through the ages feeding his life-blood into the branches, causing them to bear fruit. And the second was that of the bride, the church—preparing its members for the wedding with Christ, who is also called the Lamb of God. For in truth, Jesus paid the blood price for his bride. Until that great day comes, let us learn what it means to abide in him and bear fruit for our heavenly Father's glory in the Muslim world.

Don McCurry
President, Ministries to Muslims, Colorado Springs, Colorado

ABIDING IN JESUS:
An Introduction to Vision 5:9 and Abide, Bear Fruit

The glorious vision of every tribe, tongue, people, and nation worshiping Jesus is only possible through partnership. No solitary mission agency, no isolated church, and no independent missionary is able to fulfill this heavenly task alone. We need each other, and most significantly we need the help of the triune God—Father, Son, and Holy Spirit. As it specifically concerns the Muslim world, Vision 5:9 is at the forefront of making this kind of partnership happen. Our name comes from the multicultural worship of Jesus described in Revelation 5:9:

> You are worthy to take the scroll and to open its seals, because you were slain, and with your blood you purchased for God persons from every tribe and language and people and nation.

Our model is based on the principle of partnership—that is, the body of Christ, united and empowered by his Spirit, focused on making disciples and planting indigenous churches among every Muslim people. Our goal is that resident church-planting teams would be effectively engaging every Muslim people with the gospel by 2025.

To reach this ambitious goal requires a major effort to share resources, something that lies at the heart of Vision 5:9. However, we are not just about talking together; we are about doing together. Our members have the desire and the capacity to take practical steps to reach the unengaged and establish church-planting teams among unreached Muslim people groups. The tangible efforts of this network catalyze many diverse organizations to get church planters on the ground and become fruitful in discipling Muslims.

One tangible expression of our partnering together has been that we have periodically gathered global church planters among Muslims for a consultation. The first such gathering was in 2007 and resulted in the book *From Seed to Fruit*, which articulated fruitful practices in church-planting efforts among Muslims. A second global gathering named Abide, Bear Fruit was held in Chiang Mai, Thailand, in October 2017.

As we prayed and planned for this consultation, John 15:5 became a key thought—without abiding in the presence of Jesus, we can do *nothing*. We agreed that as part of the consultation we would spend extravagant time in the presence of Jesus, both individually and corporately. We wanted to do this to act on our conviction that this is indeed the first priority of the missionary and the base methodology of mission. While we are grateful for the continuing improvement of methodologies and missiology, we recognize that first and always we must be people of the presence of God—intimate with and obedient to the Lord Jesus Christ.

So with that as a backdrop, almost one thousand church planters gathered in Thailand to reflect, pray, and recommit to the vision of every Muslim people group evangelized and represented around the throne. This was a powerfully diverse group: 25 percent of the delegates were Muslim-background believers; 25 percent of the delegates were women; 50 percent of the delegates were from the Global South. Furthermore, this was a group of veterans, with an average experience of twenty years in Muslim ministry. We specifically recruited for this to reflect the diversity of our network.

I (Allan) am a Latin American who speaks English as a second language; and I have found that Vision 5:9, more than any other network I have been a part of, gives a voice to members from the Global South and the rest of the majority world. Without hesitation, Vision 5:9 gives leadership opportunities and appreciation to members from the Middle East, Africa, Asia, and Latin America—respecting our experience and knowledge and embracing our differences.

During our week of meeting together, we intentionally provided time in the morning for personal abiding in Jesus; and just as intentionally we provided times in our plenary sessions to abide in Jesus corporately—waiting for the Father to speak to us through the Holy Spirit. Each morning we heard a message from Scripture related to bearing fruit. As we waited on the Lord in prayer, a group of elders in the faith—each of whom had served in Muslim contexts for forty years or more—helped us discern what God was saying to us.

Several important outcomes emerged from our consultation, including ...

THE BOOK YOU ARE NOW HOLDING!

Our Global Trends and Fruitful Practices task forces teamed to produce this volume as a follow-up to the 2007 consultation book, *From Seed to Fruit*. Throughout this volume you will find first-rate missiological thought from an extremely wide range of contributors, as they give voice to missiological reflection drawn from around the world. We encourage you to use this anthology as a tool to help you strengthen your own ministry and engage in the best practices for planting indigenous churches among Muslims.

A RENEWED FOCUS ON ABIDING IN JESUS

Individually and corporately, the theme of the consultation became more than a slogan—it became a longing and a mandate for the body of Christ going forward. As one MBB testified, "I was stuck and did not know what to do, but now I know—I am to return to my context and abide in Jesus."

Over and over delegates confirmed that God clearly spoke and reordered their lives; their action step going forward is to lavish extravagant time with Jesus, allowing that rich intimacy to season and guide all that they do in church planting. We encourage you to join us in abiding in Jesus.

THE 10/10 PRAYER AND FASTING INITIATIVE

During the week that we met together, the Lord led us to consider adopting a ten-year period of 24/7 prayer and fasting in which we would ask the Lord for at least 10 percent of the Muslim world to be saved (according to Rom 10:9) by 2028. It was agreed that different mission agencies would sign up for several days in the year (as many as they felt led) and mobilize their members to fast and pray on those days for this immense harvest. This initiative was accompanied by repeated warnings from the Holy Spirit that it would be accompanied by cost. Suffering and spiritual attack are sure to follow a movement of prayer and fasting like this. When millions of Muslims begin to respond to the gospel (as we believe will happen), there will also be unprecedented martyrdom and persecution—among both MBBs and missionaries.

We all felt the weight of what we were being led to do, yet we also sensed the leading of the Lord to do it. A simple website, www.1010prayerandfasting. com, has been created for people to sign up to pray and fast. We encourage you to join us in fasting and praying, asking God that in the next ten years at least 10 percent of the Muslim world will be saved.

EXCITEMENT ABOUT NEW PARTNERSHIP OPPORTUNITIES

Time was given during the consultation for conversations about partnerships that are based on regional—or other—configurations. Our world is arranged and aligned by affinities, languages, culture, and geography. National and regional partnerships (for example, the Arabian Peninsula, Central Asia, the Sahel, etc.) are increasingly important to our networking and sharing of tools, information, and resources. We are also in the process of seeing an MBB global partnership form that will advance initiatives that are particularly near and dear to them.

We encourage you to participate in one of these; you will both be blessed and a blessing. For more information you can contact us at info@vision59.com.

CONCLUSION

The time we spent together at Abide, Bear Fruit in Chiang Mai was a beautiful, partial picture of Revelation 5:9. Muslim-background believers, Latinos, Africans, Asians, Europeans, Americans—all sharing in a commitment to our calling: to make disciples among unreached Muslim people, through the global church. At the same time, we are very aware that without Jesus we really can do nothing (John 15:5). Only through abiding in Christ can we accomplish this. However, we know there is no separation between the calling to abide in Christ and his promise to bear much fruit for his kingdom. Indeed, we cannot do one without the other. When Jesus called his very first disciples, he said "Follow me" before he said "I will make you fishers of men" (Matt 4:19 ESV). In God's mind, there is no division; when we abide in him, we will bear much fruit—to the Father's glory.

Together in that hope and joy,

Alan Matamoros, chairman, Vision 5:9
Dick Brogden, consultation chairman, Abide, Bear Fruit

A CALL TO ACTION:
The Abide Commitment

MARTIN HALL

There is a well-known African proverb, "If you want to go fast, go alone; if you want to go far, go together." In keeping with that spirit, eighteen of us gathered in February 2016 from around the world, India, Germany, Jordan, France, America, Sudan, Hungary, Malta, Algeria, and Costa Rica—among others. Some born Christian, some born Muslim. All from different missions and denominations, but united around the cross and Christ's command to take the gospel to every ethnos, every people group. We came together to pray and to plan how every Muslim ethnos/people group could be effectively engaged by church-planting teams by 2025.

Part of our agenda was to decide whether or not to host a global congress. Just over eight years earlier, the Vision 5:9 network had called an assembly of church planters among Muslims, with almost five hundred people from seventy-eight organizations responding. We had also planned for a follow-up in ten years. That date was now very close, and a decision had to be made. Was there really justification for another global meeting? What would and could it achieve? Who would, who could, and who should attend?

We asked what had changed in the Muslim world since 2007. It was clear that the last decade had brought immense changes, particularly the attempts to throw off authoritarian rule in the Arab world and the rise of a barbaric form of Islamic fundamentalism—and the chaos and disillusionment that has followed. Alongside these geographical trends, with their threats and opportunities, we saw that mission to Muslims had also changed. In 2007 the congress had focused on church planting; now we were seeing movements among Muslims right around the globe. Missions and denominations were restructuring to focus on the unreached, least reached, unengaged. There was a need for a new word for a new context; thus another consultation was in order.

So then we asked what we could learn from previous congresses. Together we agreed that the greatest failure in the past was that we did not make an effort to listen to those who knew Isla. So we suggested aiming at 25 percent of the attendees being Muslim-background believers, and at least half of the plenary speakers also being MBBs. At first, we wondered if that was achievable without compromising biblical authority.

> So we suggested aiming at 25 percent of the attendees being Muslim-background believers, and at least half of the plenary speakers also being MBBs.

Once we actually started suggesting names, we soon discovered that the only challenge would be choosing who to invite. There was certainly no shortage of outstanding MBB leaders from every region of the world. Another failure at previous congresses was diversity in age, gender, and global participation, so we set a goal of 50 percent from the Global South, 25 percent women, and 25 percent millennials. By God's grace all these goals were met and surpassed—though not without keeping them in focus and working hard to achieve them.

While the role of the younger needed to be emphasized and empowered, the Africans and Asians on our leadership team reminded us that we also needed to honor the wisdom of the elders in whose paths we have walked. Therefore, we carved out a special place for them in the consultation so that we could honor their experience and sacrifice.

As we planned, the Holy Spirit continued to impress on us the need to *abide*. Then, as we read and meditated on John 15:5, we were drawn to the promise coming out of this passage that out of abiding we would bear much fruit. So our theme became clear. Abide, bear fruit: in preaching the Word, in praying, amid suffering, to abide in Jesus and bear much fruit.

We were also keen that there should be a "call to action" coming out of this waiting on God. But that posed a dilemma. If we were to wait on God and hear from him, what would that "covenant" look like. Could we wait until the congress, listening to God as he speaks through his Word, his Spirit, and his body? Could we really go into such a big meeting without our outcomes defined? In the end, we prepared by only roughing out the main ideas for the covenant and placing a draft in the congress booklet. The details would have to wait until the Holy Spirit moved on his people collectively.

During the mornings, the whole congress—close to one thousand people—met in groups of ten to discuss and pray over the wording of the portion of the covenant tied to that day's message and theme. Then a very diverse committee looked at the feedback each day—from all 110 small groups! In the end, there was a consensus that the word covenant was too strong, so the Abide Covenant became the Abide Commitment.

That small change, from the first day's discussion, was a watershed moment. The assembly saw clear evidence that the committee would truly listen to them. Now the feedback increased as brothers and sisters from across the globe shaped what they collectively wanted to say at this historic moment. Each evening the committee pondered and prayed, discussed and conceded, over the day's group deliberations—all the while believing the Holy Spirit was leading.

This process was at the heart of the Abide congress. A thread running through every aspect: from the personal abiding time to the teaching of the Word in the morning, with its corporate abiding time—listening to God—through the afternoon with the focus on effective engagement—assessing what has been done and what remains—to the evening looking at our mission in our changing context. All was summed up in the Abide Commitment: committing both individually and corporately to abide in Jesus, to be filled with the Spirit, to preach the Word, to intercede, and to die daily.

As the congress closed, we asked those assembled to sign the commitment and come forward for prayer and to be anointed with oil by the elders and leaders. Over eight hundred people came forward, a solemn and joy-filled moment—a moment I will never forget. Praying, with oil running down our arms, for so many as they signed the commitment to abide in Christ, seeking to bear much fruit, working and praying for movements among every Muslim people group—to the glory of God and his Christ.

THE ABIDE, BEAR FRUIT COMMITMENT

For the glory of God and the engagement of every Muslim people group through effective church planting, we make the following commitment by God's grace.

1. ABIDE IN JESUS: John 15:5; Psalm 1:1–3; 1 John 4:16

"He who abides in Me and I in him bears much fruit. For without Me you can do nothing."

We commit to consistently give Jesus extravagant time and to make abiding in him our first priority and foundation of ministry.

2. BE FILLED WITH THE SPIRIT: Ephesians 5:18; Acts 2:4; 4:8, 4:31; Acts 1:8; 1 Corinthians 1:17–23; 2:1–5; John 1:1

"Be ye being filled with the Spirit... . And they were all filled with the Holy Spirit... . Then Peter, filled with the Holy Spirit, ... And they were filled with the Holy Spirit and they spoke the word of God with boldness."

We commit to seek to be continually filled with the Holy Spirit so that we boldly proclaim Christ, the Word of God.

3. _PREACH THE WORD:_ 2 Timothy 4:2; Mark 4:14; Isaiah 40:8; Acts 28:31; 2 Timothy 2:2; Matthew 28:19–20

"Preach the word! Be ready in season and out of season. Convince, rebuke, exhort, with all longsuffering and teaching... . The sower sows the word... . The grass withers, the flower fades, but the word of our God stands forever... . Preach and teach ... faithful men who will in turn teach others."

We commit to faithfully obey, boldly preach, and widely sow the whole Word of God, making disciples among every Muslim people group by lovingly demonstrating biblical truth.

4. _INTERCEDE:_ Ephesians 6:18; Acts 13:3; Daniel 9:3; 1 Thessalonians 5:17

"Praying always with all prayer and supplication in the Spirit, being watchful to this end with all perseverance and supplication for all the saints... . as they ministered to the Lord and fasted ... make request by prayer and supplications, with fasting. (NKJV)

We commit to regularly pray and fast with perseverance, individually and corporately, for church-planting movements among every Muslim people group.

5. _DIE DAILY:_ Galatians 2:20; John 12:24; Luke 9:23; 1 Corinthians 15:31

"I have been crucified with Christ; it is no longer I who live, but Christ lives in me... . Unless a grain of wheat falls to the ground and dies it remains alone, but if it dies, it produces much fruit... . If anyone desires to come after Me, let him deny himself, and take up his cross daily, and follow Me... . I die daily." (1 Cor 15:31 NKJV)

We commit to follow Jesus, taking up our cross daily for the effective engagement of every Muslim people group.

CONCLUSION

"In the love of God, by his grace, and for his glory, we commit to God and each other to abide in Jesus, be filled with the Spirit, preach the Word, intercede, and die daily, believing that every Muslim people group will experience a church-planting movement."

Signed_____ October 17, 2017, so help us God.

INTRODUCTION

*I tell you, open your eyes and look at the fields! They are ripe for harvest.
Even now the one who reaps draws a wage and harvests a crop for eternal life,
so that the sower and the reaper may be glad together. —John 4:35-36*

We live in a great hour of harvest in the Muslim world. The fruit of eternal life is being reaped from all corners of what has long been deemed to be a spiritual desert. Past generations of missionaries often spent years sowing seed, yet ended with little to show for it except faithfulness to their call. But today those who sow and those who reap are rejoicing together in many of the same places and peoples who were considered spiritual wasteland only a few decades ago.

At the same time that the harvest has greatly increased, those who share in its labors have radically changed. Today those reaping the harvest of the Muslim world are a diverse group from many different countries. Perhaps most significantly, many of the harvest workers are former Muslims themselves. The faithful sowing of God's Word is producing not only a harvest but new laborers to share in it.

And as new laborers enter the fields, they are bringing with them new ideas and creating new pathways for others to follow. In the chapters collected here, we have endeavored to capture some of these new ideas, new ways of abiding, and new ways of being fruitful. This meant gathering thoughts, ideas, and stories from diverse backgrounds in diverse places around the globe. As a result, the team who produced this book was made up of more than fifty people from many different nationalities and twenty home countries. These authors, editors, and administrators worked for over a year to capture some of the most important aspects of what God is doing among Muslim peoples in our day.

Hopefully this book will enable you to travel the world and to meet brothers and sisters you might not otherwise get a chance to meet this side of heaven (as we will all surely meet there someday). These stories, disciple-making movements, and acts of God are all a part of God's beautiful tapestry as he makes his own name great among the peoples of the earth. Although it is true that there are many obstacles to Muslims coming to Jesus, it is also true that

Jesus has overcome. And there is much good news in the Muslim world that is rarely heard, shared, or even accessible. This volume seeks to bring together the greater body of Christ to rejoice in what he is doing.

As we acknowledge his work through us in the Muslim world, we recognize that none of this happens apart from the work of God himself. The fruit is his, and the harvest is his. Jesus told us:

> Abide in me, and I in you. As the branch cannot bear fruit by itself, unless it abides in the vine, neither can you, unless you abide in me. I am the vine; you are the branches. Whoever abides in me and I in him, he it is that bears much fruit, for apart from me you can do nothing. —John 15:4–5 (ESV)

SERMONS: VOICES FROM ABIDE, BEAR FRUIT

A significant part of what God did at the consultation in Thailand came about through the preaching of his Word in some of the plenary sessions. Not only were individuals changed, but as we collectively listened and responded, these messages became part of the DNA of the Vision 5:9 network. Space prevents us from including in this book all of the plenary sermons in their entirety, but what follows is a selection from those messages. There are five sermons, each preceeding one of the sections.

–The editors

SERMON №·1

DICK BROGDEN

Scripture Reading: John 15:1-8

Abiding in Jesus must be the priority of the missionary and the base methodology of his mission. If he abides in Jesus, he will bear fruit. If not, he can do nothing. The truth is, abiding in Jesus leads to fruitfulness, while non-abiding in Jesus leads to fruitlessness. Thus, we must be certain on what abiding means and that we are abiding.

The Definition of Abiding

When writing down in Greek the Aramaic words of Jesus, John chose the word *meno* to communicate the concept of "abiding." The Latin word for *meno* is *mansio*, which is the root of the English word *mansion*, or *house*. So *meno* literally means "a place where you spend time." Therefore, the definition of *abiding* is precious and delightful extravagant time lavished on Jesus, which involves quantity and quality time.

Another essential word in this biblical passage is *ballo*, found in verse 6, and it means to "release," like when you are dropping a paper out of your hand. Therefore, Jesus is warning us that if we don't spend time with him, we can't do anything—much less make disciples.

Examples of Abiding in Jesus

My parents: They were missionaries and just retired from forty-seven years of ministry. For as long as I can remember, they have based all their years of ministry on abiding in Jesus. Every morning, from eight to ten, they would take their Bibles and sit out in the equatorial garden of western Kenya and lavish time, attention, and worship on Jesus. They planted churches, taught in Bible schools, discipled new believers, and were leaders and administrators. They were incredibly fruitful because they knew how to tithe their time.

Hudson Taylor: Taylor was a great missionary to China. What many people do not know is that Taylor did not know how to abide in Jesus when he first went to the field. After six years he was so burned out that he was ill and had to go home for five years. It was during this time that he learned to abide. When he returned to China he walked with Jesus, and it made all the difference in his life and ministry.

Helen Ewan: She was a simple British girl, born in 1910, who died at twenty-two years of age. Throughout her life, she would rise at 5:00 a.m. to abide with Jesus. During the winter, she would not turn on the heat in her little room, feeling she could be more alert in the cold. She prayed daily for the lost by name until they were saved. At university prayer meetings, people could always tell if Helen was present. They could tell when she entered the room without seeing or hearing her. They sensed the presence of God in their midst.

Temple Gairdner: He was an Anglican who worked in Egypt one hundred years ago. Gairdner was a man full of the Spirit of God. He was radically converted and deeply in love with Jesus. Gairdner's passionate intimacy was to mark him all of his life, as his strength was the practice of the presence of Christ. From that abiding, flowed a full and even tide subconscious, unceasing, holy compelling influence. Without Jesus, Gairdner could do nothing. With Jesus, Gairdner changed both Muslims and ministers.

My own story: My first assignment among Muslims started in 1992 in Mauritania. The team I was a part of had a rule that new missionaries should spend the first two weeks immersed in the new culture without much contact with the team. I knew no one, could not speak the language, and was surrounded by the heaviness of Islam. Even when the first two weeks were over and I joined the team, I was still not able to do anything significant. So I spent the time abiding in Jesus. I would wake up at 5:00 A.M. and spend two hours reading my Bible. I would pray as the sun went down, walking for two hours in the evening in the rubbish fields outside the city—singing, praying, crying, listening to Jesus, abiding in him.

We want so much to see God glorified among our Muslim friends. We are longing, groaning, to see them saved from the wrath to come graced with eternal life. We are overwhelmed by the needs without and the limitations within. We acknowledge that without Jesus we can do nothing; and we believe that if we abide in Jesus and Jesus in us, we will bear fruit, and our fruit will remain.

SECTION 1: Harvest Trends

Stefan Henger, section editor

T here is significant change in the spiritual response of Muslims to the gospel in the world today! For centuries, workers in the Muslim world have seen little fruit. This is still true in some places, but increasingly in peoples and places once cut off from the gospel there is considerable harvest. Evangelism, discipleship, church planting, leadership development, and passing the baton to new local teams continues to be a challenge, but it is happening. Still, much work remains.

Muslims and Christians alike find that the world today brings new situations and challenges that affect relations between us, challenges to living together, and opportunities. Our deepest desire for Muslims is that harvest trends bring them all new opportunities for finding new life in Christ. This section shares how this is happening—the seed of the gospel not only has borne fruit, but the fruit has been scattered and carried to new peoples and places. God is bringing forth a vast orchard, growing from the imperishable seed of the gospel and drawing from the living water.

This section provides insights into historic signposts in Muslim evangelism, as well as current trends with their opportunities and threats. The authors are from diverse backgrounds and share their experiences, wisdom, and insights to make the ministry of you and your team more effective among Muslims. As you and your team share Christ boldly, in fervent prayer and with loving relationships, these chapters will challenge your approaches and outlook. In fact, you will be challenged to the point that you will find the need for new structures and methods so that Muslims will come to know Christ. Most of all, we hope that you will find cause for celebration that leads to focused and fervent prayer, deeper love, and hope for Muslims.

—Stefan Henger, section editor

Stefan Henger, section editor, loves people and wants to give them the opportunity to hear the message of love and peace through Jesus Christ in a meaningful way. He also encourages those who want to share where Christ is not yet known. He has served through SIM and some networks by providing training, developing resources, and encouraging national leadership in different contexts.

EXTRAORDINARY BOLDNESS TO MUSLIM PEOPLES

Global Trends Task Force Plenary Presentations, Abide and Bear

Abide, Bear Fruit Global Consultation*

Jim Haney served as Director of Global Research for the International Mission Board, Richmond, Virginia, and coordinator for Vision 5:9's Global Trends Task Force from 2005 to 2018. Before that, Jim planted churches among Muslims peoples in West Africa for eighteen years. Jim has written and spoken widely on missions and missiology.

MAIN POINTS NOT TO MISS:

- Today's teams can learn from the hopes and disappointments of those who came before them.

- Today's teams must engage the Muslim world with new, sacrificial, and extraordinary boldness to give Muslims an opportunity to hear the gospel. If not, millions of Muslims will perish without a single opportunity to find hope in Christ.

* Jenn Brown, Jeff Liverman, Jeff Neely, and Jim Haney led "Global Trends" plenary sessions at Abide, Bear Fruit, Chiang Mai, Thailand, 2007

I would like to invite you to a conversation in this chapter.

I've brought a few guests with me today, from the past and present, and I've told them that God is sending you to proclaim the gospel of Jesus Christ to Muslims. They have agreed to meet with you in this chapter. So sit with us and have some tea.

The reason my guests want to speak with you is simple—they want to encourage your faithfulness to the calling God has placed on you. While countless teams have gone to Muslim peoples in the past, many teams have experienced great challenges and Satan has frustrated them. In fact, "Throughout history, Christianity has found Islam to be its most persistent, and often most successful, rival."[1]

You, the reader, are the focal point for this conversation because you live in this generation. Take counsel from the words of history because there remains a huge gap between the reality Muslims face each day and the plan God has for them through Jesus Christ. We need you and your team to be faithful to the calling God has placed on you. Ready to hear?

MUAWIA AND YEZID

My name is Muawia, and this is my son Yezid. My son and I lived many years ago. We knew the Prophet Muhammed—we saw him with our eyes. We speak to you today from words that were written about us at the time of our death. We are condemned because in our lifetime we did not believe in the name of Isa al Masih. We did not follow his way.

In our time, we knew Allah to be unique, with no relations or affection for any creature. We knew Allah as absolute sovereign and his omnipotence as impersonal.[2] There were stories of a man who came to Arabia who had the truth, but we heard that he returned to Damascus.[3] We do not know where he went. We did not hear his message. After this, but before the Prophet, some Arabs in Hirah and Kufa[4] heard a message of Isa al Masih and followed in the way. They were serious followers, and one of them named Noman abu Kamus proved the sincerity of his faith by melting down a golden statue of the Arabian Venus, worshiped by his tribe, and then he distributed the proceeds among the poor. Many of the tribe followed his example and were baptized.[5]

But even though some Arabs had become Christians by the time of the

---

1 Philip Jenkins, *The Lost History of Christianity: The Thousand-Year Golden Age of the Church in the Middle East, Africa, and Asia—and How It Died* (New York: HarperOne, 2009), 214.
2 Samuel Marinus Zwemer, *Arabia: the cradle of Islam* (New York: Fleming H. Revell Company, 1900), 171–72.
3 Galatians 1:15-18.
4 Al-Hirah, south of Kufa in modern Iraq, was a significant city in pre-Islamic Arab history.
5 Zwemer, *Arabia*, 301–5.

Prophet, Arabia became 'the mother of heresies.' Christians were to bring the gospel to us, but they were consumed with bitter quarrels. Instead, there were bishops, pastors, and missionaries who brought immorality, hypocrisies, and heresies.[6]

Then came the Prophet. We followed him, looking for power, meaning, and truth. The Prophet taught us that we were superior to immoral people like Christians through the mercy of Allah, but our lives were full of uncertainty under the absolute sovereignty of Allah. In fact, we were destitute, lost, and without hope. None of us knew the God who has called you; none of us knew the good news.

One by one we passed from the earth. As we passed, I told my son Yezid, 'When I die, take some of the hair and nails of the Prophet and place them upon my eyes and in my mouth and throat; then spread the Prophet's shirt along the coffin; if anything could bring a blessing this would.'

At my funeral, my son Yezid said, "If the Almighty forgive him, it will be because of his mercy; if he take vengeance upon him, it will be for his transgressions."[7]

Many others who followed the Prophet were lost, just as we were lost. To be Muslim is to be uncertain and hopeless.

So what does an old Muslim and his son who have since passed many years have to say to you, a new missionary of Isa al Masih? We do not know who you are. We don't care who you are. But if you have the cure for sin, don't turn away from us or spend your time in meetings. Instead, come. Stay with us; speak the truth of Isa al Masih clearly to us so that we will hear and believe.

RAYMOND LULL

As Muawia told his story, a man began to weep as he looked down at the floor. This man, a brilliant but humble Franciscan missionary to North Africa during his lifetime,[8] had come prepared to share his counsel with you, the reader, but he is overtaken with grief for lost Muslims. Finally, he looks at you and speaks quietly.

---

6 Ibid., 306.
7 Elwood Morris Wherry, Samuel Marinus Zwemer, and James L. Barton, The Mohammedan World of Today: Being Papers Read at the First Missionary Conference on Behalf of the Mohammedan World Held at Cairo April 4th-9th, 1906 (New York: Fleming H. Revell Company, 1906), 15-16.
8 Following a vision, Raymund Lull (1232-1315), from Majorca, dedicated his life to the peaceful and prayerful conversion of Muslims to Christianity.

I am Raymond Lull.[9] When I came to the seventy-ninth year of life, my friends wanted me to stay in Europe to teach, but my resolve was to die as a missionary and not as a teacher of philosophy. So when the time of my departure was at hand, I prayed, "As the needle naturally turns to the north when it is touched by the magnet, so it is fitting, O Lord that thy servant should turn to love and praise and serve thee; seeing that out of love to him thou wast willing to endure such grievous pangs and sufferings. Men are wont to die, O Lord from old age, the failure of natural warmth and excess of cold; but thus, if it be thy will, thy servant would not wish to die; he would prefer to die in the glow of love, even as thou wast willing to die for him."[10]

Dear follower of Jesus, be urgent to leave the praise and honor that men would give you to volunteer. Earnestly and urgently surrender your life to share and suffer for the salvation of Muslims. This is the kind of volunteer we need—not just believing but doing.[11]

There are many others who engaged Muslims from the time of the seventh century. Their words are recorded in many books. Let us now build on their testimonies with voices from the last century. Their words are offered here for the benefit of your calling and that of your team.

H. H. JESSUP

I would like to add to the conversation. My name is Jessup. I helped to lead the Missionary Conference on Behalf of the Mohammedan World in Cairo, Egypt, in 1906. I joined with others in Cairo to understand the extent of darkness in the Mohammedan world and to do something about it. We estimated 233 million Mohammedans in the world in that day. We can only assume that many of them have passed through the gates of hell to be condemned forever.

"Very few even among Christians are aware of the great spiritual needs of Islam. Nor is the Church at large awaken to the fact that the Mohammedan world has suffered this destitution because of her past neglect, and that present open doors are a challenge to her faith and faithfulness."[12] So I'm glad to pass on to you some encouragement for what you are undertaking, if you are truly serious about your calling to reach Mohammedans.

---

9   Other spellings used, depending on language and translation.

10   Samuel Marinus Zwemer, *Raymund Lull: First Missionary to the Moslems* (New York: Funk & Wagnalls Company, 1902), 132-35.

11   Raymund Lull was stoned to death in North Africa on June 30, 1315, after boldly entering a marketplace to share the gospel one last time.

12   H. H. Jessup's introductory paper, in Wherry, Zwemer, and Barton, *The Mohammedan World*, 14.

As those of us who attended the Cairo conference see it, you should focus in earnest on three things:[13]

1. Set apart more special laborers and give them specialized training. More than anything, they should hear the devastating stories of people like Muawia and Yezid. They must understand that Mohammedans are spiritually destitute. Unless workers know this and feel it deeply in their heart, they will not see their calling as a matter of life and death. You must train laborers to meet hostility with patience, kindness, and the presentation of Christ as the only Redeemer.

2. Organize more efficiently the production and distribution of literature for Mohammedans. During our conference in Cairo, we heard that in 1905, forty-six million pages of the Arabic were printed at the press in Beirut. Wonderful! But you and your team must find ways to get the Word of God to Mohammedans so that they can read it, hear it, and be transformed by it.

3. Systemic common arrangements for the fresh occupation of important centers. Listen to me—you cannot run from Mohammedan cities. Are you a Jonah? You cannot run from them! You must go and give your all until God raises up Mohammedan scholars, enlightened, renewed by God's Spirit, thoroughly converted to faith in Jesus, the Son of Mary, as the only Redeemer, who proclaim that the set time to favor Islam has come and that they are all called to accept Christ.[14]

Finally, challenge churches who neglect the realities that hold Mohammedans in bondage—polygamy, suppression of women, devastating divorce, hatred, and suspicion. These and other features have been ignored or even defended. My friend, Mohammedans are lost, lost, and lost, and they must see in you and your family the love of Christ that proves your discipleship.[15]

S. M. ZWEMER

Yes. Amen to that part about loving as Christ loved, Mr. Jessup. I am Zwemer. My counsel comes from those of us who gathered at the great World Missionary Conference in Edinburgh, Scotland, in 1910. Clearly, as was the case then, the church is at a turning point. If the church will not turn toward Muslims—239 million as of 1910—or if there is further delay, can there be any outcome other than absolute judgment for every Muslim? Also, what awaits the church for neglecting Muslims?!

---

13 J. Brown, "Families Engaging Muslims in Grace and Truth" (presentation, Abide, Bear Fruit, Chiang Mai, Thailand, October 13, 2017).
14 Jessup, introductory paper, 14-20.
15 John 13:34-35.

In Edinburgh, we members of the World Missionary Conference desired to send a message to the members of the church in Christian lands. Our meeting 'impressed upon us the momentous character of the present hour. We heard from many quarters of the awakening of great nations, of the opening of long-closed doors, and of movements which are placing all at once before the Church a new world to be won for Christ.' However, there was a great concern for the goal of our network that it might not be accomplished, even by God's grace. In our letter, we added, "The next ten years will in all probability constitute a turning-point in human history and may be of more critical importance in determining the spiritual evolution of mankind than many centuries of ordinary experience. If those years are wasted, havoc may be wrought that centuries are not able to repair. On the other hand, if they are rightly used they may be among the most glorious in Christian history."[16]

In Edinburgh, we understood ourselves "to be on the brink of a great new surge of missionary advance. Sadly, never again would the western missionary movement occupy center-stage in the way it felt it did in Edinburgh. For most of the mission boards and societies represented, the twentieth century would be one of remorseless decline in their operations."[17] Sadly, our resolve was impacted by Satan himself. He loaded upon us the pressures of our day—genocide, world war, pandemic, economic depression, nationalism.[18]

So what counsel can I bring to you? The hour remains momentous—your hour. My counsel? Don't waste your present hour; use your time rightly to awaken the church; do not abandon your post.

DON MCCURRY

I'm Don. In 1978, a few of us organized the North American Conference on Muslim Evangelization in Glen Eyrie, Colorado. At that time, there were 720 million Muslims in the world,[19] or nearly half a billion more than in Edinburgh in 1910. W. Stanley Mooneyham, president of World Vision International, rekindled the embers of Edinburgh with stern determination, saying, "Some conferences debate, declare and depart, other conferences change history."[20]

---

16 John Raleigh Mott and W. H. T. Gairdner, *Echoes from Edinburgh, 1910: An Account and Interpretation of the World Missionary Conference* (New York: Fleming H. Revell Company, 1910), 277–88.

17 David A. Kerr and Kenneth R. Ross, eds., *Edinburgh 2010: Mission Then and Now* (Oxford: Regnum, 2009), 314.

18 J. Liverman, "The Church at a Turning Point: If Not Now, When?" (presentation, Abide, Bear Fruit, Chiang Mai, Thailand, October 14, 2017).

19 L. Ford, preface to "North American Conference on Muslim Evangelization," in *The Gospel and Islam: A 1978 Compendium*, edited by Don M. McCurry (Monrovia, CA: Missions Advanced Research and Communication Center, 1979), 6.

20 W. S. Mooneyham, foreword to "North American Conference on Muslim Evangelization," in *The Gospel and Islam: A 1978 Compendium*, edited by Don M. McCurry (Monrovia, CA: Missions Advanced Research and Communication Center, 1979), 7.

By now the optimism of Edinburgh had waned in light of the growth of Islam and "the failings of the Church."[21] While conference attendees continued to be optimistic about new opportunities, social and political upheaval in Muslim lands, loss of access to Muslims, and ineffective methods in the evangelization of Muslims meant a growing gap between the state of evangelization among Muslims and God's plan to redeem them.

I called for a time of new beginnings. Missions to Muslims has rejected the culture of the converts and imposed that of the missionary or evangelist. This pattern of extractionism and insistence on a double conversion, first to Christ and then to the culture of the missionary or evangelist, may well be the single most important reason for a greater lack of results in work among Muslims. Today's teams must understand how Jesus related to cultures. We notice that he did not ignore the fallenness of human nature. He spoke directly about sin, error, and disobedience... . While Jesus commended what was praiseworthy in human culture and behavior, he labored in love to transform humanity.[22]

When we seek to apply the above precepts to evangelizing Muslims, we are moving into uncharted waters. You and your team must learn to conduct yourselves as Christ would relate to living Islamic cultures today—to preach the transforming gospel through "more effective approaches in evangelizing Muslims."[23] The source of missionary endeavors is the heart of God, so we must call on God to answer us—you must call on God to answer you so that you and your team become an extension of God's own heart. That's the new beginning. "Unreached Muslims need to hear His voice."[24]

FUTURE

Now, dear reader, we have had our tea together. We have listened to the voices of the ages. What will it be? What will come of these words? What will it be for the millions of Muslims who may never hear unless you act? What about the hopes and dreams of past missionary conferences with their declarations and statements? Will our churches continue their past neglect of the Muslim world, or will volunteers respond with extraordinary boldness to the call of the Great Commission, in persistent prayer, joining God in the kairos moment of movements in the Muslim world? Yes, what will it be?

---

21 Ibid.
22 "North American Conference," 13–21.
23 Ibid.
24 J. Neely, "Let Unreached Muslims Hear His Voice" (presentation, Abide, Bear Fruit, Chiang Mai, Thailand, October 16, 2017).

DISCUSS AND APPLY

- What are the strengths and weaknesses of the church today in relation to Muslim ministries, in your view?

- What would "extraordinary boldness" look like for your team? Would you give your life for that level of boldness?

BIBLIOGRAPHY

Brown, J. "Families Engaging Muslims in Grace and Truth." Presentation at Abide, Bear Fruit, Vision 5:9, Chiang Mai, Thailand, October 13, 2017.

Jenkins, Philip. *The Lost History of Christianity: The Thousand-Year Golden Age of the Church in the Middle East, Africa, and Asia—and How It Died.* New York: HarperOne, 2009.

Kerr, David A., and Kenneth R. Ross. *Edinburgh 2010: Mission Then and Now.* Oxford: Regnum, 2009.

Liverman, J. "The Church at a Turning Point: If Not Now, When?" Presentation at Abide, Bear Fruit, Vision 5:9, Chiang Mai, Thailand, October 14, 2017.

Mott, John Raleigh, and W. H. T. Gairdner. *Echoes from Edinburgh, 1910: An Account and Interpretation of the World Missionary Conference.* New York: Fleming H. Revell Company, 1910.

Neely, J. "Let Unreached Muslims Hear His Voice." Presentation at Abide, Bear Fruit, Vision 5:9, Chiang Mai, Thailand, October 16, 2017.

"North American Conference on Muslim Evangelization." In *The Gospel and Islam: A 1978 Compendium*, edited by Don M. McCurry. Monrovia, CA: Missions Advanced Research and Communication Center, 1979.

Wherry, Elwood Morris, Samuel Marinus Zwemer, and James L. Barton. *The Mohammedan World of to-day: Being Papers Read at the First Missionary Conference on Behalf of the Mohammedan World Held at Cairo April 4th–9th, 1906.* New York: Fleming H. Revell Company, 1906

Zwemer, Samuel Marinus. *Arabia: The Cradle of Islam.* New York: Fleming H. Revell Company, 1900.

———. *Raymund Lull: First Missionary to the Moslems.* New York: Funk & Wagnalls Company, 1902.

2

RISE OF THE MAJORITY WORLD
Reasons for Celebration, Caution, and Counsel

John Cheong holds a PhD in intercultural studies from Trinity International University. He is a researcher, consultant, and lecturer in missiology and teaches in various seminaries around Asia. Specializing in globalization studies and Southeast Asian Islam, he has published on this as well as on the cultural dimensions of economics and contextual theology.

MAIN POINTS NOT TO MISS:

- The harvest force from all regions of the world need each other—we should celebrate success and learn from failure.
- In partnership, there needs to be an honest and open discussion about the underlying agendas and projected outcomes for healthy relationships.

Global gatherings of Christian leaders and workers provide wonderful opportunities for the church to experience the diversity of God's people and how he works extraordinarily among us. This was the case at the recent Abide, Bear Fruit (ABF) consultation in fellowship with nearly one thousand believers and workers in the Muslim world. Many were Christ-followers from the non-West (or Majority World)—an evident sign of Christianity's shifted center from the West to the non-West. However, the Majority World's rise also invites caution and counsel, which I will discuss, in order that it grows healthily and that the church evaluates it honestly in God's mission among Muslims. The chapter also reflects the thoughts of various attendees from the consultation garnered from my interviews and conversations with them. They are not comprehensive of the Majority World attendees, but a sampling and a distillation of my own thoughts.

REASONS FOR CELEBRATION

"After this I looked, and there before me was a great multitude that no one could count, from every nation, tribe, people and language, standing before the throne and before the Lamb" (Rev 7:9).

A Celebration of People

Revelation 7:9 gives us a glorious vision of God's fulfilled mission to unbelievers. A small sense of this at ABF was to witness many Muslim-background believers (MBBs) gathered there. It was stirring to know how many Muslims, who were formerly hard to reach, had come to Christ, and to hear their powerful testimonies of transformation from despair to hope and from abandonment to fellowship and community. A Southeast Asian Indian remarked, "I never realized so many Muslims could come to Christ. Now I know nothing is impossible with God!"

As an Asian (and as a Majority World attendee), experiencing this was exciting and powerfully encouraging because for many of us who serve as religious minorities in Asia such numbers and fellowship with converts were rare. Paul's words are apropos here: "There we found some brothers and sisters who invited us to spend a week with them. And so we came to Rome. The brothers and sisters there had heard that we were coming, and they traveled … to meet us. At the sight of these people Paul thanked God and was encouraged" (Acts 28:14–15).

When Majority World believers gather, especially in mission among Muslims, we want to learn about how God works among them. We desire safe and filtered places to meet and hear MBBs. A Bangladeshi shared about the church he started among MBBs, and about families following Jesus. He excitedly showed me photos of men he discipled and of government officials touched by the gospel. I related my own joys of knowing MBBs who touched my life in my relationships with them. We shamelessly shared about our trials, sufferings, and requests for prayer.

A minister from India confessed wanting to learn how to better help expelled MBBs and find networks of safe houses for them. Prayer requests for such needs and a desire to grow were the main staple of my many encounters with other Majority World believers. I pondered about the Westerners I met who, when asked about themselves, often detailed programs they ran, evangelistic tools they deployed, statistics they generated, or their big picture/systematic plans for mission.

Majority World believers and shared lessons from their contexts, and the larger body of Christ was roundly edified. We drew strength from stories because they have an embodied, emotional, and memorable impact—often more than sermons with three-point propositions. We benefited from hearing from Westerners about the progress of the gospel and the continued commitment and sacrifices they made. Westerners also spoke about what God had done in their ministries, books they had written, or their long service in various organizations. However, Majority World attendees recounted stories about their church leading people to Christ or about individuals whom they mentored then leading others to faith. Their pride lay not in structures they established nor in books they wrote (which were few, if any), but in people.

> Majority World believers and shared lessons from their contexts, and the larger body of Christ was roundly edified.

There was a diversity of people who served in mission agencies and churches represented at ABF. We praise God and give thanks for Westerners who display genuine humility and a desire to learn and collaborate with us in mission.

A Celebration of Worship

It was amazing to attend the worship. I'm so glad I could attend! At ABF, the joyful music and uplift in worship we experienced was wonderful, reflecting the multiplicity of various peoples praising God in Arabic, French, Swahili,

> " Christianity is a singing religion. Singing is one of the ways Christians have edified and encouraged ourselves for centuries; it is key to our faith and identity.

and other languages. The reports were encouraging, detailing growing numbers of unbelievers now reached among previously unengaged people groups. They reminded us that the strength of the church is not so much in what we do first, but rather in our availability to come to love God in worship and community, and the enjoyment and encouragement we bring to one another united in Christ (John 17:20–23).

Such spiritual nourishment is especially crucial for those of us who serve in contexts where loud and joyful singing cannot occur in MBB house churches lest they draw the attention of the authorities. It reminded me that Christianity is a singing religion. Singing is one of the ways Christians have edified and encouraged ourselves for centuries; it is key to our faith and identity.

Because worship times at ABF were uplifting, the fellowship sweet, and the excitement contagious, many used social media to share their excitement with friends and family back home! However, organizers reminded attendees not to do so. Workers in the Majority World are learning that there are significant risks to sharing openly about ministry among Muslims in today's globalized world.

Securing worker identities and protecting names of converts, locations, and mission plans are all standard security protocols in many Western mission agencies. However, those in the Majority World—especially those ministering from a church-based or pastoral-evangelistic approach to Muslim ministry— are less experienced in these matters. More experienced workers from mission agencies recognize these risks and minister in bold but measured ways. However, newcomers to the work still not fully realize the security risks of announcing their presence on social media, where information could spread virally without control. This is an area where Majority World believers should learn from experienced Western missionaries and other fellow believers in mission agencies who are sensitive to security precautions.

REASONS FOR CAUTION AND COUNSEL

Caution and Counsel on Managing Missions

Evangelical conferences such as Lausanne I, II, and III and other global gatherings are fond of restating covenants or manifestos for the church to stay the course in mission. ABF was no different, as a majority of the conferees voted to adopt its covenant—a sign of a continued global consensus and commitment of evangelical mission among Muslims. Even so, this caused consternation. Some disliked using English to craft the declaration, feeling certain terms did not translate sufficiently well in their own context. One wonders why they could not be crafted into some of the majority stakeholders' languages (e.g., Arabic, Indonesian, Swahili, etc).

A few Majority World believers also privately expressed feeling "pushed" to decide there and then, without due time to process and discuss with their stakeholders later. This reaction is not unexpected in cultures where decision-making takes longer than Western norms. Future consultations must deal with this complaint.

Related to this were conference deadline-specific goals for focused engagements with hitherto unreached people groups by 2025. When delegates were asked to discuss and vote on these goals, some felt uncomfortable about this process. A Southeast Asian Chinese described it as a "constant need to push for goals [and] drive a Western agenda." He added that it was "so much management but little trust in the Holy Spirit." Indeed, the charge of "managerial missiology" continues to beset modern evangelical missions.[1]

While goal-making and strategy-implementation does not preclude dependence and trust in God's Spirit,[2] Ruth Valerio issued the following warning well over a decade ago:

> This domination inevitably affects mission thinking and practice. A South African … saw the push [in previous global congresses] from Northern mission centres as being of a globalising order, carrying the implication that the rest of the world had to accept [their] priority…. The economics of the situation made it difficult to resist or ignore, and countries in the South tended to lose the theological space to frame their own questions and make their own contribution to global mission. My friend spoke of contending against the hegemony of AD 2000.[3]

Because of Western financial heft and machinery to generate statistics and trends, Western missions thinkers tend to produce managerial-oriented missiology. Even at ABF, some Majority World believers felt that Western mission leaders still spin mission plans and use their means to support projects that do not make sense to believers in host countries. Some workshop sessions

---

1 Samuel Escobar, "Evangelical Missiology: Peering into the Future," in *Global Missiology for the 21st Century: The Iguassu Dialogue*, ed. William Taylor (Grand Rapids: Baker Academic, 2000), 101-22.
2 John Mark Terry and J. D. Payne, *Developing a Strategy for Missions: A Biblical, Historical, and Cultural Introduction* (Grand Rapids: Baker Academic, 2013).
3 Ruth Valerio, "Globalisation and Economics: A World Gone Bananas," in *One World or Many? The Impact of Globalisation on Mission*, ed. Richard Tiplady (Pasadena, CA: William Carey, 2003), 19.

were disappointing for two believers who felt that, even there, many monologue presentations implicitly spun their own agenda by allocating little to no time for discussion.

Space limits discussions on the other hurdles that we experienced. Among them are the continued high cost of attending such events and a lack of space and time to hold honest and open dialogues between Westerners and those of us who harbor doubts as to whether Western methods still apply to Majority World settings. Continued disappointments in these areas will likely lessen the appeal to join in such future global gatherings.

Meanwhile, since the theme was Abide, Bear Fruit, it would have been good for there to be more time in the program for abiding in Christ and fellowshipping with believers. "Insufficient abiding!"

Caution and Counsel on Collaboration

In addition to many new friendships being established at ABF, fresh ideas for collaboration were also discussed. We—particularly those among us who were jaded or had run out of options—greatly appreciate the energy and continued investments of time, teaching, and personnel from the West to inject new initiatives. Because collaborations are common today, it is important to examine them, for they are key in many North-South, East-West mission partnerships;[4] *it implicates cross-cultural understandings of what partnership and accountability entail, as well as people with different goals and expectations, denominations and theological traditions.*[5]

Due to the importance of resources, particularly for Majority World participants who serve in resource-poor nations, some Majority World participants at ABF were canvassing support for their ministries. It is not easy to determine if such conversations or exchanges were unabashed attempts at procuring money or status-accruing credentials for personal gain.[6] Or were they genuine initiatives seeking relationships that would generate win-win partnerships for kingdom expansion?

---

4 Space does not permit fuller discussions on partnership in mission and its implications. On this, see Phill Butler, "Is Our Collaboration for the Kingdom Effective?" Lausanne Global Analysis 6, no. 1 (January 2017), https://www.lausanne.org/content/lga/2017-01/is-our-collaboration-for-the-kingdom-effective.

5 Mary Lederleitner, "An Approach to Financial Accountability in Mission Partnerships," in *Serving Jesus with Integrity: Ethics and Accountability in Mission*, EMS series, vol. 18, ed. Dwight P. Baker and Douglas Hayward (Pasadena, CA: William Carey, 2010).

6 Western missionaries are no less susceptible to similar impulses; many involved in short-term missions have utilized their ministry photos in Third World settings to "valorize" their ventures in order to accrue ascriptions of noble-mindedness or high spirituality to present themselves as morally commendable creatures. On the practice and ethics of this, see Gabriel B. Tait, "The Missionary and the Camera: Developing an Ethic for Contemporary Missionary Photographers," in Baker and Hayward, *Serving Jesus with Integrity*.

Further suspicions arise when some Majority World believers greet Westerners with long, obsequious salutations. Interestingly, such greetings are somewhat similar to Paul's greetings to fellow believers in Scripture (e.g., Rom 1:6–12; Eph 1:15–18; Col 1:3–12). Culturally, in contexts of socio-economic inequality and status hierarchy, such greetings are normal. Backgrounding these encounters is also a patron-client mind-set common in Asia, where relationships are key in managing the unequal distribution of resources. Sometimes even experienced missionaries find it difficult to ascertain whether Majority World believers are expressing their cultural, deferential habits or they have hidden motives. Only those who have a long history of relationships with them and know their culture well might truly understand these dynamics.

Lastly, people from patron-client societies also tend to accede to those higher in status; this sometimes occurs due to a misplaced sense of honor.[7] This is evident when Majority World believers with plenty of experience in ministry give way to Westerners, even though the latter may not have visited or known about their ministry or culture.

As global conferences, involving contacts between East-West and North-South, occur with increased frequency, opportunities for ministry and resources proliferate quicker than before, and the ability for both sides to access them have multiplied. However, the access to these flows may operate asymmetrically, bypassing institutional oversight or mission committees via everyone's own personalized social media (e.g., WhatsApp, Facebook) or email to gather support and supporters more privately.[8] When this occurs, greater scrutiny and ethical questions regarding healthy partnerships apply.

What is good accountability? Do Western norms still apply where top-down, patron-client rules operate? How much is too much or too little? As Majority World believers grow in strength and numbers and more partnerships increase, it becomes imperative for both sides to ask hard and honest questions about partnerships and how they can be better configured so that we can all co-labor more wisely as good stewards and servants in God's kingdom.

Lastly, a new consideration that must now be recognized with the Majority World's rise is the underbelly of unconscious or unspoken nationalist mind-sets they bring in mission. When Westerners ran missions, their enterprise was often entangled with the crusading or civilizational projects of their nations,

---

7 John Cheong, "Polycentrism in Majority World Theologizing: An Engagement with Power and Essentialism," in *Majority World Theology*, EMS series, vol. 26, ed. Allen Yeh and Tité Tienou (Littleton, CO: William Carey Publishing).

8 Peter Horsfield and Paul Teusner, "A Mediated Religion: Historical Perspectives on Christianity and the Internet," Studies in *World Christianity* 13, no. 3 (2007): 292.

demonstrating that they were not immune to nationalist forces. Similarly, it would be naïve to expect Majority World believers to escape this influence. Recent examples of mission from China and Singapore have shown our susceptibility to running ministry objectives under nationalist or ethnocentric impulses.[9] As ministry and mission continue to expand into new peoples and places, the plurality of unspoken nationalist mind-sets will create the potential for disagreements arising from cultural biases. This challenge must be met by challenging bias with the Bible, which is the basis for authentic Christian faith and practice.

CONCLUSION

As the Majority World grows in strength and in the power of our own local-global networks forged from new relationships through such global gatherings, the "cumulative effect of these numerous smaller intimate groupings offers an alternative conglomeration of Christianity equal to the more visible centralised large church embodiment of Christianity."[10] The increasing reality is that "Western missionary initiative remains the most visible but are no longer the most dominant or consequential."[11]

Presently, the Majority World's rise signals a wonderful and healthy development in twenty-first-century mission. However, many mission movements among us still remain

> fundamentally unstructured, spontaneous, and clandestine. For this reason, the analysis of its scope and potential impact remains complicated, and its largely inchoate nature also means that even the best assessments will remain partial and provisional for some time.... .

> Prominent features associated with the Western missionary project are largely absent, including the entrenched territorial (and one-directional) structure of missions, the instrumentality of para-church mission societies, the complicated relationship with colonial dominance, and the projection of cultural superiority [such] that the burgeoning South-North element is church-based, self-evidently incarnational in its witness, and closely exemplifies New Testament patterns (demonstrated in its dependence on individual inventiveness, emphasis on spiritual power, use of house churches, reliance on tent-making ministries, and disconnect from empire).[12]

9   See Simon Chan, review of Tan-Chow, May Ling, *Pentecostal Theology for the Twenty-first Century: Engaging with Multi-Faith Singapore*, H-Pentecostalism, H-Net Reviews, December, 2007, http://www.h-net.org/reviews/showrev.php?id=13966; and James Sung-Hwan Park, "Chosen to Fulfill the Great Commission? Biblical and Theological Reflections on the Back to Jerusalem Vision of Chinese Churches," *Missiology* 43, no. 2 (September 2014): 170.
10 Horsfield and Teusner, "A Mediated Religion," 293.
11 Jehu Hanciles, "Migration and Mission: The Religious Significance of the North-South Divide," in *Mission in the 21st Century: Exploring the Five Marks of Global Mission*," ed. Andrew Walls and Cathy Ross (Maryknoll, NY: Orbis, 2008), 127.
12 Ibid., 129.

Due to this, any ongoing collaboration between Westerners and us in ministry must remain humble and open to dialogue and correction. Though our rise may be celebrated, we should not be unrealistically optimistic[13] regarding its promise—the road is paved with our fallen nature. Paraphrasing Paul, we can only trust that he who began a good work in us will accomplish it in the day of our Lord Jesus (Phil 1:6).

DISCUSS AND APPLY

- Where do you see potential partnerships across regions that will help share Christ with those who have not yet heard the gospel?

- What are some of the pitfalls of partnerships you have experienced, and (how) have you overcome them? Where do you need to seek an honest discussion with this partner?

---

13 Teams must be ready to encounter many barriers for the cause of Christ, and breakthroughs and movements will come only through the one who puts fruit on the vine.

BIBLIOGRAPHY

Butler, Phill. "Is Our Collaboration for the Kingdom Effective?" *Lausanne Global Analysis* 6, no. 1 (January 2017). https://www.lausanne.org/content/lga/2017–01/is-our-collaboration-for-the-kingdom-effective.

Chan, Simon. Review of Tan-Chow, May Ling, *Pentecostal Theology for the Twenty-first Century: Engaging with Multi-Faith Singapore*. H-Pentecostalism, H-Net Reviews. December, 2007. http://www.h-net.org/reviews/showrev.php?id=13966.

Cheong, John. "Polycentrism in Majority World Theologizing: An Engagement with Power and Essentialism." In *Engaging Theology, Theologians, and Theological Education from the Majority World*. EMS series, vol. 26, edited by Allen Yeh and Tité Tienou. Pasadena, CA: William Carey (forthcoming).

Escobar, Samuel. "Evangelical Missiology: Peering into the Future." In *Global Missiology for the 21st Century: The Iguassu Dialogue*, edited by William Taylor, 101–22. Grand Rapids: Baker Academic, 2000.

Hanciles, Jehu. "Migration and Mission: The Religious Significance of the North-South Divide." In *Mission in the 21st Century: Exploring the Five Marks of Global Mission*, edited by Andrew Walls and Cathy Ross, 118–29. Maryknoll, NY: Orbis, 2008.

Horsfield, Peter, and Paul Teusner. "A Mediated Religion: Historical Perspectives on Christianity and the Internet." *Studies in World Christianity* 13, no. 3 (2007): 278–95.

Lederleitner, Mary. "An Approach to Financial Accountability in Mission Partnerships." In *Serving Jesus with Integrity: Ethics and Accountability in Mission*. EMS series, vol. 18, edited by Dwight P. Baker and Douglas Hayward, 27–47. Pasadena, CA: William Carey, 2010.

Park, James Sung-Hwan. "Chosen to Fulfill the Great Commission? Biblical and Theological Reflections on the Back to Jerusalem Vision of Chinese Churches." *Missiology* 43, no. 2 (September 2014): 163–74.

Tait, Gabriel B. "The Missionary and the Camera: Developing an Ethic for Contemporary Missionary Photographers." In *Serving Jesus with Integrity: Ethics and Accountability in Mission*. EMS series, vol. 18, edited by Dwight Baker and Doug Hayward, 321–40. Pasadena, CA: William Carey, 2010.

Terry, John Mark, and J. D. Payne. *Developing a Strategy for Missions: A Biblical, Historical, and Cultural Introduction*. Grand Rapids: Baker Academic, 2013.

Valerio, Ruth. "Globalisation and Economics: A World Gone Bananas." In *One World or Many? The Impact of Globalisation on Mission*, edited by Richard Tiplady, 13–32. Pasadena, CA: William Carey, 2003.

3 | GOSPEL ADVANCE AMONG MUSLIM PEOPLES

Jim Haney served as Director of Global Research for the International Mission Board, Richmond, Virginia, and coordinator for Vision 5:9's Global Trends Task Force from 2005 to 2018. Before that Jim planted churches among Muslims peoples in West Africa for eighteen years.

Jim has written and spoken widely on missions and missiology.

MAIN POINTS NOT TO MISS:

- A common agenda, clear and consistent definitions, and shared measurement systems are necessary for the collective impact of a network on vision and key results.

- God is bringing a harvest that is beyond our expectation and beyond our knowledge.

Since 2005, the Global Trends Task Force has served the Vision 5:9 network to monitor and evaluate the state of gospel advance among all Muslim people groups. This chapter will provide an overview of the fruit we have seen.

VISION 5:9 OBJECTIVES

The primary objective of Vision 5:9 clearly states why Vision 5:9 exists. "Vision 5:9 *exists to see effective church-planting efforts among all Muslim peoples. By the grace of God, we aspire to see this accomplished by 2025.* "[1]

The secondary objective of Vision 5:9 must be undertaken before the primary objective is possible. "Vision 5:9 seeks to engage all unengaged Muslim unreached people groups (100,000) by the end of 2012."[2]

VISION 5:9 OBJECTIVE LEVELS

The two objectives imply three levels needing attention:

Level 1—Unengaged Muslim Unreached People Groups (UMUPGs)

Because UMUPGs exist, we must understand what they are, who they are, and what it means to engage them. Clearly, they are lacking something—they are among the most deprived peoples of the world. Imagine going through an entire lifetime without a single opportunity to know that God is love, God is provider, God is alive and cares, and God cares for each person in the world. People living in UMUPGs will never know what it means to be transformed by a loving God unless we are faithful to answer God's call to engage them with the gospel.

The Global Trends Task Force has defined each of these terms—"unengaged," "Muslim," "unreached," and "people group." Common definitions are important to a network like Vision 5:9 because we want to be very specific about what we seek to accomplish by God's grace.

Unengaged: A people group is unengaged until all four of the following criteria have been met.[3] Before a people group can be considered engaged, there must be evidence of:

1. An apostolic (pioneering) effort in residence,
2. A commitment to work in the local language and culture,
3. A commitment to long-term ministry,
4. Sowing in a manner consistent with the goal of seeing a church-planting movement (CPM) emerge.

---

1 Vision 5:9 Strategic Plan
2 Ibid.
3 Jeff Liverman, "What Does It Mean to Effectively 'Engage' a People?" *Mission Frontiers* (November-December 2006), 10-12.

Muslim: A people group is a Muslim people group when a plurality[4] of those living in the people group are adherents of Islam. The same concept can be applied to a country, city, affinity bloc, people cluster, people, or place. Therefore, a Muslim community is any group of people where more people call themselves Muslims than any other religion.

Unreached: A people group is considered unreached (UPG) when there is no indigenous community of believing Christians able to engage this people group with church planting. Technically speaking, the percentage of evangelical Christians in this people group is less than 2 percent.[5]

People Group: For strategic purposes, a people group is the largest group through which the gospel can flow without encountering significant barriers of understanding and acceptance.[6] In addition to this common strategic definition, people groups may be identified in any number of ways by outsiders, by insiders, by a community to which they belong because of historical and cultural distinctives—there are many ways to identify and subdivide people groups.

So while these descriptions sound very technical, they help us to know the specific needs of people groups we serve.

Vision 5:9 is focused on engaging the larger UMUPGs. This is not because they are more important than smaller UMUPGs; it is because they are identifiable and often concentrated in communities. For example, it is very difficult for a team to engage a small, dispersed people group, especially when that people group may speak a language different than their heart language. On the other hand, if the larger UMUPGs can be engaged, they may inform our strategy to reach the smaller people groups and even help us find them.

Level 2—Engaged Muslim Unreached People Groups (EMUPGs)

After a UMUPG is engaged as defined above, it can be considered an engaged Muslim unreached people group (EMUPG)—at least one team has begun to implement a church-planting strategy. However, we all know that one team is not enough to share the gospel broadly throughout a people group. Still, initial engagement is an important step, even when there is only one team.

---

4 There are more Muslims than any other religious tradition.
5 http://peoplegroups.org/.
6 http://peoplegroups.org/294.aspx#310.

Every team must begin somewhere. In Matthew 4:23, we read that Jesus was going about Galilee, teaching in their synagogues, proclaiming the gospel of the kingdom, and healing every kind of disease and every kind of sickness among the people. In Acts 13:4, we read that Paul and Barnabas left Antioch, went down to Seleucia, and from there sailed to Cyprus. When a people group moves from the level of UMUPG to EMUPG the work has only begun, but at least with an EMUPG we no longer pray for the first teams to come; we pray for the team to multiply disciples and churches so that the engagement flourishes under the power of the Holy Spirit.

Today we are thankful for engaged people groups that were unengaged and unreached when Vision 5:9 began in 2002. We are also thankful that as people groups are engaged, the multiplication of disciples and churches provides new teams for wider impact.

Level 3—Effective Church Planting

While we have been careful to be clear in definitions for how we determine whether a people or place is a UMUPG or EMUPG, the final level has not been defined. Instead, we turn our attention to the quality of what we want to see because of God's work in a people group that has been effectively engaged.

In January 2016, the Global Trends Task Force met in San Francisco and gave serious thought to what we wanted to see among every Muslim people group. Rather than creating a definition, we just considered God's Word regarding what his church is to be. We also considered how movements might be evaluated. We thought about the following question: "How will we evaluate whether we have accomplished our network goals in the year 2025?"

The Holy Spirit led us to a description, not a definition, of effective church planting. We agreed on the following description for assessing effective church planting.

> A people group has *effective church planting* when there are groups characterized by: "Repentant, baptized and reproducing disciples of Jesus Christ joined by the Holy Spirit who regularly meet together for doctrine, fellowship, communion and prayer." (Acts 2:38–47)[7]

---

7 Italics added for emphasis. This is the primary objective of Vision 5:9; this is the fruit we want to see in the harvest. We want to see effective churches planted in every Muslim people group. Churches with these qualities will multiply and honor God.

In short, all the meetings, passport applications, support raising, persecution, diseases, border crossings, tears, and trials are about this one thing—to be faithful to proclaim the gospel of Christ so that *by the Holy Spirit* those living in Muslim people groups become a great family in Christ. We have the perfect picture of what the church is to be. For Muslims, we hope for a community sharing a new identity in Christ as those who are loved in his divine plan of salvation. What we see in Acts 2 is the new *ummah* of Christ-followers, and we have the privilege of introducing Muslims to the wider *ummah* of the global church.

We tasted this wider *ummah at the* Abide, Bear Fruit global meeting in Chiang Mai in 2017. Believers from diverse religious backgrounds and from many languages, peoples, tribes, and nations gathered together for worship, healing, anointing, training, and fellowship. This global conference included diversity in gender, age, nationality, ministry, and calling. Having witnessed this event, I believe that this global conference gave us a sense of family and identity made possible by a loving Father who calls us brothers and sisters. So while we were not a church, we realized our strong connection within the universal church that is the body of Christ.

Before moving on to the report on gospel advance among Muslim peoples, one final definition is necessary. This definition is important because it helps us to identify who we are in faith and practice, and it helps us to introduce Muslim-background believers (MBBs) in the new *ummah* to a worldview that brings a grateful acknowledgement their relationship to the Father.

Evangelical:[8] An evangelical Christian is a person who believes that Jesus Christ is the sole source of salvation through faith in him, has personal faith and conversion with regeneration by the Holy Spirit, recognizes the inspired Word of God as the only basis for faith and Christian living, and is committed to biblical preaching and evangelism that brings others to faith in Jesus Christ.

Therefore, an evangelical church is a church that is characterized by these same beliefs and principles. Some churches that are not considered evangelical in faith and practice may contain members who are evangelical.

Now let's look at gospel advance among Muslim peoples over the last ten years.

---

8 This definition is common in missions research and is quoted by Operation World, IMB, Finishing the Task, Joshua Project, and other partners. Note the personal nature of this definition and that this implies the nature of evangelical faith and practice, not just religious affiliation.

GOSPEL ADVANCE AMONG MUSLIM PEOPLES—A CHANGE ANALYSIS

In Luke 10:2 (ESV), Jesus tells his followers, "The harvest is plentiful, but the laborers are few. Therefore pray earnestly to the Lord of the harvest to send out laborers into his harvest."

The harvest does not come when the first fruits appear; it comes when the harvest is plentiful. The Lord is looking for and expecting a plentiful harvest among every language, people, tribe, and nation. He says to us in Matthew 28:19–20 (ESV), "Go therefore and make disciples of all nations, baptizing them in the name of the Father and of the Son and of the Holy Spirit, teaching them to observe all that I have commanded you. And behold, I am with you always, to the end of the age."

With this reminder of what we are about as a network among Muslim peoples, let's look more closely at the changes that have been reported to the network. First, how are we doing as we seek to engage every unengaged Muslim unreached people group that is at least one hundred thousand (100K) in population?

Number and Population of UMUPGs

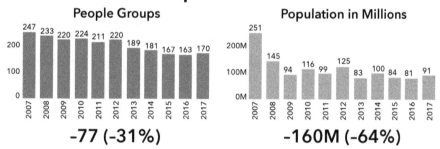

Since 2007, the number of UMUPGs of 100K has decreased from 247 to 170, and the population living in UMUPGs of 100K has decreased from 251 million to 91 million. This results in a -77 change in UMUPGs of 100K and a -160 million change in UMUPGs of 100K population. The accompanying two graphs show steady progress in our work.

While we have not engaged every UMUPG of 100K and above as we attempted by 2012, we have made significant progress in the decrease in the number of UMUPGs and especially in the decrease in the population living in UMUPGs. The reason that there has been a greater decrease in population is because the UMUPGs we have engaged have been the larger ones.

Why are we only looking here at those of 100K and above? First, our 2012 goal was focused on this population size. Second, we believe that by engaging and establishing effective church planting in these larger people groups, they can join us as partners in engaging those less than 100K. In these larger people groups, we seek to build capacity of local believers so that they can engage their neighbors. However, we should not assume that near-culture partners have cross-cultural competencies. In fact, one of the reasons people groups remain Muslim is because near-culture Christian people groups lack the cross-cultural skills to lovingly communicate the gospel to them.

However, let's be careful not to celebrate too early. While we rejoice that UMUPGs have been engaged by teams and these teams have seen the first fruits of believers and churches, we cannot celebrate these who are orphaned when engaging teams leave. When engaging teams leave a people group, the first disciples have little opportunity to be mentored and trained so that they become mature believers in healthy churches.

Now let's look at the reasons why UMUPGs are added to the list and why UMUPGs are removed from the list. Since 2007, when there were 247 UMUPGs of 100K, we've added 104 UMUPGs of 100K. The accompanying graph shows some of the reasons we have added UMUPGs to the list.

Reasons for Additions to List

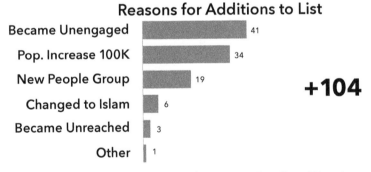

Since 2007, when there were 247 UMUPGs of 100K, we've removed 181 UMUPGs of 100K. The accompanying graph shows some of the reasons we have removed UMUPGs from the list.

Reasons for Removals from List

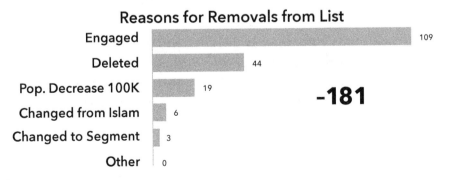

The map shows the changes to the Vision 5:9 list of UMUPGs of 100K since 2007. The color and size of the dark gray dots indicates people groups that were not on the list in 2007 but are now. These PGs need to be engaged. The medium gray dots indicates people groups that were on the list in 2007 but are no longer. These dots show progress. The light gray dots indicates people groups that were on the list in 2007 and still are. Either these PGs are unchanged, or we have not received a report showing how they have been engaged.

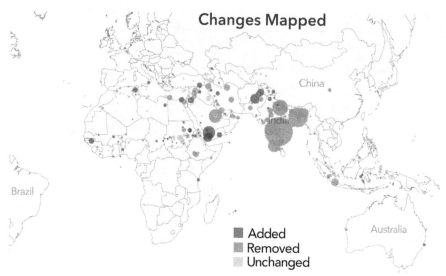

The number of UMUPGs on the list changes from month to month. One of the reasons for this is the movement of teams in and out of people groups. We need to pray earnestly that the Lord of the harvest will not only send workers but that workers will remain.

In summary, we began with 247 UMUPGs that were at least 100K in population in 2007. Since then, we added 104 (see addition reasons chart) and we removed 181 (see removal reasons chart). Therefore, at the time of the Abide, Bear Fruit global event in Thailand, there remained only 170 UMUPGs with a population of a 100K to engage with church-planting teams.

It is quite possible that some of the 170 UMUPGs with a population of 100K are also engaged, but further reports and assessments are needed to make sure that church planting is underway. We need well-documented reports to really know whether Muslim Unreached people groups are currently engaged with church-planting teams.

> It is quite possible that some of the 170 UMUPGs with a population of 100K are also engaged, but further reports and assessments are needed to make sure that church planting is underway.

We must make the remaining UMUPGs of 100K, with a total population of 91 million people, our engagement priority. These 170 UMUPGs represent 84 percent of the total population living in all UMUPGs. The other 16 percent of the UMUPGs are much smaller people groups and could be engaged and reached by the 170 that are proximal and near-culture to them.

So let me say this again. Engaging and establishing disciples in the largest UMUPGs is the best way to engage the remaining smallest UMUPGs around them.

In the last ten years, a good number of these PGs have been added to and removed from our list of UMUPGs more than once as teams engage, move away, etc. We are looking for teams that will have a long-term engagement presence, especially so that long-term relationships are developed with Muslims.

We need teams that will complete the missionary task among the UMUPGs they are engaging: entry, evangelism, discipleship, healthy church formation, and leadership development. Finally, they will be prepared to engage others near to them, joining with us in the expanding harvest force.

God is helping us to get to engagements, but these engagements are often very fragile. While we can rejoice that there only remain 109,000,000 living in all remaining Unengaged Muslim Unreached People groups, we estimate that there are nearly 1.6 billion Muslims living in Muslim Unreached People Groups that are engaged but underserved.

ENGAGING THE UNENGAGED | ESTABLISHING WITH THE UNDER-ENGAGED | ENLISTING THE REACHED

To summarize, to reach our goal we need advancement as follows:

1. We need Engaging teams—peoples and places need their first pioneering teams to enter people groups and to implement church-planting strategies.

2. We need Establishing teams—peoples and places already engaged need evangelism, discipleship, healthy churches, and effective leaders. But we cannot stop with this.

3. We need Enlisting teams—people groups no longer unreached need to be enlisted in the Great Commission. We need to pass the baton, so that the ever-increasing harvest force goes to the final frontiers of lostness.

There is a vast potential harvest force beyond our comprehension within Muslim people groups around the world. We must engage the unengaged with their first teams. After the first teams arrive and they are engaged, we must establish churches until they are reached and can be enlisted in the harvest force. While this is the goal, we cannot engage, establish, or enlist in our own power; rather, we faithfully serve so that the Lord of the harvest will provide the fruit in his time and as he remains faithful to the promises he has made.

As God reaches into the remaining people groups of the world, we get to follow him and see his glory revealed among the nations. We can be confident that he will transform the nations by his grace and for his glory.

DISCUSS AND APPLY

- How many UMUPGs have teams from your organization or church engaged in the last ten years? What is the situation of those people groups today? List them and write beside each what needs to happen:

  –*Engaged or Re-engaged* (Needing teams to engage with a pioneering effort in an appropriate language for the long term in a way consistent with seeing a CPM emerge)

  –*Established* (Needing teams already present to boldly evangelize, make disciples, plant healthy churches, develop committed leaders)

  –*Enlisting* (Needing teams already present to enlist established disciples and churches so that they hear the call of the Great Commission and engage those remaining to be engaged and reached near to them)

- How can your church or organization engage and establish churches among one or more Muslim unreached people groups for the long term—until those they have engaged are engaging themselves?

BIBLIOGRAPHY

Liverman, Jeff. "What Does It Mean to Effectively 'Engage' a People?" *Mission Frontiers,* November–December 2006, 10–12.

People Groups, http://peoplegroups.org/.

OPPORTUNITIES AND THREATS IN THE MUSLIM WORLD
A Case Study

Pam Arlund spent ten years in Central Asia as a church planter and Bible translator working among a previously unengaged people group. Pam's heart is to train and send church planters to share Jesus with other unreached people groups: those who would never have any chance in their lives to hear about him. To this end, she trains and coaches disciples who make disciples based on simple biblical and research-based best practices

MAIN POINTS NOT TO MISS:

- New trends in our world are threats and opportunities alike—it all depends on our reflective response to the call of faithfully sharing the gospel with Muslims.
- You and your team must understand opportunities and threats in our generation to be wise and effective in engaging and reaching Muslim peoples.

Doing a SWOT (Strengths, Weaknesses, Opportunities, and Threats) analysis before attempting new projects has become a widespread practice in many countries. Such an analysis often yields positive and beneficial planning insights.

Jesus seems to encourage such thinking when he asks the question, "Who would begin construction of a building without first calculating the cost to see if there is enough money to finish it?" (Luke 14:28 NLT). Jesus also went on to ask, "Or what king would go to war against another king without first sitting down with his counselors to discuss whether his army of 10,000 could defeat the 20,000 soldiers marching against him?" (Luke 14:31 NLT). Jesus seems to imply that the answer to either question is "No one." No one would take on important projects without counting the cost. Jesus finishes the discussion by saying, "So you cannot become my disciple without giving up everything you own" (Luke 14:33 NLT).

This brief survey will look at threats and opportunities for Muslims coming to Jesus.

Truly there are many threats in this world. Jesus promised there would be. However, in each threat there is also potential opportunity. In the end, to pull back from the task because of the threats would be a misunderstanding of the exercise. Furthermore, Jesus gives specific encouragement when analyzing threats. He said, "I have told you these things, so that in me you may have peace. In this world you will have trouble [threats]. But take heart! I have overcome the world [created opportunity]" (John 16:33).

MUSLIM MIGRATION

Likely the largest migration of Muslims in history has occurred in the last decade. Most of the migration has happened due to the war in Syria (beginning in 2011) and ongoing political and social unrest in many countries, but most notably Iran and Afghanistan. This trend has changed how and where Muslims live and how they perceive themselves. It has also created entirely new levels of refugee and diaspora ministries.

The Middle East has received far more Muslim refugees than any other region on earth. Countries like Jordan, Lebanon, and Turkey have opened their borders to many Syrians, in particular. Forty-one percent of Syrians who have fled the country went to other places in the Middle East.[1]

---

1 Phillip Connor, "Most Displaced Syrians Are in the Middle East, and About a Million Are in Europe," Pew Research Center, January 29, 2018, http://www.pewresearch.org/fact-tank/2018/01/29/where-displaced-syrians-have-resettled/.

Although Europe as a continent is only about 5 percent Muslim, in many European countries an overwhelming majority of the Muslims are new arrivals.[2] In Germany, for example, almost four million Muslim immigrants have arrived in a relatively short period of time, causing Angela Merkel to give speeches before the German Bundestag asking people to realize that "Islam has also become a part of Germany."[3]

Compared to Europe, the United States has a small Muslim population and has received fewer Muslim refugees. Nevertheless, beginning in the early 2000s the United States allowed hundreds of thousands of Muslim refugees to immigrate to the country.[4]

In addition to Europe and the US, Africa has received many Muslim refugees. Uganda has received the largest number of official Muslim refugees, flowing mostly out of Sudan and South Sudan. Nigeria has seen an increase in refugees, although these are on the move because of internal threats such as those posed by Boko Haram. On the eastern part of the African continent, Somalis roam illegally on the fringes of society and are moving into cities for new opportunities. There are no reliable statistics on refugees in Africa, but numbers are certainly higher than officially reported.[5]

In both Europe and the US there has been dramatic backlash due to this rise of Muslim immigrants. Angela Merkel was booed in the Bundestag for her open-door policy to immigrants, and many European countries either passed or seriously debated laws restricting how Muslim women could dress in European countries.[6] By the end of 2018, the US had enacted new laws causing a dramatic decrease in Muslim migration into the country, apparently reaching the lowest point since the 9/11 terrorist attacks.[7]

---

2 Conrad Hackett, "Five Facts About the Muslim Population in Europe," Pew Research Center, November 29, 2017, http://www.pewresearch.org/fact-tank/2017/11/29/5-facts-about-the-muslim-population-in-europe/. It is difficult to know for sure exactly when these immigrants arrived due to the controversies surrounding census-taking in Germany in previous decades. But it seems likely that roughly four million Muslims have arrived in Germany since 2011. (See https://www.bbc.com/news/world-europe-22727898.)

3 David Frum, "Competing Visions of Islam Will Shape Europe in the 21st Century," The Atlantic, May 2, 2018, https://www.theatlantic.com/international/archive/2018/05/akbar-ahmed-islam-europe/559391/.

4 Sarah Feldman, "Muslim Refugees in the U.S. On the Rise, Till Now," Statista, June 29, 2018, https://www.statista.com/chart/14502/muslim-refugees-in-the-us-on-the-rise/.

5 Phillip Connor and Jens Manuel Krogstad, "Record Number of Forcibly Displaced People Lived in Sub-Saharan Africa in 2017," August 9, 2018, Pew Research Center, http://www.pewresearch.org/fact-tank/2018/08/09/record-number-of-forcibly-displaced-people-lived-in-sub-saharan-africa-in-2017/.

6 Ariana Monique Salazar and Scott Gardner, "Most Western Europeans Favor at Least Some Restrictions on Muslim Women's Religious Clothing," Pew Research Center. September 17, 2018, http://www.pewresearch.org/fact-tank/2018/09/17/most-western-europeans-favor-at-least-some-restrictions-on-muslim-womens-religious-clothing/.

7 Phillip Connor and Jens Manuel Krogstad, "The Number of Refugees Admitted to the U.S. Has Fallen, Especially among Muslims," Pew Research Center, May 3, 2018, http://www.pewresearch.org/fact-tank/2018/05/03/the-number-of-refugees-admitted-to-the-u-s-has-fallen-especially-among-muslims/.

In countries where Muslims have resettled, Christians have had varied reactions. Many have reacted out of suspicion and fear and reacted only to the threat they feel Muslim immigrants present. Others have reacted to new Muslim neighbors as an opportunity to engage Muslims with the good news and love of Jesus. In every country where we can gather information, many Muslims who have been engaged with the good news have responded favorably. From refugee populations, literally thousands (likely much higher) of new Muslim-background believers (MBBs) have come into the kingdom. Many new churches have been planted, and Muslim-background believers are boldly remaining close to home to share Christ with their families. In some countries in the Middle East that closely monitor missionary work among their own native populations, governments are tolerant of missionary assistance among refugee populations provided these are conducted through approved programs and approaches.

In all, teams are finding an unprecedented opportunity to share Jesus with Muslims on the move. Unfortunately, news outlets rarely if ever publicize the good news of unprecedented numbers of Muslims coming to Jesus, but every missions group of any background who has engaged Muslim refugees tells wonderful stories of Jesus being discovered by Muslims.

As Muslims migrate to places that are historically Christian, the potential for social unrest is a threat. Migrant populations that do not find a welcome (or lose welcome due to specific incidents, cultural misunderstanding, or the bad behavior of a few) may gather into ethnic enclaves or ghettos and become violent, resulting in isolated Muslim communities. In turn, original populations may become unresponsive to these areas of their cities. For example, there are Muslim communities (e.g., sections of Dearborn, Michigan, or London) in which shadow governments are operated by Muslim leaders who impose their authority over civic governments. Additionally, churches and Christians are becoming unresponsive to the needs of immigrants, looking at them with suspicion.

In the end, the greatest threat to Muslim immigrants is the neglect and unresponsiveness of those who know Jesus. The integration of Muslim immigrants into our communities is not just important for the peaceful settlement of immigrant population; it is necessary for Muslims to understand the love of Christ by the church of Christ.

Communities that receive Muslims will probably never be the same again. But rather than responding in isolation and anger (out of threat), we need eyes to see the unfolding opportunity before us. Here is an opportunity to create generations of Christians who enjoy learning about cultures, honoring people as human beings created in the image of God, and training children to love those different than them in the name of Jesus. It's a chance for believers to grow in Christ and for Muslims to discover Jesus.

Crises of any kind, whether man-made or natural, create opportunities. As Christians respond in love with food, kindness, care, and authentic relationship, there is opportunity. In such crises, however, there is also the danger of creating "rice Christians" (i.e., people who follow Jesus only for the food or money they receive). This can also lead to long-term unhealthy dependence on outsiders if only handouts are given. But as believers help refugees learn the language, acquire jobs, and contribute to society, there is an opportunity to demonstrate the love of Christ by spending time with Muslim families.

COMMUNICATIONS REVOLUTION/SMARTPHONES

For the first time in human history, two-thirds of the world are connected by cell phones, and the number continues to climb. Likely 75 percent of the world will have a mobile phone by 2020.[8]

Smartphones have created unprecedented opportunity for the gospel. People can access the gospel through their phones, even in countries where access comes at great risk. Some are leveraging social media to invite people to engage with Jesus. Because Internet access provides anonymity, Muslims are daring to engage with followers of Jesus and download ministry resources in innovative ways. Churches are meeting over the Internet, coaching and pastoral care are happening over long distances, baptisms are done remotely, and church planting and disciple-making training are conducted through smartphone apps.

Considering these opportunities, we have an open door to reimagine church and think about a connected, global community of believers.

Through microSD cards, cell phones provide access to materials for people who are not connected to the Internet. These cards give people access to Bibles, pastoral training, and worship music even if they are not connected to the Internet. They are small and easily transportable, and many countries have relatively cheap phones with speakers good enough for group listening. There are reports of families in unreached people groups acquiring their first cell phone so that they can gain access to such materials. They are willing to buy the SD cards with their own money and to use their phones first and foremost as

---

8 Rayna Hollander, "Two-Thirds of the World's Population Are Now Connected by Mobile Devices," Business Insider, September 19, 2017, https://www.businessinsider.com/world-population-mobile-devices-2017-9.

discipleship tools, and seem to use them only secondarily as phones! SD cards can also be destroyed or hidden if persecution comes. When using SD cards, seekers and believers do not need to worry about government monitoring of their Internet traffic.

However, smartphones represent a threat—they are addictive to young and old alike, especially as air time becomes less expensive and widespread. Christians and Muslims can find common ground in realizing the threat posed by the Internet and the access to information it provides.

COSMOPOLITANISM/LIBERALISM

As people move to cities and the world has become increasingly connected, there has been a new wave of liberalization in traditionally Muslim areas. For example, Saudi Arabia is allowing women to drive and is no longer legally enforcing laws regarding veils. In many Muslim countries, secular political parties are on the rise.[9] *Muslims and Christians alike are victims of secularization that challenges our values and threatens our families by promoting and advertising sex outside of marriage, alcoholism, and divorce.*

Cosmopolitanism has created an opportunity to be in shared spaces with Muslims that has never existed before. As more Muslims (including women) are found in work spaces, shopping malls, coffee shops, bars, and other urban landscapes around the world, there is a chance for friendship and engagement. And, as with secular Westerners, we can expect that these lifestyles will sadly and eventually lead to emptiness and brokenness outside of Christ. There is an opportunity for believers from similarly secular cultures to understand Muslim brokenness better than ever before. As secular lifestyles converge in many ways, many (but not all, of course) cultural barriers to understanding deep heart-level issues begin to converge across the world. As secularism spreads globally, believers can sense a global opportunity.

It will be important in these environments to make sure that Jesus-followers do not simply begin to sound like conservative Muslim clerics. This might happen if believers emphasize legalistic behaviorism rather than living lives of a certain style out of an overflow of love for Jesus. To enter into the brokenness without simply sounding like warmed-over Islam might be difficult for some believers.

9 Nicolas Pelham, "Roll Over, Religion," in *The Economist: The World in 2018*, edited by Daniel Franklin. Singapore: Times Printer, 64. Available at: http://www.theworldin.com/article/14440/edition2018roll-over-religion [Accessed 18 Oct. 2018].

EASE OF TRANSPORTATION

The world is now connected in the greatest transportation network ever seen on earth. Not only do all major cities—which house huge chunks of the world population—have airports, but many of them now have more than one. In addition, roads are better than ever before. (Although all of us are probably now thinking of the last really terrible road we traveled!) It is probably not surprising that many traditionally Muslim countries now have excellent roads and airports as well.[10] *Globally, twenty-five million kilometers in new roads are expected by 2050.*[11]

There is an opportunity for believers to use these transportation networks to get to the last places and peoples on earth that have not heard about Jesus. There is also an opportunity to have global interconnectedness of believers like never before. This means that no people group and no Muslim should be inaccessible to believers carrying the good news.

On the other hand, such ease of transportation makes ill-conceived and ill-designed short-term missions possible and even tempting. This is not to say that all short-term trips are unproductive. But there is a threat that ease of transportation will increase the temptation to go without doing the proper learning first. It will also increase the temptation to not invest long term into communities and build deep relationships. Some will decide to go back and forth (which is not always bad), but at the expense of knowing and being known deeply.

There is also a threat as roads open new areas to new ideas and other outside influences. Not all outsiders are kind or have the best interests of the local at heart. Some new roads blaze their way into marginal lands or special ecosystems. Sometimes exploitative entities utilize the same roads that carry good news. In the face of such threats, believers can become advocates and help traditionally isolated peoples navigate the changing world coming from the outside. This can lead to opportunities to love and guide in the name of Jesus.

ISOLATIONISM

Seemingly the opposite of the previous point, there has been a trend to make immigration and receiving of long-term visas for outsiders very difficult in some countries. Some of these countries that make visas and long-term residence more difficult still have a lot of Muslims who have not yet had a chance to meet Jesus—countries like India, China, Chad, Sudan, Nigeria, Iran, etc.[12]

---

10 "Roads Quality—Country Rankings," TheGlobalEconomy.com., 2015, https://www.theglobaleconomy.com/rankings/roads_quality/.

11 "Global Road Maps," Global Road Map, https://www.global-roadmap.org/global-road-maps/.

12 "Ten of the World's Hardest-to-Get Visas," Wanderlust, February 10, 2018, https://www.wanderlust.co.uk/content/10-of-the-worlds-hardest-to-get-visas/.

This can present a threat, as it gets harder and harder to place long-term missionaries into these countries. In some cases, no matter what marketable skill one has to offer, teams are finding it hard to remain among a people or place long enough to significantly engage and reach them.

The opportunity here is that local believers are getting the chance to rise into leadership very quickly. For many of these countries, local believers are taking the good news to the unreached peoples within their countries. Cross-cultural missionaries are helping local believers catalytically through coaching ministries. There is an opportunity for the global family to have more equitable partnerships as locals carry the gospel to their people group and beyond while helping the rest of those who desire to come alongside them to learn fruitful practices that work in their settings. These same practices may be applied by local believers when they return to their homelands or migrate to new places.

PERSECUTION

Persecution is on the rise globally.[13] India, China, Sudan, and other countries have long-standing policies and restrictions that severely limit the life, liberty, and future of individual believers and churches. While persecution is difficult, Scripture tells us to expect it and prepares us to endure it.

One of the hallmarks of disciple-making and church-planting movements is that nearly all of them experience persecution. When believers persevere, their bravery and blood identify with the life of Christ and encourages believers and churches to persevere and grow in trust and dependence on God.[14] As local believers are both wise and brave, there is great opportunity for Jesus to be lifted high. It seems likely that both foreign missionaries and local believers will be tortured, imprisoned, or killed for their faith in the future. If nothing else, Jesus promised this in Matthew 24 as he described the unfolding of the end of time. Jesus told us to expect this.

The threat is that believers will shrink back and will love their lives so much as to shrink from death. When this happens, the beauty of Jesus begins to shrink in comparison to the things of this world. There is great opportunity when believers bravely and wisely stand and serve despite the cost.

---

13 Ashlyn Webb and Will Inboden, "Religious Persecution Is on the Rise. It's Time for Policymakers and Academics to Take Notice," *Foreign Policy*, July 23, 2018, https://foreignpolicy.com/2018/07/23/religious-persecution-is-on-the-rise-its-time-for-policymakers-and-academics-to-take-notice/.
14 Jerry Trousdale and Glenn Sunshine, *The Kingdom Unleashed* (Murfreesboro, TN: Thomas Nelson, 2015).

There is danger that some Christians will not send their missionaries to love Muslims due to danger. To them, the advice of Ralph Winter is highly relevant: "Risks are not to be evaluated in terms of the probability of success, but in the value of the goal."[15] The goal, Jesus being worshiped by all the peoples of the earth, is worth everything.

CONCLUSION

This last point completes the circle. True disciples, as defined by Jesus (Luke 14:33), are to be willing to give up all that we own to follow him. In each of these global trends that form the backdrop of the present work of Jesus on earth, there are great threats and great opportunities. The difference between whether these trends will be good or bad for the advancement of the kingdom of Jesus will lie in the reaction of the followers of Jesus on earth.

Loving in the name of Jesus is not easy. He never promised it would be. Loving Muslims boldly and leveraging the opportunities of this present time and place in which we have been placed is our unique opportunity. These opportunities may only be given for this generation. May we seize them with grace and confidence in him no matter what the future may hold.

DISCUSS AND APPLY

- Which of these threats and opportunities affects your ministry the most? How are you addressing this to share Christ with Muslims?

- What is Jesus worth to you to engage in ministry to Muslims? What does it mean to be wise as serpents and harmless as doves (Matt 10:16) in your context?

BIBLIOGRAPHY

"Challenging Missions Quotes," Joshuaproject.net, https://joshuaproject.net/assets/media/handouts/challenging-missions-quotes.pdf.

Connor, Phillip. "Most Displaced Syrians Are in the Middle East, and About a Million Are in Europe," Pew Research Center, January 29, 2018, http://www.pewresearch.org/fact-tank/2018/01/29/where-displaced-syrians-have-resettled/.

Connor, Phillip, and Jens Manuel Krogstad, "Record Number of Forcibly Displaced People Lived in Sub-Saharan Africa in 2017," August 9, 2018, Pew Research Center, http://www.pewresearch.org/fact-tank/2018/08/09/record-number-of-forcibly-displaced-people-lived-in-sub-saharan-africa-in-2017/.

———. "The Number of Refugees Admitted to the U.S. Has Fallen, Especially among Muslims," Pew Research Center, May 3, 2018, http://www.pewresearch.org/fact-tank/2018/05/03/the-number-of-refugees-admitted-to-the-u-s-has-fallen-especially-among-muslims/.

---

15 "Challenging Missions Quotes," Joshuaproject.net, https://joshuaproject.net/assets/media/handouts/challenging-missions-quotes.pdf.

Feldman, Sarah. "Muslim Refugees in the U.S. On the Rise, Till Now," *Statista*, June 29, 2018, https://www.statista.com/chart/14502/muslim-refugees-in-the-us-on-the-rise/.

Frum, David. "Competing Visions of Islam Will Shape Europe in the 21st Century," *The Atlantic*, May 2, 2018, https://www.theatlantic.com/international/archive/2018/05/akbar-ahmed-islam-europe/559391/.

"Global Road Maps," Global Road Map, https://www.global-roadmap.org/global-road-maps/.

Hackett, Conrad. "Five Facts About the Muslim Population in Europe," Pew Research Center, November 29, 2017, http://www.pewresearch.org/fact-tank/2017/11/29/5-facts-about-the-muslim-population-in-europe/.

Pelham, Nicolas "Roll Over, Religion." *The Economist: The World in 2018*, edited by Daniel Franklin. Singapore: Times Printer, 64. http://www.theworldin.com/article/14440/edition2018roll-over-religion.

Rayna Hollander, Rayna. "Two-Thirds of the World's Population Are Now Connected by Mobile Devices," *Business Insider, September 19, 2017, https://www.businessinsider.com/world-population-mobile-devices-2017–9.*

"Roads Quality—Country Rankings," *The Global Economy,* 2015, https://www.theglobaleconomy.com/rankings/roads_quality/.

Salazar, Ariana Monique, and Scott Gardner, "Most Western Europeans Favor at Least Some Restrictions on Muslim Women's Religious Clothing," Pew Research Center. September 17, 2018, http://www.pewresearch.org/fact-tank/2018/09/17/most-western-europeans-favor-at-least-some-restrictions-on-muslim-womens-religious-clothing/.

"Ten of the World's Hardest-to-Get Visas," Wanderlust, February 10, 2018, https://www.wanderlust.co.uk/content/10-of-the-worlds-hardest-to-get-visas/.

Trousdale, Jerry, and Glenn Sunshine, *The Kingdom Unleashed* (Murfreesboro, TN: Thomas Nelson, 2015).

Webb, Ashyln, and Will Inboden, "Religious Persecution Is on the Rise. It's Time for Policymakers and Academics to Take Notice," *Foreign Policy, July 23, 2018, https://foreignpolicy.com/2018/07/23/religious-persecution-is-on-the-rise-its-time-for-policymakers-and-academics-to-take-notice/.*

5

THE FAITH OF BELIEVERS FROM MUSLIM BACKGROUNDS
A Case Study

Abu Suleman Yahiya is a consultant, trainer, and facilitator of church planting and mission mobilization in Pakistan. His special interests include religious transformation in South Asian history and its correlation with the contemporary period, contextualization, and the state of human rights, diversity, and interreligious relations.

MAIN POINTS NOT TO MISS:

- Even in very difficult circumstances there are ways of sharing Christ with those who are opposed to it.
- Learn to share Christ with Muslims through the stories of believers from Muslim background.

Pakistani Christian history begins with church planting by Saint Thomas in the Punjab, Northwest, and South of India in the first century.[1] Through the following centuries, missionaries made inroads and met with heartbreaking setbacks. Christian numbers declined due to persecution and killings.[2]

Under the Sikhs, hostility toward Christianity continued as the British Empire's occupation in the subcontinent created tension. Missionaries in British India faced opposition from both British civil and military personnel, as well as from Indian nationalists.[3] A Christian community developed, producing contextualized Christian literature for United India. The division of India and Pakistan, with great bloodshed and violence, changed the multicultural and multireligious landscape of Pakistan into a more homogeneous Muslim state.

POST-PAKISTAN EXPERIENCE: THE CHANGING LANDSCAPE OF INTERRELIGIOUS TOLERANCE

Within Pakistan, Muslim religious organizations influenced political, legal, and social matters. Systematic discrimination and persecution of non-Muslim minorities began with enactment of blasphemy laws. Religious literature produced by local converts and missionaries during the British period was destroyed by local Christians fearing retaliation with escalating violence and Islamization of the state.[4] Many upper-class Christians migrated to other countries. The majority of Christians from low-caste Hindu backgrounds were forced to do menial labor. Therefore, to be Christian or convert from Islam meant downward mobility.

Dawood Ahmed says that Muslim converts face severe persecution—particularly by society, and more generally by the state. While the local church is fighting decay, stagnation, and denominational divisions, it still survives in the middle of religious hatred and discrimination in this Islamic state and grows daily. Read on for extraordinary stories of Muslim-background believers (MBBs) living and secretly practicing their faith in Pakistan.

STORY OF ABBAS

Allama Akbar Abbas, a fifty-eight-year-old man living in Pakistan, was born into a Sufi Muslim family of the *Naqashbandi*—a major Sunni spiritual order of Sufism with thousands of followers. As a boy, Abbas saw a newspaper article about building radios. While marketing for supplies, Abbas met Mr. Davis, a British missionary newly arrived in Pakistan, who helped the boy find supplies and offered him some biblical storybooks.

---

1 B. Ullah, *Saint Thomas the Apostle of India* (Lahore: National Council of Churches in Pakistan, 2010), 36-76.
2 B. Ullah, *Christianity in Moghul Empire* (Lahore: National Council of Churches in Pakistan, 2010), 555.
3 Jeffrey Cox, *Imperial Fault Lines: Christianity and Colonial Power in India, 1818-1940* (Palo Alto, CA: Stanford University Press, 2002), 1.
4 Farahnaz Ispahani, *Purifying the Land of the Pure: Pakistan's Religious Minorities* (Noida Uttar Pradesh: HarperCollins India, 2015), 215.

In the following weeks Abbas and his mother read stories that became lifelong favorites, such as Abraham and Old Testament prophets. One day Abbas's mother said, "Son, it seems this book quotes some verses from Christian Scripture, and I am unable to understand it." The books became forbidden reading. After Abbas learned to read, he retrieved the books and began his study.

As a teen, Abbas purchased the Holy Bible and sought out the missionary, but Mr. Davis had moved. No one preached the Word to him, except the Holy Spirit. After accepting Christ as his Lord and Savior, he spent the next six years studying Scripture at his home, visiting the local church, and preaching the Word—alongside Christian workers from a parachurch organization—among Muslims.

Twelve years had passed since Abbas's first encounter with Mr. Davis. Now a grown man, he attended a Bible study summer camp organized at one of the hill stations in the northern part of the country. Leading the Bible study in that camp was Mr. Davis, the same British missionary who had given Abbas Christian literature twelve years before. Mr. Davis started telling his story, how twelve years before he came to reach this country for the Lord but his ministry had not been fruitful. He said with a heavy heart, "Today is my last day in the country, as I am flying this evening to Jordan for good."

Abbas recognized him and wept. He addressed the missionary, "How can you say that your ministry was not fruitful? Remember me? I am the same boy who met you many years ago, and you gave me Bible stories. I am the fruit of that seed which was sown by you. And now that seed has grown into a big tree that produced many other trees."

Both wept as they hugged each other. Abbas's friends told Mr. Davis that Abbas was a brave soldier of Christ who had led many Muslims to Christianity.

The missionary told everyone, "Now I cannot say that my ministry was not fruitful in this country, as I can see the fruit of this work now." The missionary was not able to see the transformation of a seed into an orchard, because it took twelve years for the seed to become an orchard.

DISILLUSION AND FEAR OF THE LOCAL BELIEVERS

Abbas said, "Local Christians did not work with me out of fear of preaching the gospel to Muslims; the majority are cowards. I challenged local Christians, saying that Christ died for them. Look at fanatic Muslims who blow themselves up as martyrs, while Christians will not even come out of their homes to preach the gospel to Muslims."

There were many occasions when Abbas faced isolation and discouragement from local believers. He exclaimed, "If someone had merely preached to me, I would have gone back to my previous faith; but I, myself, accepted Christ after understanding his power and truthful nature."

Sometimes Abbas feels alone in the field of ministry. He does not have resources to address the needs for Muslim people who come to talk to him about God, repentance, and other religious matters. "Also, my Muslim relatives took away my property and business," Abbas recalled. "They attacked me and tried to kill me." A dagger scar remains on his face.

Abbas said, "Almost twenty years ago I set a target to reach twenty-five Muslim families for the Lord. And now I have reached twenty-four families, so one is still missing, and God will provide me that family soon. My two sisters also accepted Christ, and they faced severe persecution, as one of the sisters was divorced by her husband because she and her children are also believers."

Abbas added, "When I accepted Christ I was engaged to a Muslim girl, but her family learned about my conversion and refused to give their daughter to me in marriage. But now I think that it is better to be alone and serve the Lord, as he said that the person who does not marry can serve him in a more effective way. I will continue to serve the Lord until my last breath."

Now Abbas lives with his eighty-five-year-old mother, who is also a strong believer in Christ. He runs a small business and has a prayer room in his home, where many people from the community visit him daily. He prays for them and teaches about repentance, is well-versed in Islamic scriptures and traditions, and knows the local context. He talks to people according to their understanding and needs, uses the Qur'an and the Bible to convey his message of forgiveness of sins and salvation, and has said he always keep this Scripture in mind: "Behold, I am sending you out as sheep in the midst of wolves, so be wise as serpents and innocent as doves" (Matt 10:16 ESV).

Muslim people argue with him, but Abbas says the Holy Spirit guides his responses. He sows the seed of eternal life every day and has gathered a group of believers from Muslim backgrounds.

STORY OF ARIFA

Arifa, a sixty-three-year-old woman living in Pakistan, is the only surviving child of nine in her family. She said, "I was chosen by the Lord from my mother's womb, who called me by his grace for his service."

As a Muslim, Arifa never hated people from other religions because God gave her a loving heart. Her husband always told her not to eat with Christians (considered untouchables by most Muslims), but she always replied, "They are all humans—How I can hate them?"

In 1987, Arifa taught Urdu and Islamic studies in a private school about ten kilometers from her residence. Traveling on a local bus every day with her two daughters, Aarzoo and Aqsa, was difficult—but the only available driver was a Christian, Mr. James, a teacher in another school, who provided car service to students and teachers to earn some extra money.

One day Arifa said to Mr. James, "You are a good person. Why don't you accept Islam?"

He replied, "We both are teachers; therefore, we should have a special discussion on this topic. But I wonder why you said it this way. Suppose I say that all the Muslims would go to hell, and all the Christians would go to heaven. Then what would you have to say?"

She immediately replied, "No. This is impossible."

Mr. James asked, "If you say that you believe in the Torah, the Zaboor (Psalms), and the Injeel (Gospels), then why do you not read those books?"

Arifa instantly responded, "Those books have been corrupted and changed by the Christians and Jews."

He replied, "The Qur'an says that the Word of God cannot be changed, then how is it possible?"

Discussions about Islam and Christianity continued for the next ten years in daily discussions. During that time, Arifa shared these discussions with her parents, who warned her that her husband could divorce her for discussing such things. Mr. James later led Arifa to a Bible study group offered by a senior Muslim-background believer, Mr. Naqvi.

On Good Friday, Arifa visited her mother and announced she was going to attend a special prayer service at Mr. Naqvi's. Her mother was ill and replied to Arifa, "You are the reason for my sickness, because I am afraid that your husband will divorce you one day when he finds out."

Arifa replied that she would pray to Jesus for her mother's healing. That night, her mother had a dream. She saw herself, along with a huge multitude, standing in front of one of the very famous shrines. All the people were waiting for a holy wise man to come and heal them. She saw a holy man in a white robe coming to her, and he told her that she was already healed; she should not stay at that place anymore. After saying these words, he went to the other people.

Arifa took her mother to Naqvi's house, where she recounted the dream. He told her the man in white was Jesus—the way, the truth, and the life; the only way to salvation; and the only mediator between God and humans.

Arifa and her parents became regular members of this Bible study group. In the early 1990s, both parents came to faith in the Lord and were baptized by Mr. Naqvi. Arifa, along with her two daughters, Arzoo and Aqsa, and her son, Saqib, were advised to wait until her husband had come to faith. Arifa tried to share the gospel with her husband, but he became angry.

Arifa's husband, a police officer, strictly watched over her and the children, especially on Sundays. He was not aware of the conversion of his family. The children were facing serious identity issues: they claimed to be Christians among Naqvi's Bible study group, but in school and with extended family they acted like Muslims. They wanted to study "civic education" in place of "Islamic studies," but they could not because only non-Muslims could take that course. They had a sense of dual belonging.

During those years, Arifa's husband was deputized to another city about four hundred kilometers away from their hometown. During a visit home, he asked the children to take him along to their evening class. Not knowing what to do and under great pressure, they led their father around the city, pretending to have forgotten the house. Their father got angry, but they thanked God that the Bible study group was not found.

Finally, Arifa and her three children were baptized. Mr. Naqvi often talked to an uncle at Arifa's parents' house, who refused to accept the Lord until he was hospitalized. Mr. Naqvi and a pastor visited ICU, where the uncle accepted the Lord and was immediately baptized. He lived for twenty-four more days, and then he went to be with the Lord.

In 1998 Mr. Naqvi also went to be with the Lord, a loss for the Muslim-background believers' fellowship that was growing every day. Arifa and her children had lost their spiritual leader, who was like a loving father to Arifa and a grandpa to her kids.

ENCOUNTER WITH FEAR AND DISCOURAGEMENT

During those years when Arifa's huband was still deputized in another city, Arifa's daughter Aqsa visited the local church. Some of her schoolmates who attended the church noticed her—a Muslim girl—there. Aqsa was afraid of reprisal, so her family decided to send her to a Christian school that was far from their neighborhood so that her former classmates and relatives would not know.

In 2003, Arifa's husband accused them of becoming infidels—"the Christians." Out of fear, some Christian groups requested that Arifa and her children not come to Bible study or visit their houses for a while. The family was isolated. Arifa's husband left her and gathered his relatives and decided to take Arifa and her children to the mosque to consecrate their Muslim faith. Arifa and the children were in a serious situation; they would have to announce their Muslim faith by renouncing their Christian faith.

They prayed and discussed this issue with some people from a parachurch organization, who took the family to a safer location. The presence of God was with them, as some Christian men came with a truck in the middle of the night and transported the family to safety. Arifa lived in this safe place with her children and her mother, who had become one of the bravest evangelists in the city, writing contextualized pamphlets and distributing them on public buses. She openly shared her faith with many before she went to be with the Lord in 2018.

For the last sixteen years, various Christians have both helped and discouraged Arifa. Mr. James, the teacher/van driver, continued to help the family until his death in 2004. Arifa said that the faith and commitment of Mr. James led her and some family members to Christ. If Christians would show Christlikeness in their daily lives, then many would come to faith in Christ.

When the children finished their education, there were challenges in finding marriage partners for them. But they remembered the words of Mr. Naqvi: "Always focus on Christ and do not put your eyes on the Christians in terms of what they do to you." Eventually, all three of the children married into Christian families, and they live happy lives, without forgetting to share their faith every day.

Their father, now retired from the police, has started visiting them; they pray for him to come to faith. They open their house to offer Bible study for Muslim-background believers, like Mr. Naqvi did in the past. Their faith and lives speak volumes.

CONCLUSION

The work of the Lord within the community is not limited to these stories. There are many small church-planting movements going on in the mountains, deserts, villages, and megacities of this country. The people are receiving dreams, visions, and wonders as God is gathering a flock of believers from different tribes, languages, and people groups. I have directly recorded a couple of stories where people went for PhD work in the UK or the USA and returned as believers.

There are many challenges to these believers. Local Christians suffer from poverty, despair, and fear; they confine themselves to the church building, sharing the gospel only with traditional Christians. Muslim-background believers face many challenges in Pakistan, the biggest being lack of fellowship. Most mission agencies working in Pakistan lack a follow-up–based program and strategies for new believers. Their focus is outer confession and baptism, and they disappear in the face of sorrows and sufferings.

God helps the Muslim-background believers in ways we can't understand or imagine. We are coworkers with God; we must obey God and not abandon our brothers and sisters who follow Christ. The seed is growing into an orchard in God's time, to be watered and cultivated through prayers and preaching until the harvest.

DISCUSS AND APPLY

- Listen to stories of believers from Muslim background and write them down as an encouragement to you and others in the ministry to Muslims. Make sure not to endanger them by sharing their real names and locations, nor to glorify their lives instead of Christ living in them.

- What does it cost to follow Christ in your context? How can you encourage yourself to be a bold witness for Christ, and how can you help believers from Muslim background as well?

- What are the characteristics of teams that stay—teams that don't disappear in the face of sorrows and sufferings?

BIBLIOGRAPHY

Ahmed, Dawood. "The Two Faces of Religious Persecution in Pakistan." *DAWN*, August 7, 2012. https://www.dawn.com/news/740453.

Ali, Mubarak. *Akbar Ka Hindustan*. Lahore: Tarikh Publications, 2016.

———. *Badalti Hui Tarikh*. Lahore: Tarikh Publications, 2016.

Cox, Jeffrey. *Imperial Fault Lines: Christianity and Colonial Power in India, 1818–1940*. Palo Alto, CA: Stanford University Press, 2002.

Ispahani, Farahnaz. *Purifying the Land of the Pure: Pakistan's Religious Minorities*. Noida Uttar Pradesh: HarperCollins India, 2015.

Ullah, B. *Christianity in Moghul Empire*, Lahore: National Council of Churches in Pakistan, 2010.

———. *Saint Thomas the Apostle of India*. Lahore: National Council of Churches in Pakistan, 2010.

Walker, G. C. *Gazetteer of the Lahore District 1893–94*. Lahore: Sang-e-Meel Publications, 2006.

6 | THE LOVE OF FAITHFUL FAMILIES

Sue Eenigenburg has been involved in cross-cultural ministry for over thirty years. She loves seeing the body of Christ work together to fulfill the purposes of God for his glory.

Naveed and Sara have been working among Muslim unreached people in South Asia for twenty years, serving the Lord as a family. They are passionate to reach people who don't know about Jesus and are both church planters. They want to see thousands of home churches in their area.

Linda Simon is a wife, mother, and medical doctor. With her family, she has served in Central Asia among one of the world's largest unreached Muslim people groups. She has a passion to share the love of Christ with Muslim women and to encourage women workers to thrive in the calling God has given them.

MAIN POINTS NOT TO MISS:

- There are many advantages for families (and single missionaries) living and sharing Christ with Muslim families.
- Blood is the bond of physical families, but so it is with the spiritual family as well. This new family in Christ needs to welcome those who have lost their previous family.

What is truth? Who is my neighbor? Who is my family? Jesus declared life-changing truths as he answered these questions. When we believe and act on these truths, we can better partner with him in mission. This is our aim as we explore how he sees family and how that manifests itself in our cross-cultural witness.

When we think of family, our physical family is what usually comes to mind. It could be parents, siblings, a spouse, children, grandchildren, grandparents, aunts, uncles, cousins, and in-laws. God created physical families and works through them: he established the first marriage through Adam and Eve (Gen 2:24) and told them to be fruitful, and he sets out to redeem humanity through the family of Abraham (Gen 12:1–4). When Jesus considers family, he broadens the definition to include spiritual relatives, highlighting our identity in the family of God. Jesus points out this spiritual family in Mark 3:31–35:

> Then Jesus' mother and brothers arrived. Standing outside, they sent someone in to call him. A crowd was sitting around him, and they told him, "Your mother and brothers are outside looking for you."
>
> "Who are my mother and my brothers?" he asked.
>
> Then he looked at those seated in a circle around him and said, "Here are my mother and my brothers! Whoever does God's will is my brother and sister and mother."

As we look at the love of faithful families in the context of cross-cultural witness to Muslims, we must examine both physical and spiritual family. We see the need to minister as a nuclear family and reach out to other families. As the body of Christ, we also represent a bigger family, a spiritual community that loves and serves one another, testifying of our eternal home. Not only are we sent in physical and spiritual families, but the gospel is also received in and flows through a family context. Physical families are united by blood, but spiritual families are also united by blood—the blood of our Savior who redeemed our souls.

PHYSICAL FAMILY

The call to apostolic witness from our sovereign Lord, who knows the context of our lives and orders our steps, is for the whole family.

Gospel Extended

The story of Noah shows us that God's calling was not just upon Noah but his entire family. God's plan for Noah included his salvation, his wife's, his sons', and his son's wives'. God's calling to Abraham was similar—Sarah was to conceive;

Isaac was to be sacrificed. By God's grace Isaac was spared. The New Testament shows the importance of family unity that honors God in passages such as Ephesians 6, which carries forward the intent of the Ten Commandments, and then Jesus goes beyond biological families to extend the context of family when he says, "For whoever does the will of my Father in heaven is my brother and sister and mother" (Matt 12:50).

Families are called as a family, sent as family, and equipped as family. This is a holistic view of our lives and a freeing truth. We can rest in God as he takes care of us and we can be encouraged to involve our family in our witness.

Linda shares how this is even true for children, from her experience in a more restricted area:

> I was praying for new ways for my daughters to make friends, and God sent me a patient who needed daily care. I invited her to come to my house each day for her medical procedure. Imagine my surprise when she arrived the first day with three daughters the same ages as my three. For two months they were daily visitors at our house, playing with our daughters. Through that time, we all grew close as families in a natural way.

In addition to being cared for, it is easy to see that children open doors to relationships. They are approachable, lighthearted, and nonthreatening. God uses their childlike faith to reach others.

Among Muslims, a whole family can be reached most effectively by another whole family. In some Muslim cultures with strict gender segregation, there are limitations. Women are secluded in homes, behind veils, and under scrutiny of male family members. In conservative Muslim settings, this makes it nearly impossible to reach them, unless contact is made through the whole family, with men reaching men and women reaching women.

Naveed and Sara share their experience in South Asia:

> At the beginning of our ministry we were in the habit of meeting our single friends in parks and hotels, but not in their homes. As we discipled them, we challenged them to share with their families. This proved to be so difficult that we shifted our approach to family-to-family. We and our children spent time with the men, women, and children. We built family relationships. After making this change we saw whole families come to the Lord. One example is Mr. Shahid's family.
>
> Mr. Shahid came to the Lord twenty-three years ago. His family was Muslim, and he found it very difficult to share Christ with them. Our family started to

visit his family five years ago. Sara regularly spent time with his wife, mother, and other women in the extended family. Mr. Shahid said that in the twenty-three years he has known Christ, these five years have been the most fruitful for his family. The faithful love and kindness of our family reaped fruit, and now his family, his brother's family, and others are more open to Jesus. His family members say that his nephews are imitating the way he follows Jesus—they listen to the Bible most of the time and talk about Jesus. His mother listens to the Audio Bible daily, and his sons remember Bible verses.

We see the infinite wisdom of God in sending whole families to reach families. This story not only shows the power of the witness of a family, but also begins to reveal the way the gospel can spread through a family.

Gospel Received

In Muslim societies, trust is often found only within the family. An example of this is that marriage often happens within extended family. This keeps resources within the family, as well as matters of the heart that cannot be entrusted to outsiders. Because of this strong family bond, new fruit can often ripen and take root safely within the context of extended family. Households of faith can withstand outside pressures, worship with one another, and encourage one another in the faith.

In conservative Muslim communities in Central Asia, the church is growing along family lines. Just like in the book of Acts, house churches provide the context for fellowship and worship.

Naveed and Sara share how they go about introducing a person and a family to Jesus in their context, and how the gospel is received:

> We encourage our friends in South Asia who are beginning to follow Jesus to stay with their family. One key to enable new believers to stay in their home is to have the seekers include their family in their spiritual journey early on, even before they become believers. That is, whenever a Muslim requests to study the Bible, we ask him to consider how his parents would feel about it. We encourage him to be open with his family from the start by having a Bible study in his home.

> It is prudent that the goal is simply learning about Jesus, rather than challenging religious beliefs. In this context, having a Bible study in which they learn about the prophets and about Jesus is not a threat and may lead to the salvation of their family.

> Not long after a friend began learning about Christ by meeting with Christians and reading their books, his neighbors began noticing. This was quite

extraordinary in his village. Despite this, he quietly remained in his family. Soon they observed that he became more obedient to his parents and more loving to his family members, friends, and relatives. The villagers pressured his future father-in-law not to allow his daughter to marry him because he had become a Christian. However, his character had impressed his father-in-law enough to take the risk. After their marriage, the man's wife accepted Jesus as her Savior. Now the whole family follows Christ. His father is an imam in a mosque, and he loves to read the Bible with us because he saw the positive changes in his son.

This hints not only to methods that have worked in this context and the transformation that can happen through families, but also to the possibility for displeasure by the community at the decision to follow Christ.

Many Muslim people possess a group identity, in family and in the wider community. They tend to be group decision makers rather than individualistic ones. Women are particularly bound by "community think" and identity. As people enter the kingdom, extreme pressure from the community can be exerted on the new believer, as the story above illustrates. This unbearable pressure can be endured in the context of family. It is amazing how often the lasting fruit in Muslim communities has sprung up from within extended families. God uses the family structure to extend his kingdom through trusted connections.

Because of the religious and cultural constraints that bring persecution to new believers, great wisdom must be sought as new believers come to faith.

It is ideal when families come to faith, since they can be a source of encouragement and strength to each other during persecution. We now turn to examining the spiritual family of God, which provides strength both to the witness of the gospel and to new believers who enter the family of God—especially when they face hostility from their physical family.

SPIRITUAL FAMILY

Believers in Jesus are a spiritual family where all are welcomed into a household of faith. As Paul says in Ephesians 2:19, we are "no longer foreigners and strangers, but fellow citizens with God's people and also members of his household." We have been given the title of "children of God" (John 1:12). How does our collective identity as a spiritual family impact our witness to Muslim neighbors and friends and their identity when they come to faith?

Gospel Extended

Not everyone who is called by God to cross-cultural ministry comes with a family. Single cross-cultural workers have much to offer as members of the family of God. Many single coworkers have much broader networks than those who are married. Because of the high value of family, Muslim neighbors adopt singles into their family. They are often invited to weddings, funerals, birthdays, and holidays with extended family members, where they have many opportunities to share their faith. Singles reflect the gospel as they live out their calling, modeling the all-sufficiency of Christ in every area of their lives in cultures that are normally dependent on people to fulfill those needs.

Single and married people working together also have an opportunity to model spiritual family through celebrating together, supporting and encouraging one another, and giving children and adults extended aunts, uncles, brothers, and sisters. These healthy, pure relationships between brothers and sisters in Christ are often unheard of in host societies.

We must continue asking ourselves questions: Could we do more to model spiritual family within cultural appropriateness and without losing our reputations? How could we be more demonstrative in our roles as brothers and sisters in Christ? What does spiritual family look like in our cultural contexts? Do we adopt relational cultural norms based mainly on fear and innuendo in the community?

Another example of spiritual family witness comes from a single woman living and working in the Muslim world. In the following story, she shares how moving in and living with a biological family made a difference in her life and work. With this change, her individual or personal evangelism became "household evangelism," especially as others in her community could see that she lived her faith in the context of family. Living with her new family, she lived like those in her host culture; not as a single person living alone but in a household that was extended and multigenerational.

> During my first three years, I spent hundreds of hours a month sharing Jesus. Eventually, my one-on-one relationships deepened to the point that many I had met brought me home to meet their families. I became daughter, sister, cousin, auntie, and granddaughter. But I knew my ministry was missing something.

I knew that I was missing that love visible in the space between believers. I began praying for God to bring some semblance of community around me. I imagined that my one-on-one relationships could lead many ways instead of just one—me to her household, her to my household, my household to her household. A few months after I began praying, a family of six, who were in my host city for the same reason I was, invited me to live with them.

We asked big questions to neighbors and researched and took care not to ignore the cultural implications of our convergence. With the blessing of our neighborhood, I moved into my new home. Our household became one that looked like those around us—nuclear family and extended family under one roof, all doing life together. Approaching outreach as a household instead of a single going at it alone changed my ministry in far more dramatic ways than I'd envisioned. Local Muslim households I'd become part of while I was alone became households we invested in deeply together. We suddenly were able to reach entire households at once: our head of household to theirs, mother to mother, sister to sister, children to children.

Modeling spiritual family opens doors to minister to physical families and invites them into a spiritual family. It also opens doors to the lonely, the outcast, the widow, or the divorcee. Those who need family can find it in households reaching out to them! In the book of Deuteronomy, Moses shared God's heart for the aliens, the widows, and the orphans as he called on his people to take care of them and provide for them. He was asking them to be family for them.

Gospel Received

There are times when families will not come to faith together. Wisdom is needed in how new believers engage with their families so they do not unnecessarily insult their family and increase resistance to the gospel. However, even in situations where great wisdom is used, some new believers are ostracized because of their faith. They lose their jobs and their families. They need community.

As the body of Christ, how can we model a family that is stronger than blood to our Muslim neighbors? How can we hold out to them the strong bonds of Jesus' blood family? Surely the family of God can captivate the hearts of our Muslim friends and provide the community they need.

What would this spiritual family look like to a Muslim friend who knows Jesus? Linda and Sue share:

> I (Linda) remember when a new believer was severely burned by her mentally ill husband, and at the same time he committed suicide. As a refugee and new believer, she found herself alone and fighting for her life. She and her nine

children had no one in the city to help her. The family of faith quickly sprang into action to care for her in the hospital and her children at home. Even now, twenty years later, this family of God is all she has.

I (Sue) met with my team regularly—we were married, single, national, or expat believers, loving and caring for one another. We prayed for each other, encouraged each other, worshiped and looked in God's Word together. When a young single woman, the only believer in her family, was facing persecution from her physical family, we stood with her as spiritual family. Whenever she went to her home, her family searched for Christian literature or Scripture, and if they found it they would burn it and threaten her. They wanted her to marry a Muslim man to bring her back into alignment with their family religion. Man after man came to the house only to be rejected by her, as she wanted to marry a follower of Jesus.

Finally, after her father threatened her with death, her mother took her to the religious sheikh as a final appeal. Our sister didn't know what to do. Should she go? Should she run? She looked to her spiritual family for help. As we prayed, we all felt she should go. As her family, each one of us fasted and prayed for her on the day she went with her mother to the sheikh. He explained that every person has a *qarina in the spirit world, and hers was jealous. He told them to stop pressuring her to marry, leave her alone, and eventually the qarina would be appeased. She came back not only rejoicing that God took care of her, but bolder in her faith.*

No decisions like these were made lightly, but as a family we prayed and trusted our heavenly Father together.

"By this everyone will know that you are my disciples, if you love one another" (John 13:35). Our Muslim friends will see a bigger picture of what the family of God can be as the gospel breaks down cultural barriers and invites them into the eternal family of God with people from every tongue, tribe, and nation.

CONCLUSION

When Jesus was dying on the cross, he fulfilled his responsibility to care for his physical parents as the oldest son. He did so by handing over the care of his mother to his disciple John, not one of his half-brothers (John 19:25–27). He recognized and possibly was demonstrating the broader, stronger bond of eternal spiritual family.

Whether bound by physical or spiritual family ties, individually and together we are constrained to share the gospel with those who are lost. We must lovingly offer this promised adoption through faith in Christ to all. John writes in his

Gospel: "Yet to all who did receive him, to those who believed in his name, he gave the right to become children of God—children born not of natural descent, nor of human decision or a husband's will, but born of God (John 1:12–13)."

As those who were once enemies of God, we have now become his children. We are a part of God's family, sharing eternal citizenship with our spiritual brothers and sisters. As part of this eternal family, may we share this good news with others—person to person, family to family, and household to household—so that he will bring the increase of lasting fruit for the glory of his name.

DISCUSS AND APPLY

- What do Muslim families in your context look like? What are the ways to come close to them and become part of one of these families? Start engaging them as a single person or whole family, while praying for them as well.

- Who is your family? Jesus challenged us to think about our family. Certainly we have our biological family. Some have spouses. Some have children. How can singles engage with and through their family? How can those with biological families engage with and through their family rather than each going their separate way?

7 PRAYER: THE FUEL FOR CHANGE

Tamara is the international coordinator for the *30 Days of Prayer for the Muslim World* prayer guide. She and her husband, Jeff, have served with Youth with A Mission for thirty years. Jeff is the director of operations for Vision 5:9, while Tamara is the network administrator.

MAIN POINTS NOT TO MISS:

- Fervent prayer changes the world of Islam—we find more movements to Christ after ongoing prayer efforts than ever before in history.
- Spiritual battles require spiritual means.

For almost fourteen centuries, Islam and Christianity have been engaged in a spiritual battle to capture the allegiance of men and women across the world. For most of that time, Islam has emerged as the clear victor, sweeping tens of millions of Christians Islam. During the first 350 years of Islam's history, Christian populations from the Middle East to Spain were conquered by Islamic armies and later converted to Islam, with few exceptions—while movements to Christianity were few and far between.

In 2014, David Garrison, well-known author and student of the work of God among Muslims, published the findings of several years of research into movements of Muslims to Christ in his book *A Wind in the House of Islam*.[1] Dr. Garrison's discoveries about the number of movements were astonishing, awakening the body of Christ to the big picture of what God has been doing in the Muslim world. Prayer has played and will continue to play an important and necessary part in breakthroughs leading to movements in the Muslim world.

History records that in the year 982 twelve thousand Arab Muslim men (presumably with their families) sought baptism and were converted to Christianity. Records in the twelfth and thirteenth centuries show large numbers of conversions to Christianity two more times, in what is today Lebanon and Libya, respectively. For the next six centuries, however, there is not a single recorded movement of large numbers of Muslims to Christ—while Islam grew unabated.

The first modern-day movement of Muslims to Christ occurred in 1870, in the remote island of Java. This was followed a decade later by a second movement in 1890–1920 in Ethiopia. The twentieth century began with the global distraction of two world wars and a great and global depression. Not until 1967 do we begin to see another movement, this time of more than two million Muslims, again in Indonesia, who were baptized into hundreds of Christian churches.

It was not until the last two decades of the twentieth century, however, that we began to see a significant change in the pattern. Movements broke out in Algeria, Soviet Central Asia, Bangladesh, and Iran. And then, the twenty-first century began, and in the first fourteen years, Muslim movements to Christ multiplied in places where Christ had never previously been preached.

---

1 Monument, CO: WIGTake Resources, 2014. David Garrison called a "movement" as the confirmed baptism of at least one thousand new believers, from the same group of people, who have turned from Islam to faith in Christ.

Since the turn of the century there have been sixty-nine new Muslim movements to Christ using Dr. Garrisons research criteria! The sixty-nine new Muslim movements account for 84 percent of all movements of Muslims to Christianity ever recorded. We are now living through the greatest and most wide-reaching turning of Muslims to Christ in history!

A COINCIDENCE?

In 1993, a group of leaders from a global mission organization gathered for a meeting in the Middle East. They were drawn in prayer to acknowledge their lack of focus on the Muslim world and challenged to be more inclusive in their efforts to see the gospel message reach all peoples, including Muslims.

In response, some of those leaders began an annual prayer event, focused on praying for Muslim people every day for thirty days during the month of Ramadan. This event became known as "30 Days of Prayer for the Muslim World."[2] A prayer guide was produced, helping users to learn more about Islam's beliefs and different Muslim cultures and directing prayer toward some of the least-reached Muslim people groups in the world. Participation in the guide grew, other Christian organizations became involved in helping to translate and distribute it, and today—in 2018—the guide is translated into over thirty languages with estimates of up to one million participants each year.

When Dr. Garrison's research was published, it was impossible to overlook the connection between the time that "30 Days of Prayer for the Muslim World" began to mobilize the body of Christ to pray for Muslims and the sudden growth of movements to Christ in the Muslim world. In this same quarter century, there have been concerted efforts of prayer and more movements to Christ than in all of the history of recorded missions. As believers, we cannot think that this is a coincidence.

PRAYER CHANGES THINGS

Additionally, as part of Dr. Garrison's research, more than a thousand Muslim-background believers from these movements were asked, "What did God use to bring you to faith in Jesus Christ?" Many of the answers that emerged emphasized the significance of prayer and reflect answers to the prayers suggested in the "30 Days of Prayer" guide for Muslims to receive revelations of Jesus.

A Muslim-background believer in North Africa was asked, "Why do you think so many of your people are now having dreams and visions of Christ?"

2 https://www.pray30days.org

She replied, "I believe the prayers of people around the world have been ascending to the heavens, where they have accumulated like great monsoon clouds. Today, they are raining down upon my people miracles of grace and salvation."[3]

According to 2 Corinthians 10:4, prayer is one of the divine weapons given to us to do battle in the spiritual realm. And the work of the Holy Spirit is engaged by our prayers to convict and direct the world toward the truth, as Jesus described in John 16:8–14. Through the prayers of so many in the last two decades, we have seen this happening in the Muslim world. Will it continue to happen?

"30 Days of Prayer for the Muslim World" is not the only prayer event focused on Muslims. Vision 5:9 has developed a prayer calendar, the "10/10 Initiative,"[4] to facilitate an ongoing commitment to prayer, and many of Vision 5:9's partner organizations have their own information and events to mobilize and inform effective prayer for the Muslim world.

This recently recognized connection between persistent prayer and the surge of movements to Christ is not a conclusion, but rather a beginning. It is an inspiration to engage in hopeful prayer, with the assurance of even more movements spreading throughout the Muslim world. This evidence that abiding in God's presence in prayer on behalf of the Muslim world bears fruit— such fruit!—should motivate the body of Christ to even greater commitment and support of such prayer initiatives.

DISCUSS AND APPLY

- Consider joining one of the prayer movements, praying regularly for the Muslim world, and even participate in fasting when and where possible. Pray by name for the local Muslim leaders, as well as for the families you know.

- Mobilize your church for prayer: share regularly about the needs and how God answers prayer, distribute prayer resources to believers, and invite believers into your home and church for prayer. The links below will help with practical material.

PRAYER LINKS

- Prayercast: https://prayercast.com
- 30 Days of Prayer: https://www.30daysprayer.com
- 10/10 Initiative: https://1010prayerandfasting.wordpress.com
- Many mission organizations have prayer resources regarding prayer for the Muslim world.

3 *30 Days of Prayer for the Muslim World*, 2015 edition, 39.
4 https://1010prayerandfasting.wordpress.com/home/vision-1010/

8 | ORGANIZATIONAL THREATS AND OPPORTUNITIES

Martin Hall is a founding member of Vision 5:9, serving on the international leadership team. He has worked with OM among Muslims for thirty-nine years and is presently OMUK's (OM in UK) Muslim Ministries Ambassador, a role he shares with his wife. Martin is the adjunct Islamics lecturer at Regent's Theological College and a cultural coach to the senior management of many major brands.

John Becker served as International Coordinator of the Vision 5:9 network for ten years. He is now the Global Strategy Director for AIM International and VP for Global Networking and Partnership for GACX (Global Alliance for Church Multiplication). He has been serving Muslim peoples in Africa, Europe, and North America for the past twenty-five years and currently lives in California with his wife and four children.

MAIN POINTS NOT TO MISS:

- As the Muslim world has changed and still is undergoing change, so mission organizations need to change as well to effectively reach out to Muslims.

- It takes bold evaluation and a commitment to sharing Christ where he is least known to rekindle the passion of the past pioneers for a future of harvest in the Muslim world.

The member organizations in the Vision 5:9 network represent many different structures, cultures, and purposes. Some began recently, while others formed over a century ago. But all organizations are at risk of failing to change when change is required. God calls us to follow him and his calling, not our organizational structures. Yet many groups have failed to reach their potential in the harvest field because of the fear of change or reluctance to evaluate themselves and try new things.

This chapter will highlight two long-term Vision 5:9 member organizations—Operation Mobilization (OM) and Africa Inland Mission (AIM)—which have boldly pursued organizational change to be more effective at engaging and reaching Muslim people.

The Muslim world has changed; missions has changed. Has your organization changed to adapt to the threats and opportunities that could impact your efforts at reaching unreached Muslims? Here are the stories of two organizations that have evaluated the threats to their success and embraced the opportunities for more fruitfulness.

The Tailwinds and the Headwinds– OM's Journey to Keep Their Its Calling

MARTIN HALL

"Are you OK?" the guide asked as he saw me choking up.

He had closed the door on me in a tiny prison cell in the Apartheid Museum in Johannesburg, South Africa. Unexpectedly, this took me back to 1979, when I spent time in a Turkish prison cell during my first year in Operation Mobilization (OM). I had joined OM because its members would do whatever was required to share the good news with those who had not heard, even if it meant ending up in a prison cell.

Forty years later (and still safely out of prison), I am writing about how OM realized that we risked losing that calling and the opportunities we had to keep it.

Operation Mobilization began in 1957 with a strong focus on sharing the good news, especially with the unreached, whatever the cost. The 1960s was a revolutionary decade, an era of passionate beliefs with a willingness to follow those beliefs whatever the consequences. OM rode that tailwind and people joined—seeking community, willing to sacrifice, wanting to put their faith into action. This took us all over the world to share the gospel with as many people as quickly as possible.

A tailwind is a wind blowing in the same direction an aircraft or ship is traveling. Tailwinds can change direction, so a good pilot seeks them out to find the ones that are helpful in getting to the destination faster, with less resistance. Traveling into a headwind is the opposite of this. This analogy relates to OM as we seek to identify global trends that we can move with while not taking our eye off our destination.

Over the first forty years, OM established itself in 110 countries and visited many more with OM ships. We attracted pioneers and entrepreneurs and started hundreds of ministries and projects. As the evangelical church embraced social justice, we expanded into compassionate ministries, justice, arts, and sport. As the pioneers added ministries, our settlers added structure to keep us together.

Toward the end of 2013, Lawrence Tong was appointed as the international director of OM with a call to innovate. In 2015, I asked Lawrence about OM's role in Vision 5:9 and the goal of placing effective church-planting teams among all unengaged Muslim peoples by 2025. Lawrence said, "Imagine if our next project goal was not a ship or a building but to reach one hundred unreached peoples!"

OM began with a passion for those who had never heard the gospel. However, by 2015 our focus on unreached people groups had become rather vague. Was it possible to refocus on our original calling again, with all our creative, compassionate, and justice ministries?

In 2015, finding ourselves with over five decades of "add-ons" in both mission and structure, we asked ourselves two questions:

1. What is our mission?

2. Does our structure serve our mission, or are we serving our structure?

To answer these questions, we started with a year of deep consultation within OM. Interviews were offered to all senior leaders and members, asking about how OM was structured, what our mission was, and where we thought change was needed. The results were very revealing. We found fifty-four different OM mission statements around the globe! Some were just variations on a theme, but some were quite different. With structure focused around local operations that attracted pioneers and entrepreneurs, this was not surprising.

We also found numerous layers of decision making in our structure, potentially taking several years to authorize change. Again, not surprising when you have spent decades "adding on" structure to keep up with your pioneers.

Of course, this is a simple description of the situation. We had conducted strategic reviews and restructuring at times, but our corporate culture had generally left us running in many directions—doing lots of great ministry, but often with structures we served rather than structures that served us. The interviews showed that most OM leaders did not understand how OM worked or how to effect change through our structures.

It was clear that change was needed.

A proposal was made to have one global mission statement, which became: "We want to see vibrant communities of Jesus followers amongst the least reached." A second proposal followed—to totally restructure so we could enable OM to fulfill that statement.

The process of getting to this point was transparent, using different communications tools to avoid any one person dominating the discussion and inviting questions from all. This transparency gave ownership of the change to the organization. I was amazed to see that 97 percent of our leaders voted for adopting these proposals. Transparency and inclusion were keys to moving forward in one mind.

Much has been left out of this reflection, but it is important to note that other important elements of our journey included prayer, silent retreat, and a sense of celebration, along with diligent preparation and presentations by OM leadership. Our leadership meetings in 2016 were a surprise for me—at times more like a worship meeting than a business meeting. But why shouldn't business be our worship? Of course, there were concerns about where some of our ministries would fit within the new mission statement. Yet we agreed together that if those that have never heard are to have the chance to hear, we must change radically.

Three years on, OM is moving from being a broad, multi-focused mission to having a single focus of "wanting to see vibrant communities of Jesus followers amongst the least reached." We need many ministry expressions to achieve this, and all our teams have been required to state how they are working toward that goal. Rather than exclude our compassionate and creative ministries, it has refocused and refreshed them, as indeed it has the whole movement. Personally, I feel again that passion that inspired me to risk everything to join. We are finding the tailwind that will carry us to our destination.

If tailwinds are the opportunities that will take us forward, headwinds are threats that will stop us from making progress. In mission, we must adapt to take full advantage of tailwinds in global trends, rather than press on against a strong headwind and see our perseverance as a virtue.

The biggest threat to accomplishing our mission is our relationships. Relationship is the heart of God. We are called to hold to truth, living out what we preach, but too easily we "bite and devour each other" when we disagree (Gal 5:15). The challenge of placing effective church-planting teams amongst all unengaged Muslim peoples will only be accomplished by working together, and the opportunities for partnership have never been greater. Our mission statement says what we want to see happen, but not that we must do it—it is enough to see our mission accomplished by someone else, through partnership.

One of the strongest tailwinds we need to be following is the growth of the proximate church: the believers who are geographically and culturally close to the unengaged or least reached. I was recently visiting an OM team who is planting churches among a cluster of unengaged Muslim unreached people groups (UMUPGs). While there, the leader got a call from an exploratory team he had sent out; they had found two local Christians close to one of the UMUPGs who were eager to be trained in church planting, which our team provided. So far, they have planted twelve churches amongst unengaged Muslim people groups. The proximate church will go further and faster; we just need to lend a helping hand.

Jesus warned us about the greatest headwind, or threat, that we face: "The harvest is plentiful but the workers are few." But he gave us a simple answer: "Ask the Lord of the harvest, therefore, to send out workers into his harvest field" (Matt 9:37–38).

As Vision 5:9 looks at our part of that harvest field—effective engagement of all Muslim peoples—we must begin by applying Jesus' simple answer: praying for more workers. We also need to recognize the tailwinds, or opportunities, in that prayer: the mobilization of the church in the Global South. The challenge is to find new sending structures that can send thousands of workers into the harvest field. Our present structures, dependent on raising support, cannot achieve this alone. Expatriate and migrant workforces, a global trend of our time, can be a tailwind for sending out workers if we can embrace the secular as sacred in our mission.

In OM we are returning to our calling, but within a twenty-first century context. This was unachievable with our old structures, so we have rebuilt them from scratch. Understanding which global trends are tailwinds that we need to travel with is vital if we are "to see vibrant communities of Jesus followers amongst the least reached."

Learning and Growing in Focus and Fruit– Organizational Change in Africa Inland Mission
JOHN BECKER

Lanny Arensen, then international director for AIM, returned from the Singapore 2002 mission conference, Advancing Strategies of Closure among All Unreached Peoples,[1] with cautious enthusiasm. He had participated in the Muslim Peoples track,[2] and I remember him saying, "Let's check this out, John!" to the invitation to participate in follow-up conversations led by Vision 5:9 in England. The purpose was to discover the state of the gospel in the Muslim world and learn what church-planting strategies are bearing fruit.[3]

At that meeting with leaders from ten organizations, everyone was initially very reluctant when asked to share where their teams were serving. However, a community of trust and interdependency began to develop. In a way, the network provided positive peer pressure that helped organizations like AIM make courageous, and sometimes costly, changes to better serve the remaining task.

In AIM, we were struck by the enormous amount of work remaining. Africa Inland Mission was founded in 1895 by Peter Cameron Scott, a man with a vision to create mission stations from Mombasa to Lake Chad. He died of blackwater fever in his first year, having walked 2,600 miles placing workers in four locations.[4] This vision for the unreached parts of Africa continued to be our mandate.[5] But 120 years later the vision still seemed out of reach. Of the 3,700 unique ethnic people groups in Africa, 1,000 of them, over three hundred million people, still had no viable gospel witness.

Though we hadn't lost our priority of church planting among the unreached, we had gained a growing number of wonderful, fruit-bearing ministries that did not serve the remaining task. We became aware of our need for collaboration and the opportunity we had to change. Learning where others were engaging the

1 http://www.missionfrontiers.org/issue/article/singapore-021.
2 http://www.ijfm.org/PDFs_IJFM/20_1_PDFs/05%2013s02reportfixed.pdf.
3 http://www.missionfrontiers.org/issue/article/what-must-be-done
4 Dick Anderson, *We Felt Like Grasshoppers* (Crossway Books, 1994), 17-22; https://dacb.org/
   stories/kenya/scott-petercameron/.
5 http://www2.wheaton.edu/bgc/archives/GUIDES/081.htm.

Muslim world and seeing fruit was stimulating. Learning how others were mobilizing, training, and deploying teams to meet their organizational priorities for the unreached was faith-stretching. AIM's involvement in the Vision 5:9 network started moving us toward organizational change.

Significant influence came through the Fruitful Practices Task Force, which wanted to know how churches were being planted in the Muslim world. Vision 5:9 member organizations were asked to collect case studies and evaluate how their teams were succeeding in planting churches. We took the opportunity to call our first AIM church planters' consultation. Bringing together leaders and church planters revealed that we needed to increase our efforts at church planting and be more consistent in training toward fruitfulness.

We also began serious organizational restructuring. We created regions with appointed, rather than elected, leaders, so that we could use our resources more effectively and extend our work into new areas in North Africa and the Horn of Africa, where many of the unreached peoples were.

Possibly the greatest advance came in clarifying our vision. We set a clear statement and priorities: "With priority for the unreached, Christ-centered churches among all Africa's peoples."[6] We also needed a simple definition of "church" to measure progress more effectively. We realized that our previous measurement was so idealistic that it was not realistic. In fact, we realized that none of us could honestly say that we were currently in a church that fully measured up! So we created a definition of church that focused more on discipleship and less on structure: "an assembly of disciples who know and reflect their identity in Christ expressed through corporate worship and mission."[7]

We also adopted the Vision 5:9 definition of "engagement,"[8] so that we could better track our progress on identifying the unengaged and our work among them.

Sharpening our vision and creating new priorities led to some inevitable, but painful, pruning. We were a one-thousand-member organization serving in about thirty-five nations with many legacy ministries.[9] Luke Herrin,

6 AIM international council minutes, Bristol, England, November, 2007.
7 AIM definitions, 2008.
8 Vision 5:9 Global Trends definitions: a pioneer church-planting effort resident; a commitment to work in the local language and culture; a commitment to long-term ministry; a commitment to sow and train in a manner consistent with the goal of seeing multiplication of disciples or a church-planting movement.
9 Including office staff, mobilizing regions, and short-term workers.

AIM's international director, courageously set about creating a framework for ministry that defined our preferred culture: service, sacrifice, suffering, seeking, and submission; and a central ministry focus: disciple-making among UPGs of Africa, mobilizing churches and believers to missional disciple-making, equipping leaders for African churches, and serving and supporting those engaged in these activities.[10] All AIM members and new initiatives would need to fit into the framework.

This decision was costly to many who felt devalued and forgotten. There were many long conversations and a process to adopt the framework or begin the process of transitioning ministry. Though we are still on this journey, the process has been invigorating and we are experiencing great fruit. As the following graph shows, the overall number of AIM members serving unreached people groups has risen from 24 percent in 2007, when we first started to collect this data, to nearly 50 percent! This is a real change in our mission direction and culture.[11]

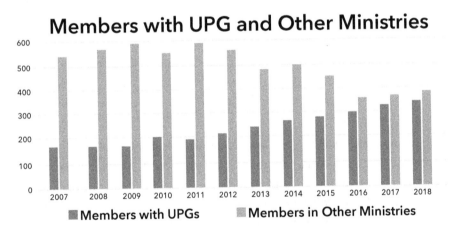

Members with UPG and Other Ministries

■ Members with UPGs   ■ Members in Other Ministries

We have encouraged each other by holding ourselves accountable to reason for existence. Foremost, has been our growing posture of prayer. We corporately pray and fast and have doubled our efforts to invite others to pray for Africa.[12] Generous abiding with the Lord is discussed and practiced together and modeled by leaders.

---

10 AIM Member Handbook, 2018.
11 See the following graph. (% determined by "members with UPGs" divided by "members with UPGs" plus "members in other ministries) x 100)
12 www.prayafrica.org.

We created shorter-term goals and specific measurement tools to chart progress toward our priorities.[13] The data is encouraging—consistently trending up in almost every category and in every year. We now engage eighty UPGs and are seeing increases in baptisms and new churches. AIM members are more consistently and intentionally sharing their faith daily.[14]

Regarding measurements, Luke Herrin shared this in his last monitoring report:

> Collecting and analyzing data is good stewardship.... Good stewardship requires that we measure our impact: How is the Lord using us? What of significance is being accomplished? The data should guide us as we consider how to proceed. We need to carefully pray, think, plan, and measure progress to be more fruitful in God's kingdom.[15]

We recognized the priority of partnership and that the harvest force is in the harvest field. AIM has always had fruit-bearing partnership with African ministries. However, we are now on our greatest journey yet—and that is to meaningfully increase our African membership. There are 180 million evangelicals in Africa, in countless indigenous organizations, with hundreds of leaders who have global impact. We've begun to listen and learn more actively and establish fruit-bearing partnerships. AIM was thrilled to help dozens of Muslim-background African workers attend the Abide, Bear Fruit Global Consultation on Ministry to Muslims in 2017.

Our most relevant question now is how we can serve the African mission movement to most effectively reach our vision and fulfill our mandate. This servant posture is forcing us to rethink our funding structures, our team approaches, needed skill sets, and a host of other things. Although this is unsettling, it has opened exciting opportunities for strategic involvement such as the Go North Initiative,[16] which seeks to mobilize and equip Sub-Saharan church planters to North Africa.

Surely it is an exciting era of mission collaboration! Recognizing the danger in not adapting, AIM is ready to be at the center of what God is doing as we continue to depend on and abide in him, taking new opportunities so that we might bear much fruit from among all the peoples of Africa, so that Christ is glorified everywhere.

---

13 http://eu.aimint.org/about/vision2020/.
14 Forty-four percent of AIMers share their faith daily, according to 2018 data.
15 AIM monitoring report, May, 2018.
16 Also known as S2NP—South to North Partnership.

DISCUSS AND APPLY

- What is the task you are facing, and what's it like? What are the changes that occurred since the organization began? How is the organization facing these changes, and is it still effective in its task? Where would it need to change?

- It takes bold evaluation to assess the effectiveness of your ministry and organization. Would you like help in doing so? If so, please contact Jim Haney at jimrayhaney@gmail.com.

- Is your organization or team aligned with what God is doing in the Muslim world? If not, what can you do to address barriers to your alignment with him?

BIBLIOGRAPHY

Africa Inland Mission, International—Collection 8, Wheaton, Billy Graham Center Archives, viewed on 1 May 2019, https://www2.wheaton.edu/bgc/archives/GUIDES/081.htm.

———.Definitions, AIM, Bristol, England, 2008.

———.Member Handbook, AIM, Bristol, England, 2018.

———.Minutes, AIM, Bristol, England, 2007.

———. Monitoring Report, AIM, Bristol, England, 2018.

———.Pray Africa, AIM, Bristol, England, https://prayafrica.org. 2019.

———.Vision 2020, AIM, Bristol, England, https://eu.aimint.org/about/vision2020, 2019.

Anderson, D. *We Felt Like Grasshoppers.* London: Crossway Books, 1994.

Becker, J. "What Must Be Done?" *Mission Frontiers*, http://www.missionfrontiers.org/issue/article/what-must-be-done, 2017.

Parsons, G. "A Report on Singapore 2002," *Mission Frontiers*, 20:1, http://www.ijfm.org/PDFs_IJFM/20_1_PDFs/05%2013s02reportfixed.pdf. 2003.

Smith, S. "Vision for a Refugee Kingdom Movement," *Mission Frontiers*, 31, http://www.missionfrontiers.org/issue/article/singapore-021,2016.

Vision 5:9, Global Trends Task Force 2006, Definitions. Adopted from Liverman, J. "What Does it Mean to Effectively 'Engage' a People?," *Mission Frontiers*, http://www.missionfrontiers.org/issue/article/what-does-it-mean-to-effectively-engage-a-people.

9

ASSESSING KINGDOM MOVEMENTS FOR MUSLIM PEOPLES

Jim Haney served as Director of Global Research for the International Mission Board, Richmond, Virginia, and coordinator for Vision 5:9's Global Trends Task Force from 2005 to 2018. Before that Jim planted churches among Muslims peoples in West Africa for eighteen years. Jim has written and spoken widely on missions and missiology.

MAIN POINTS NOT TO MISS:

- Movements are what God is doing to establish his kingdom. When we look at his movements, we see his kingdom unfolding whether in a place, a people, or a person.

- We play our part in kingdom movements by proclaiming the gospel of the kingdom through the whole world as a testimony to all nations.

In Matthew 24:14 (ESV), Jesus said, "This gospel of the kingdom will be proclaimed throughout the whole world as a testimony to all nations, and then the end will come." This verse establishes our agenda for proclaiming the gospel of the kingdom and Jesus' promise that there will be a day when we can no longer proclaim.

There is a clear distinction between our part and God's part. Our part is to proclaim the gospel of the kingdom faithfully throughout the whole world as a testimony to all nations. God's part is to be with us to the end of the age, and then he will establish his kingdom forever. It seems reasonable that if you and I are to work toward kingdom movements, we should take some time to understand the depth of the kingdom and to put its principles into practice. The kingdom is much more than baptisms and generations of churches.

Jesus helped his disciples focus on the kingdom—his kingdom. Without a clear understanding of his kingdom, how would they ever proclaim "this gospel of the kingdom"? They expected the Messiah to come and restore their kind of kingdom—the kingdom of Israel. They begged and pleaded with him to give them their kind of kingdom, even as he ascended into heaven.[1]

However, Jesus taught that his kingdom is different—those who follow Jesus should be busy sowing in all the soils, persevering among the tares, maturing like the mustard seed, spreading like the yeast, forsaking everything owned to gain a treasure and pearl of great price, obtaining righteousness through Christ to be gathered into his net.[2] The kingdom takes time to understand, and kingdom movements come according to God's timing, not ours. If we don't understand the kingdom, we don't understand the gospel of the kingdom. We do not want movements unless they are kingdom movements.

Let's think together then about assessing kingdom movements, whether disciple-making movements or church-planting movements. We should think together about the essentials of what it means to be a transformed disciple of Jesus Christ and the essentials of what it means to be a church of Christ-followers. When we listen to God by taking instruction from Scripture about his kingdom, we can assess whether the people groups our teams are engaging are experiencing kingdom movements.

---

1 Acts 1:6 shows us that the question the disciples asked Jesus before he ascended was about the kingdom of Israel.
2 Parables of the kingdom in Matthew 13.

ENGAGEMENT

Before the year 2000, "workamong" was the preferred term for missionary activities. A list was kept showing which people groups had missionaries working among them and which did not. "Workamong" implied that whatever work was underway among a people group by missionaries was missionary work. While a lot of good things were accomplished by missionaries over the years, a more specific term was needed to focus teams on making disciples. As a result, *engagement* was a term adopted by IMB in 1999 to keep teams focused on *implementing church-planting strategies*[3] among the peoples of the world. People groups without teams implementing church-planting strategies and with insufficient believers to carry out this task for themselves became UUPGs—unengaged, unreached people groups.

In 2006, Jeff Liverman suggested four essential elements for effectively engaging Muslim people groups:[4]

1. Apostolic (pioneering) effort in residence,
2. Commitment to working in the local language and culture,
3. Commitment to long-term ministry,
4. Sowing in a manner consistent with the goal of seeing a church-planting movement (CPM) emerge.

Vision 5:9 adopted the definition as a great starting point for teams. These criteria suggest that teams live among the people they seek to engage, they are sensitive to language and culture, they come to stay and make a home, and they avoid hindrances that might prevent a movement from emerging.

Additionally, these elements reflect how Christ first engaged our world. He was sent by God to live with man. He came and spoke our language. He lived with careful attention to the cultures of his day. He worked to see a movement emerge, just as word spread about his ministry. He was committed to a long-term ministry among those he loved. And most of all, he showed his faithfulness in the long term by ministering to disciples then and now through the presence of the Holy Spirit. Jesus came to live among us, and those who engage well live among the people groups they engage with a deepening burden and love for them.

---

3 See "What is an Unengaged People Group," IMB Global Research, http://peoplegroups.org/294. aspx#307.
4 Jeff Liverman, "What Does It Mean to Effectively 'Engage' a People?" *Mission Frontiers* (November-December 2006), 10-12.

ASSESSMENTS

In his parable of the persistent widow, Jesus assures us that God will bring about justice for his elect who cry out to him day and night. He will not defer help indefinitely. In fact, "He will give justice to them speedily." But this is followed by a haunting question: "Nevertheless, when the Son of Man comes, will he find faith on earth?" (Luke 18:7–8 ESV).

We are obliged to meet a lost world with the gospel of the kingdom so that the injustice of living a life without Christ is met with loving teams—willing to present the gospel of the kingdom, engaging and reaching people groups with the message of the cross. We are told to watch, to work, to prepare, to proclaim, and to ask for his kingdom to come on earth as it is in heaven. When the Son of Man comes, we want him to find faith on earth in every people group of the world.

We undertake assessments to make sure his message of love is reaching every language, people, tribe, and nation. Thus assessment teams look for evidence of the kingdom in every people of the world. That's why we carry around lists of people groups, and verify that reports about them are valid and current; and that's why we advocate for those who are perishing without Christ.

ENGAGEMENT ASSESSMENTS

Engagement assessments are conducted to evaluate a team's entry into a people group and to make sure that the essential elements for effectively engaging a people group are present.

These assessments:

1. Accurately describe the history, nature, and extent of involvement by one or more teams in one or more people groups or population segments.
2. Accurately describe the results of involvement by one or more teams in one or more people groups or population segments.
3. Identify effective and ineffective strategies and practices and clarify how such provide opportunities and obstacles for future involvement.
4. Determine the degree to which the involvement of one or more teams is contributing to effective engagement among one or more people groups or population segments.

An engagement assessment is conducted by a team in a way that is culturally appropriate. They listen carefully to those they interview to understand what Christ is doing in their lives. Assessments should be conducted respectfully and in a way that provides a safe opportunity to listen.

Ultimately, assessment teams must answer two questions for every people group reported as engaged:

1. Did the assessment team find evidence of engagement by one or more teams?
☐ Yes ☐ No

2. How effective is the engagement?
☐ Highly Effective ☐ Effective ☐ Somewhat Effective
☐ Ineffective ☐ Highly Ineffective

In order to answer these questions, those who want to conduct an engagement assessment must select a team leader to take responsibility for the assessment, and he or she must call together a team of mature believers, experienced in church planting, ready to listen, and knowledgeable of the context of the engaged people group.

Once a team has agreed to conduct an assessment, they must determine the best methodology for moving ahead. Methodologies should consider the best way to gather narratives and numbers from believers and leaders.

To me, testimonies of believers are highly significant. With these, the numbers have little value. Remember when Jesus turned the water into wine in John 2? He told the servants to fill six large jars with water. Some estimate that this could have been as much as 150 gallons of water. Then he turned the water into wine, and the wine itself was of the highest quality. It is the combination of "six large jars" and "high quality," along with an instant result, that was most remarkable. The relationship between numbers and narrative is critical to establishing the context for understanding the nature and extent of God's activity among a people group. One of the greatest parts of an assessment, therefore, is hearing evidence of wonderful manifestations of God's power in the lives of believers and churches.

Assessment teams should interview the engagement team as well as representatives of the people group reported to be engaged—church planters, pastors, members, elders, men and women. After interviews are completed, members of the assessment team will sit together and discuss their findings, and these sessions lead the team to a consensus regarding what they have heard. Ultimately the assessment team documents what they learn—especially effective and ineffective strategies—so that their findings are clearly documented and communicated to the engagement team.

In addition to deciding on a methodology, assessment teams should carefully consider the reliability of the many and varied information sources they utilize during their work. Often, teams will find information from different sources that seems to conflict. Teams need to press on to resolve apparent anomalies until they are resolved. The final report must include a brief discussion of sources used by the team and an evaluation of their reliability. The two primary sources for information for an engagement assessment are members of the engagement team and believers from the people group they are engaging.

Assessment teams must make sure that the assessment is conducted in a way that does no harm, ensuring that the team's presence, organizational identity, and activities do not jeopardize the safety of individuals or ongoing ministry where the assessment takes place. For example, those conducting assessments must be careful to provide a safe place where those being interviewed can freely talk.

In one assessment conducted in South Asia, the safest way for believers to talk freely was to invite them to a safe location in a large city. The team rented a hall, interviewed those invited, and provided refreshments as they shared their stories. In an assessment in East Asia, the team determined that they could interview in local churches if they did not stay in any location for more than an hour. In another assessment in East Africa, the assessment team trained near-culture church planters to conduct interviews and then report back what they found.

Assessment teams must make sure that they have taken every possible measure so that people can share what Christ is doing in their lives without feeling threatened and afraid. The goal is to provide a safe place where those interviewed can testify about what God is doing in their lives. Assessment team members often separate leaders, pastors, church members, men and women, and interview each group separately. Then, when all interviews have been conducted, the assessment team compares their findings.

Assessment teams must be careful to avoid asking long lists of questions. It's easier to begin by asking those who may have traveled a long distance just to share their story about God. As you might expect, some who share are new believers. They likely will not be able to explain the deeper truths of following Jesus. Others, such as pastors and church planters, are likely to be more mature in their faith, and they often have amazing understanding and commitment to the Lord.

Assessment teams should be careful to facilitate dialogue and avoid pointed and embarrassing questions. When we ask people to share what God is doing in their lives, they love sharing what God is doing. When we ask questions that they cannot answer, we shouldn't be surprised by inconsistent numbers or contrived answers offered to make the assessment team happy with their report. This latter point is particularly true in cultures that are highly relational.

Assessing kingdom movements is about identifying changes and transformations in believers. If the gospel of the kingdom is proclaimed but there is no evidence in transformed lives, the kingdom may have come near, but it has not come in. Pioneering teams live among people, share the gospel in a way that is appropriate in language and culture, and stay until they see fruit, by God's grace—transformed hearts, wills, affections, emotions, purpose, and relationships.

There is a lot of joy in conducting an engagement assessment if it is done the right way. Remember, when we are listening to people who have been impacted by the gospel of the kingdom, we are not just gaining an understanding about how well they have been engaged; we are seeing the glory of God in the lives of those he is transforming into his likeness.

As the assessment team ends each day, they should sit together and discuss two questions:

1. Did the assessment team find evidence of engagement by one or more teams?
   ☐ Yes ☐ No

2. How effective is the engagement?
   ☐ Highly Effective ☐ Effective ☐ Somewhat Effective
   ☐ Ineffective ☐ Highly Ineffective

The team may share any notes that they have made to support their feedback to the whole team. Also, it is good to use this time at the end of the day to thank God for what has been shared and to intercede for needs that are apparent.

One of the most exciting things in an engagement assessment is to discover things about what God is doing. What we learn from assessments adds to our own understanding of who God is and how much he loves us. Assessment teams hear firsthand that "even the demons are subject" to those who are sent by Jesus.

Ultimately, as the gospel of the kingdom is shared and evaluated, we who engage the peoples of the world have the privilege of preparing the bride for the Groom who is coming. Jesus will come when he is ready, and our work is to prepare his bride, the church.

CHURCH-PLANTING MOVEMENT ASSESSMENTS

While we can control how we engage people groups through faithful teams who share the gospel of the kingdom, we cannot predict where the imperishable seed of the gospel will fall and where we will see fruit. There are times when the gospel of the kingdom, abundantly sown, does not result in any observable harvest, but there are other times when what is sown in good soil "bears fruit and yields, in one case a hundredfold, in another sixty, and in another thirty" (Matt 13:23 ESV).

Church-planting movements (CPMs) are rare in the Muslim world. Again, the fruit of a CPM among any Muslim people group is the transformation that is evident in the stories of multiplying disciples of Jesus Christ. Church-planting movement assessments must consider the same aspects that are important to engagement assessments—team composition, methodology, security, and the purpose of the assessment. When these elements are carefully put in place, the assessment team can begin to listen to the stories of those who have been transformed.

Of course, transformation takes time—stories reveal the imperfections of every believer in Christ. While some who are interviewed in CPM assessments show great maturity and beautiful stories of faith, others are just beginning their journey with Christ. As CPMs spread, the gospel of the kingdom undergoes spiritual attacks—Satan is not going to let a movement spread without challenging it on all fronts. He will use anything to stop a kingdom movement. Assessment teams can help believers identify both opportunities and obstacles to kingdom movements. As these are discovered, there is time for praise, confession, repentance, and supplication that show ultimate dependency on the Lord of the Harvest.

When we assess a movement and people share their journeys with us, their stories may be quite similar to accounts we read about in the Gospels, Acts, or Paul's epistles. Why shouldn't it be this way? God is still active in the lives of believers today. At the same time, just as the early churches had problems, assessments reveal similar problems today. We can be grateful for a description of some of the issues faced in the early church because we can learn from these and apply them to our own lives.

Ultimately, the assessment team thanks God for the essentials of disciples and New Testament churches that are multiplying, while asking for God's help for where these essentials are lacking. Movements are fanned by the power of the Holy Spirit if the Holy Spirit is providing the movement, but movements collapse when there is wrath, anger, bitterness, competition, mixed beliefs, jealousy, and the flesh—when believers are not submitted to our Lord.

While we want the gospel of the kingdom to be preached to the whole world as a witness to all peoples, unfortunately great harm has come to people groups when something other than the gospel is spreading. It is the work of the assessment teams to listen carefully in love so that issues can be addressed lovingly and with great patience.

DISCUSS AND APPLY

- What are the New Testament essentials of a kingdom movement?

- What are some of the qualities of the kingdom that you see among Muslim-background believers that you know? Do you see evidence of transformed disciples? Of healthy churches?

If you would like to be trained to conduct an engagement assessment or movement assessment, serve on an assessment team, or suggest where an assessment is needed, please contact me at jimrayhaney@gmail.com.

BIBLIOGRAPHY

Garrison, David. *Church Planting Movements*. Monument, CO: WIGTake Resources, 2004; http://www.churchplantingmovements.com.

Haney, Jim. "Assessing Church Planting Movements." *Mission Frontiers*, March–April 2011, 14–16.

10 THE HOPES, DREAMS, AND PRAYERS OF YOUNGER WORKERS IN THE MUSLIM WORLD

Michael Kaspar relates to and collaborates with nongovernmental organizations (NGOs) and church leaders as Director of Global Initiatives with visionSynergy. He loves stories, questions, and celebrating the good work others do, as well as integrating God's Word in whatever he does. Michael has served as catalyst for the Vision 5:9 network and is a Catalyst for Ministry Collaboration with the Lausanne Movement. He also served with OM in several leadership roles for more than a decade.

MAIN POINTS NOT TO MISS:

- The next generation needs to be involved with their specific skills on all levels as they share the burden for the Muslim world with their mentors and role models.

- Young leaders are committed to disciple making among unreached Muslim peoples, using the biblical methodology of abiding in Christ, sharing Scriptures, and praying for breakthroughs among Muslims.

"Now when David had served God's purpose in his own generation, he fell asleep." —Acts 13:36

Thinking back to your childhood, when was the first moment you remember hoping for something? Was it a favorite food? Was it to see a favorite person? When you hope for something, desire for a future reality fills you.

A younger generation of Christ-followers serving among Muslim peoples are pouring out their lives for the gospel, sometimes in very difficult and hostile areas. They are cross-cultural workers, near-culture workers, and Muslim-background believers. In this chapter, we will feel the heart of this generation under age forty by observing their hopes, breakthrough ideas, and prayers.

This next generation carries deep convictions about demonstrating love for God, abiding in Jesus, enjoying God's Word, and doing significant work in the world—especially among unreached and unengaged Muslim peoples. They possess genuine love for Muslims and a belief that prayer and fasting is critical in life. They have a vision for creativity and collaboration to see breakthroughs in difficult areas and a keen awareness that their lives will likely include suffering.

What may differ from the generation before them is a native ability to use technology, a more natural tendency to collaborate to accomplish work, a globally connected orientation, and a view that work and ministry must be integrated. Like all generations, this generation of Christ-followers in the Muslim world stands on the shoulders of others. We innovate, in part, on the investment of those before us. And we share in the celebration when we accomplish together what cannot be accomplished in a single generation.

Many of the hopes and dreams identified have been written in journals and cried out in prayers long before they made it into this chapter. They are hopes tested by actual lives and sacrifices. With input from people currently living mostly in Muslim-majority contexts, these hopes fall into four categories:

1. Hopes for my relationship and walk with God
2. Hopes for my local relationships with Muslims
3. Hopes for the global church in the Muslim world
4. Hopes for breakthrough ideas in the Muslim world

Input was gathered and interpreted from four sources within the Vision 5:9 network:

1. An evening with the younger generation (under age forty) of the Abide, Bear Fruit Global Consultation on Ministry to Muslims (121 people from over seventy nations, including many MBBs)
2. A panel of younger workers and discussion together (20 people from all continents)
3. Two surveys of younger workers in early 2018, with about one hundred responses
4. Various conversations with younger-generation workers and leaders

The perspective of "we" represents all the Christ-centered people longing to see Jesus' kingdom come in the Muslim world—those intentional about making disciples or planting churches.

Recently, an older steering team member of the Vision 5:9 network, who has more than twenty-five years of experience among Muslims, made this observation: "These [younger-generation] brothers and sisters are peers. They are giving their lives alongside us." These younger-generation workers are no less committed or dedicated than those who have invested decades. We are part of one body—the body of Christ in the Muslim world.

HOPE #1: FOR MY RELATIONSHIP AND WALK WITH GOD

We want our lives to be marked by abiding in Jesus and bearing fruit. The theme at the 2017 global consultation was "Abide, Bear Fruit" from John 15:5, which says, "I am the vine; you are the branches. Whoever abides in me and I in him, he it is that bears much fruit, for apart from me you can do nothing" (ESV). One evening, 121 younger-generation leaders gathered in a room with great excitement. Some, at that point, had already lived and worked among Muslims for more than a decade, while others came with just a few years of experience.

Connections with like-hearted church planters and disciple makers in the same age range made the room buzz. There was an appropriate weight of the opportunities to seize and the challenges to overcome in the years ahead. How would this group stick together, learn from one another, and cross-pollinate what is working in the years ahead? Would we gather decades from this day and look back to celebrate what God has done in us, through us, and for us in the Muslim world? Perhaps this small gathering was similar to the age of attendees at the Student Volunteer Movement (1886) or the Lausanne Congress (1974), when most attendees were in their twenties, thirties, and forties.

We got acquainted, prayed together in small groups, and discussed what we—as a younger generation—could uniquely contribute to making disciples among all Muslim peoples. Through all this, we strongly affirmed that we want our lives to count for Jesus, and to do this, we must abide in Jesus.

We want our generation to be known for abiding, preparing the way for future generations after us. As a younger generation of Christ-centered church planters, disciple makers, and leaders in the gospel going to the Muslim world, we affirm and declare that we want our lives to align with the Abide, Bear Fruit commitment.

What does abiding and bearing fruit look like? We identified it as a vibrant walk and friendship with God that includes listening, trusting, enjoying, and responding to him. Abiding in Jesus may lead a person to be aware of his or her natural gifts and abilities, talents, situation, calling, and temperament. Our lives are much like the servants in Matthew 25:14–30. We are entrusted with talents, and we must steward them well.

In addition to abiding in Jesus and bearing fruit, we want our lives to be marked by embracing our calling and obeying God. One younger-generation church planter writes, "I hope to continue in Christ and in his calling to South Asian Muslims in the next decades." Others said they want to have no hesitation with God and fully obey his call. One Muslim-background believer said, "I want to step into the calling God has on my life." We want deep discipleship in the growth of the church, which honors evangelism and prioritizes making disciples. This includes being deeply rooted in faith, God's Word, and walking in God's Spirit. One younger church planter said, "Let's identify what the characteristics of a disciple are, and then try to step into these." Another respondent said, "We must be deeply rooted in Christ so we can be bold—not out of pride, but out of assurance that I am doing what God has called me to be and do."

Many identified a need to trust God, not ourselves. One disciple maker said, "We must enjoy Jesus because he is glorified in this trust. It is his mission, and we are privileged participants."

Specifically, we must embrace a theology of suffering. We will have opportunities to trust God during suffering and find our deepest joy in God. This will be part of God's plan in the Muslim world. Many people shared about their current suffering, as today more people are suffering for their faith in Jesus than at any other point in history. We did not identify the specifics of what a theology of suffering must require, but we know that embracing the joy of Jesus will be a significant part.

Finally, we agreed that our identity must be found in Christ for all these hopes to become reality. May God have his way in this generation of Christ-followers.

HOPE #2: FOR MY LOCAL RELATIONSHIPS WITH MUSLIMS

We all want Muslims to know and worship Jesus. We want unengaged Muslim peoples to enjoy the peace and assurance of life that Jesus promises. There are many tools and methods of evangelism, but one worker identified that if a relationship is not a vital part in seeing Muslims become fully devoted followers of Jesus, then all the tools or methods will not work.

We identified some areas we want to include in our work in the years ahead. First, we desire to live incarnationally. Jesus, as he moved into the neighborhood, is our model of incarnation (John 1). We want to learn the language and cultural contexts by living with and among Muslims. For example, we want to be aware of honor and shame dynamics in making disciples. Paying attention to the type of Muslim group and individual is critical. What may be true for one group may not be true for another. For example, the Fulani people of West Africa are a closed-culture people with different ways of relating than many other Muslim groups.

Second, hospitality and face-to-face relationships seems critical to healthy relationships with local Muslims. In many Muslim cultures, friendships and trust don't happen until after a meal is shared. We must eat together to know one another.

Third, there is a strong desire for being mentored and mentoring others. We identified this as similar to discipleship—you learn from others about following Jesus and you help others follow him.

The fourth area of relating to Muslims is in courageous boldness. Our generation desires to attempt new things and to pursue neglected peoples where there are no Christ-followers. This takes an unashamed passion, faith, courage, and strength that we must embrace from our relationship with God.

HOPE #3: FOR THE GLOBAL CHURCH IN THE MUSLIM WORLD

We hope to see significant growth of the church, especially in the Muslim world. There are still more than a thousand remaining unengaged Muslim people groups and millions of Muslims who do not know a single Christ-follower.

We do not have stories of people coming to us from unengaged, unreached peoples because there are no Christ-followers among them. To see change and an established, healthy church in the Muslim world, we believe this will include the following:

- More women and majority-world leaders influencing the global church
- Muslim-background believers taking leadership
- Prioritization of the local church at the heart of missiology
- Open-source resources and utilization of technology
- Unity and collaboration in the body of Christ
- Living with humility and love; treating all people with respect
- Continuing existing Christ-centered work and life

We hope that as we make disciples cross-culturally, we partner with the local church and are mindful of the local context. This is challenging and slower, yet we believe lasts longer and honors others.

HOPE #4: FOR BREAKTHROUGH IDEAS IN THE MUSLIM WORLD

As we see God's kingdom unfold, there will likely be creative, breakthrough ideas implemented by groups of people. There is a collaboration movement in our world releasing creativity and ability to implement seemingly impossible challenges, all because of God's people working together.

We hope to remind our generation to preach the love of God, share faith in Jesus by declaring and living it out, walk in humility and authentic relationships, and endure suffering. We must be people of prayer, seeking to break spiritual strongholds in us, in others, and in the Muslim culture in the spiritual realm. We must seek out and pay attention to movements of repentance, reconciliation, and radical generosity. We hope there will be waves of Muslim-background believers engaging in seeing the gospel of the kingdom go forth. As we see new initiatives, we want to support them and serve others launching into new work.

We hope to embrace a holistic approach to ministry, no longer dividing all of life and gospel ministry into what is secular and sacred, work and ministry, or full-time Christian workers and the rest of the body of Christ. For example, Christ-followers who are not full-time pastors or missionaries make up 99 percent of the world's Christians. But how can the 99 percent be message-bearers of the good news and disciple makers? As we see shifts in these areas, we want to support initiatives that recognize that every believer, not just pastors, has a responsibility make disciples among unengaged, Muslim unreached people groups.

There is another divide we hope to reconcile: the tension between meeting spiritual needs and physical needs. John Piper provided a statement to navigate this tension during the 2010 Lausanne Congress on World Evangelization in Cape Town, South Africa: "We Christians care about all suffering, especially eternal suffering." As the church grows in the Muslim world, we will see physical suffering and spiritual suffering. We must pay attention to both and respond. Piper went on to say, "If we do not, we have a defective heart or a defective view of hell." In light of this, we must develop holistic approaches to church planting and disciple making.

Technology is a tool that has shaped evangelism for decades, and we hope to utilize it to shape discipleship as well. For example, every weekend there is a Somali church meeting online nearly every hour. Online disciple makers are investing in others from thousands of miles away—taking interest, teaching the Scriptures, and enjoying the benefits of technology.

Many breakthrough ideas have been presented, and to accomplish them we need small teams of people across the world pursuing them at local and national levels. Some of these include workshops on writing worship songs in key cities, online forums to identify persons of peace, prayer movements in gateway cities with Muslim-background believers (MBBs) taking primary leadership, serving MBB fellowships well as they become mission senders, and utilizing the common "languages" of sports, technology, arts, and business.

We hope to invest in diaspora ministry. We now have open access to people groups who formerly were beyond the reach of the church and are now neighbors.

We hope to pay attention to the more than 80 percent of the world that prefers oral communication methods like storytelling.

We hope to keep looking for men and women of peace. One brother left Abide, Bear Fruit and returned to his home country. He prayed and found a person of peace, who attracted more people. Then he began a fellowship of believers. This kind of work happens through intentional praying and relationships.

We hope to incorporate more collaboration. We can do more together than we can accomplish independently. It is noteworthy that this is a process and skill to be learned and developed. Collaboration in the body of Christ, when done well, encourages everyone who participates and will help make significant progress in the Muslim world.

While this is not a new idea, it is important that in a conversation about new ideas, one church planter said we must "stick to Scripture"—meaning that we need to keep God's Word at the center of who we are and what we do. If Scripture is not a part of the new initiatives we launch, we need to rethink them and incorporate God's Word deliberately.

HOPE #5: SCRIPTURE PRAYERS FOR LABORERS IN THE MUSLIM WORLD

Finally, this Scripture prayer for workers in the Muslim world is adapted from selected Scriptures submitted by disciple makers under the age of forty in the Muslim world:

> Lord, we make it our ambition to preach the gospel, not where Christ has already been named, lest we build on someone else's foundation, but as it is written, "Those who have never been told of him will see, and those who have never heard will understand." (Rom 15:20–21 ESV)

> We always desire and need your help to pray in the Spirit that words may be given to us in opening our mouths boldly to proclaim the mystery of the gospel, for which we are ambassadors in chains, that we may declare it boldly. (Eph 6:18–20 ESV)

> Let our manner of life be worthy of the gospel of Christ, so that others may hear of our standing firm in one spirit, with one mind striving side by side for the faith of the gospel, and not frightened in anything by our opponents. For it has been granted to us that for the sake of Christ we should not only believe in him but also suffer for his sake. (Phil 1:27–30 ESV)

> May our Father in heaven be glorified as we abide in the vine and bear much fruit. (John 15:4–8)

> We thank you, Jesus! You are worthy to take the scroll and to open its seals, for you were slain, and by your blood you ransomed people for God from every tribe and language and people and nation (Rev 5:9 ESV). We look forward to the great multitude that no one can number, from every nation, from all tribes and peoples and languages, standing before the throne and before the Lamb, clothed in white robes, with palm branches in their hands. (Rev 7:9 ESV)

Upon asking the question, "If you were regularly praying a Bible passage for church planters/disciple makers in the Muslim world, what Scripture would you choose to guide you?" These are some further responses: These Scriptures were mentioned in response to the question, "If you were regularly praying a Bible passage for church planters/disciple makers in the Muslim world, what Scripture would you choose to guide you?" Here are some further responses:

2 Chronicles 7:14; Isaiah 11:10; 1 Peter 4:11; John 17:11; Ephesians 6:18–20; Philippians 1:27–30; Romans 15:20–21; 2 Corinthians 6:2; Malachi 1:11; Psalm 2:8; Ephesians 3:16–19, Genesis 17:18, John 15:8; Acts 13, Genesis 12, Matthew 28, Revelation 5:9; Revelation 7:9; 2 Timothy 2:2; 1 Thessalonians 2:1–12 (especially 2:4); Isaiah 64:4; Philippians 2:1–11; John 15; Isaiah 66:1–2; 1 Corinthians 15:58; Acts 16:13; Luke 10:10; John 17:11, 20–26; Romans 1:15; Jeremiah 20:9; Acts 4:20; Matthew 5:9; Matthew 10:39; Matthew 6:33; and Philippians 3:8–11.

As a collective of Christ-followers making disciples and planting churches in the Muslim world, we are deeply thankful to God for the gift of generations before us who mentor, invest, and send us forth. We eagerly embrace what God is planning in the Muslim world.

DISCUSS AND APPLY

- What do you hope for your life and ministry in relation to your Muslim neighbors?
- What do you hope for in relation to the global church? What breakthrough ideas has God given you, and how will you obey God's command for your life?

SERMON №2

DEBORAH LEE

Scripture Reading: Ephesians 6:18

God desires all people to come in touch with the saving knowledge of Jesus Christ. The Almighty wants all the saints to grow in their spiritual maturity into Christlikeness. Although we also know there is a spiritual battle going on. Our enemy, the devil, fights against this plan of God from happening in our hearts and hearts of our Muslim friends. He doesn't want to see God moving among the families of the nations. So the Bible shows us the way to fight this battle, and that is to pray.

Through prayer, we come to know God and we get to know his desires. We all know that we have to pray, but we often stop praying when the tribulations of life come. Then we lose our faith, and we focus on the challenges rather than in the promises of God. That is the battle that we all fight.

Prayer and intercession are an essential part of the missionary life. The Bible teaches that Jesus Christ went to the Cross, was buried, rose again on the third day, and is now sitting above, at the right hand of God, interceding for us (Rom 8:34). Also, Hebrews 7:25 highlights his role as our intercessor when it says that God is able also to save forever those who draw near to him through Jesus Christ, since Jesus always lives to make intercession for them, for the people.

As we persevere in prayer, we will see people being set free from the devil's control in their lives. We will see people leaving the dominion of darkness and coming into the kingdom of God (Col 1:13).

To persevere in prayer, we must grow in the knowledge of God. As we feed ourselves with the Word of God, our minds will be renewed and faith will be produced in our hearts. Then we will not be distracted or lose heart, but persevere in prayer.

Earlier in Ephesians 6, we find that the believer is fully armored to fight the spiritual battle. We must never forget that. And since this is a spiritual battle, we need to understand the ways that prayer is a weapon against the enemy. And in our main text, Ephesians 6:18, Paul goes on to say that we should pray with "all prayer." What does it mean to pray with all prayer? It is praying with every part of the totality of communication with God. Everything we do in prayer for the nations is an act of spiritual warfare.

When we see a breakthrough in one area, we are likely to get breakthroughs in other areas as well, because the enemy we are fighting is the same and often uses similar strategies. Moreover, for each battle we fight, we must stay vigilant and persevere in prayer.

As we serve the kingdom of God and do his work, we will face a lot of challenges. If we act as if the task could be fulfilled in our own strength, we will certainly be burdened and weary. But the Word of God tells us to hope in the Lord in Isaiah 40:31: "Those who hope in the Lord will renew their strength … will run and not grow weary."

David delighted to sit in the presence of God and consult the Lord before making any move. He was a man who learned the importance of spending time in God's presence: "Better is one day in your courts than a thousand elsewhere" (Ps 84:10). We learn from David that prayer is a relationship with God. It is a daily spiritual exercise for the believers to know the Lord in intimacy and understand his ways. If we persevere in God's presence and receive from him a specific task to fulfill, no matter how hard it is, God will accomplish his will through our lives.

As people living in a fallen world, we need to continually remind ourselves that our battle is not against flesh and blood, it is against principalities, rulers, principalities, and powers of darkness (Eph 6:12). Therefore, we must take on the full armor of God by feeding ourselves with the Word of God. As we grow in the Word and pray in the Spirit, we will continue to grow as disciples.

Our faith is always declared through our worship in the midst of storms of our lives. We choose to find our strength in our God, and our God alone—nothing else. Through prayers, we will witness God bringing down the enemy's strongholds in our hearts first, and in the hearts of the people that we are praying for. Let us persevere in prayer. We will witness God's will being done on earth as it is in heaven. We will see the eternal fruit of souls been harvested among the nations.

As harvesters, we know that we must plow the field to have food at the harvest (Proverbs 20:4). This section highlights different aspects of the harvest field. Each chapter highlights some of the deep aspects of identity that Muslims worldwide are currently grappling with. Many Muslims are in transitions and change (as is the earth itself). Many Muslims have had to change as they became refugees and moved to new lands to start new lives. Other Muslims (particularly women) have had their lives changed as the modern world has come to them through media, the Internet, global business, and a global exchange of ideas.

As a result, this section looks at Muslims in transition: refugees, new residents in new places, city dwellers, nomads, women, and those who are taking their first steps in obedience to Jesus. In each case, those who love Jesus and Muslims are also in transition—adapting and changing, going through the doors Jesus opens in their time and their place.

It is likely that many of these same trends are playing out around you as well. My hope is that in these pages you will find insight and inspiration to go afresh to the fields that are ripe for harvest (John 4:35). Truly the harvest is not at some distant time in the future, but is now—if we only have eyes to see it.

—Pam Arlund, section editor

SECTION 2: Harvest Field

Pam Arlund, section editor

11

URBAN MUSLIM PEOPLES:
Transitions and New Ethnic Streams among the Least Reached: A Case Study

Minh Ha Nguyen, does missiological research at International Mission Board focusing on globalization, urbanization, and migration. In 2009 he started International Community Church, a house-church network that reaches people groups from Asia, Africa, and the Middle East living in Richmond, VA. He is a PhD candidate at Southeastern Seminary.

Marko Pretorius serves as the Executive Director of the All Nations hub in Hamburg, Germany. In 2013 Marko and his wife, Maxie, both architects, joined All Nations in response to a call for workers needed on the Jordan-Syria border. They love cities and the opportunities they offer to reach the unreached.

MAIN POINTS NOT TO MISS:

- Recent instability in some Muslim countries has led to a wave of Muslim peoples pouring into the cities of the world.

- There is an unprecedented opportunity to embrace urban Muslim peoples in the cities of the world and introduce them to a Jesus-centered community.

Urbanization, migration, and diversity are complex and touch on a variety of aspects affecting twenty-first century lives. More than half of the world's population now live in cities, and by 2050 the number will rise to two thirds.[1] Migrations, both within the same country and across international borders, drive much of this growth. Of the current 258 million international migrants, 95 percent have moved to cities. Six in ten refugees find temporary shelter in urban areas, while a third live in camps that are so large that they are cities in themselves.[2] Bidi Bidi in Uganda and Kakuma and Dadaad in Kenya have populations in the hundreds of thousands, each with its own hospitals, schools, and places of worship.[3]

These megatrends are observed among the Muslim peoples too. Syria, Afghanistan, and Sudan—all predominantly Muslim countries—are the three top countries that saw the greatest number of refugees seeking shelter in countries and cities within the same region or across the globe.[4] Nearly half of the world's refugees, as well as six in ten internally displaced people, come from Muslim countries.[5] Finally, a large number of Muslim migrants have arrived in cities in Western Europe and North America, making them some of the most diverse places on earth. London, for example, now has 467 mosques, whereas fifty years ago there were only twenty mosques in all of the United Kingdom and Wales.[6]

Migration is therefore not only an urban affair but a religious one as well. However, there is very little research on Islamic cities and how to engage migrant Muslims in urban contexts. This chapter aims to draw attention to the complexity of Muslim migration to new urban centers, and the need to think contextually and biblically about reaching them with the good news.

---

1 United Nations, 2018 Revision of World Urbanization Prospects, 2.
2 International Organization for Migration, World Migration Report 2018, 32. Robert McKenzie: "Refugees don't just come to nations; they move to cities," Brookings Institution, https://www.brookings.edu/blog/metropolitan-revolution/2016/10/03/refugees-dont-just-come-to-nations-they-move-to-cities
3 United Nations High Commissioner for Refugees, Statistical Yearbook 2016, 102.
4 International Organization for Migration, World Migration Report 2018, 33-34.
5 Kirsten Zaat, "The Protection of Forced Migrants in Islamic Law," United Nations High Commissioner for Refugees, Research Paper 146, https://www.unhcr.org/research/RESEARCH/476652cb2.pdf
6 Muslims in Britain, "UK Mosque/Masjid Directory," http://mosques.muslimsinbritain.org/maps.php#/town/London. British Religion in Numbers, "Registered Mosques, 1915-1998," http://www.brin.ac.uk/figures/registered-mosques-1915-1998/

Stories of Transitions: From Damascus to Beirut

Due to the war in Syria, a woman named Um Bidea moved to Beirut with her family. One day Mary and John, followers of Jesus, met her begging on the streets. Mary and John started a business with her, which provided income and an opportunity for the three of them to spend time together. Mary and John felt that somebody caring for this family was very important, but somebody that understood their language and culture to such a degree that they could pick up nuances and underlying meanings was crucial. So, they had spent a lot of time learning language and culture. The complexity of various different religions and ethnicities living side by side, combined with the need to work, gave "outsiders" the opportunity to engage and influence Um Bidea and her family. As a result, both Um Bidea and her sister came to faith and were baptized.

One morning Um Bidea and her sister announced that they had baptized a man named Abu Ahmed. When the Syrian civil war reached the suburbs of Damascus in 2012, Abu Ahmed joined the Syrian army. During this time he witnessed horrific things. After two years of fighting he developed severe amnesia, which led to him fleeing with his family to Beirut. They found a small apartment in a poor neighborhood, and Ahmed collapsed in a comatose state for months.

While Abu Ahmed had been sick, his family cared for him as best they could. He is Sunni by birth, with roots in a family tribe that stretches over many generations. Due to his family structure, his days started with early morning calls to prayer. Fridays were for rest and worship at his community mosque, which was the hub for all social, spiritual, and political activities. Even now, though the family lives in Beirut, they don't see themselves as a single isolated family unit but as a tribe, linked to others through kindship.

When Abu Ahmed first began to follow Jesus, he was still suffering from amnesia, but one morning Jesus miraculously healed his amnesia!

From the time of Abu Ahmed's healing, John and Mary encouraged the small emerging church to grow, share, and shape community within their family and tribe—understanding that ultimately that was the only place they would experience true belonging.

ISLAM AND URBANIZATION

Islam was born an urban movement. Mecca and Medina were two of the most influential trading cities of seventh-century Arabia.[7] Additionally, Mecca was not only the birth city of Muhammad, Islam's founder, but also the place where he received the visions and revelations that became the Qur'an. Opposition in Mecca led to the *hijrah,* the migration of the first converts to the small northern town of Medina. Here Muhammad built the *ummah,* the community of those who shared the Islamic faith. He began to organize the city to be a place that supported community life with the purpose of worshiping God and applying the Islamic code (*shariah*). According to Hisham Mortada, an Islamic urban scholar with expertise in old Muslim cities, Medina's urban pattern became the planning standards that were later followed in most traditional Islamic cities—an urban model where Muslims, Jews, Christians, and others share the same city but not the same areas (*khittahs*).[8]

Islam is not only urban, but an urbanizing movement. Middle Eastern cities in the Islamic period were essentially a product of the Islamic religious ideals.[9] F. Benet, an urban sociologist, writes, "Islam is a predominantly urban religion which thoroughly reshaped the urban structures of the worlds it conquered."[10] Additionally, since Islam values knowledge and created centers of learning everywhere it went, urbanization came into being as universities and other learning centers attracted many to them.[11]

How has the church responded to this urban and urbanizing Islamic movement? Though Christianity also began as an urban movement in the shadow of the Roman Empire, it had become, a few centuries later, rural and isolationist in its orientation.[12] This was due in part to the Barbarian invasions of the fifth century and the Islamic conquests of the seventh century. As armies entered the cities, Christians fled to the countryside. Later crusades only further separated Christians and Muslims.

To effectively engage Muslim peoples, the church must seek to understand the Islamic city and have deep love for the cities, with all their peoples. This understanding and love for the city, on the one hand, must be couched in

---

7   Robert Bickert, "Evangelizing African Traditional Religion Migrants in Urban Contexts in West Africa: A Case Study of Freetown, Sierra Leone," *The Mediator* 8, no. 1 (April 2011): 58-63.

8   Hisham Mortada, *Traditional Islamic Principles of Built Environment* (London:Routledge Curson, 2003), 58.

9   Ahmad Bilal, "Urbanization and Urban Development in the Muslim World: From the Islamic City Model to Megacities," *GeoJournal* 37, no. 1: 113-23.

10 Mortada, *Traditional Islamic Principles*, 54.

11 Al-Hewar Center for Arab Culture and Dialogue, "Universal Islamic Declaration of Human Rights," http://www.alhewar.com/ISLAMDECL.html

12 Bickert, *The Mediator*, 61.

> To effectively engage Muslim peoples, the church must seek to understand the Islamic city and have deep love for the cities, with all their peoples.

a theology for the city grounded in the biblical story arc from the creation of the garden of Eden (Gen 2:8) all the way to the "Holy City, the new Jerusalem" as the dwelling place where God meets his people in Christ Jesus (Rev 21:2–3). Such theology for the city, on the other hand, cannot ignore the fallen nature of mankind in rebellion and sin against God, seeking to build cities to preserve themselves and oppress others rather than glorify the Creator.

Stories of Transitions: From Kabul to Hamburg

Azad loves asking questions, learning, and educating others. In many places these traits would be celebrated, but unfortunately Azad grew up under Taliban rule in Kabul during the Soviet-Afghan war in the 1980s. Azad received a traditional Islamic education, reciting portions of the Qur'an in Arabic even though he did not understand the language. Under the Taliban, Azad received regular beatings if he disobeyed Islamic law.

From an early age, Azad sought to understand. He would approach his imam with questions and ideas, but he was punished for his inquisitive nature. Azad eventually gave up on Islam as a path to knowing God and decided to focus on his career, although he continued to pray at the local mosque so as to not upset the local power structure.

With a desire to educate fellow Afghanis, Azad created an educational institute in downtown Kabul. It quickly became a success. In addition, the institute gave Azad the opportunity to have debates with employees regarding Islam. One day, however, a religious mob from his mosque, led by a disgruntled ex-employee, attacked him at the school. He received multiple blows to the head, lost consciousness, and nearly died. Friends and family smuggled Azad to Tajikistan and then on to Ukraine. In the Ukraine there was another attempt on his life. But he was helped by a local businessman and ultimately made his way to Germany.

In Germany, Azad met Scott. "I heard a foreigner speaking English," Azad recalls. "I wanted to practice my English, so I walked over to meet him."

Scott introduced himself as a follower of Jesus. "We had coffee together and he listened to my story. I could ask him questions about his religion without him being offended. Some he would answer, and to others he would say that he did not have the answer, but that Jesus loved me."

Scott and Azad quickly became friends. Scott would have him over for dinner and Azad would translate Jesus stories for other refugees. "Afterward we would just hang out. I still had many questions, but I saw so much joy and peace in his life. To see a person live like that had a huge impact on me."

Azad found his answers in the gospel. "I was baptized in a little plastic bath and continued sharing with other Farsi-speaking refugees. Many more believers were added and we continue to grow. I am so grateful to Scott, who did not keep this great love to himself."

ISLAM AND MIGRATION

Islam was also born a migrant movement. It is worth noting that it is the *hijrah*, the migration of Muhammad and his followers from Mecca to Medina—not the birthdate of Islam's founder nor the date of the first revelation of the Qur'an—that marks the beginning of the Islamic calendar (*Anno Hegirae*). Good Muslims are encouraged to migrate from where they live in order to spread the Islamic faith, to escape persecutions, or, if they live in a non-Muslim country, to leave and join the Muslim community.

How has the church responded to migrant Muslims moving into neighborhoods in traditionally Christian cities? Muslim migrants arriving in Western cities often face anti-immigration sentiments and stereotypes (many of which are not accurate). Though a small number migrate in order to spread Islamic fundamentalism and extremist ideologies, the vast majority of Muslims migrate because they want a better life for themselves and their children.

To effectively engage Muslim peoples, the church must engage them in transitions—fully understanding the causes and motivations of their migration and rejecting the settler protectionist mind-set. The church must invite Muslims to become disciples, who would in turn make disciples among other Muslim migrants in the city as well as share with their family and friends in their home countries. Christian hospitality and sacrificial love must be extended toward strangers. Cross-cultural outreach is often harder when we are in our own country rather than abroad because there is an ethnocentric expectation of "When in Rome, do as the Romans do." In other words, if they come to our country they have to learn our language and adopt our way of life. While natural, such expectation is counterproductive as far as the gospel is concerned because it implies that migrants have to learn the national language in order to hear the gospel. If learning a new language is perceived to be too difficult for believers, however, the national church in the city could partner with the migrant Christians to reach Muslim peoples. These migrant believers often already have the linguistic and cultural experience and also live close to the Muslim migrant peoples who need to hear the gospel. Such partnership could result in a true, accepting, and loving community within the diversity of the body of Christ.

Stories of Transitions: From the Nuba Mountains to Uganda Madina

Shadin grew up, along with her seven siblings and extended family, as a Nubian Muslim in the Nuba Mountains of northern Sudan. In 1972 Madina and her family moved from Sudan to Uganda, which was under the reign of Idi Amin. Not trusting the Ugandans' loyalty, Idi Amin brought Nubian men and their families from Sudan to supplement the Nubian army.

Madina's father, a staunch Muslim, married two wives and only spoke Arabic before moving to Uganda. Poverty forced them to integrate, mix with "infidels," and learn the local dialect. Madina could see the effects of this on their family and how they practiced Islam. As they engaged with Ugandans, their values were challenged, which then influenced Madina's worldview.

When she was nineteen, Madina married a Muslim man from Uganda. But after marrying two more wives, he became very abusive and started neglecting Madina and her six children. She felt confused and afraid, but her culture didn't allow her to discuss what was going on at home.

During this time, Matthew, a Ugandan follower of Jesus, started serving her community in search of "people of peace," as described in Luke 10. Madina would go to town to weave with some of the local ladies. Through these women, Madina met Matthew. He wisely pointed her to Jesus, telling her that Jesus was the only one who could help her.

Matthew regularly met with Madina and some of her friends, sharing stories about Jesus. Eventually Madina decided to be baptized, and today she leads several small churches in her area. Although she faces a lot of persecution, Madina continues to grow and has decided to stay within her community to share the new life she found in Jesus.

> To effectively engage Muslim peoples, the church must engage them in transitions—fully understanding the causes and motivations of their migration and rejecting the settler protectionist mind-set.

ISLAM AND COMMUNITY

Ummah, the Islamic community or nation, is the uniting source of not only religious and cultural identity but also of social and political authority.[13] As such, the Islamic ummah is more than an order or way of life but encompasses everything that makes up the Islamic city and society. Some Islamic scholars even argue that the "Constitution of Medina"—the first Islamic city—was designed to regulate the social and political life not just for Medina but for all other Islamic cities as well.[14]

Ummah is not only cultural and religious, but also social and political. Ibn Khaldun, a fourteenth-century social thinker and Muslim historian, maintained that the most important factor in the rise and growth of Muslim urbanization was the substitution of religious affiliation for kinship as the rationale for social organization. Riaz Hassan writes, "The social solidarity based on religion is the most powerful force in the creation of civilized culture which is centered around the life in cities."[15]

Christian missionaries working among Muslim people groups in urban areas need to be aware of the multifaceted nature of *ummah*. In Western cities where Muslims are in the minority, the local mosque often functions as a religious, cultural, social, and sometimes political center.

The role of the mosque helps highlight some of the differences between the Islamic concept of *ummah* and the Christian concept of community. For example, Christians value unconditional relationships free from obligation in a way that Muslims generally do not. Also absent from the concept of *ummah* are values such as grace, love, and freedom from social control. Last but not least, the Islamic *ummah* and the Qur'an do not make reference to the image of God in man, which gives every individual intrinsic value, worth, dignity, and freedom—even the freedom to rebel against the Creator.

Missiologically speaking, the concept of *ummah* provides the church one of the best opportunities to engage in dialogue and enter into relationship with

13 Ahmad S. Dallal, Yoginder Sikand, and Abdul Rashid Moten, "Ummah," Oxford Islamic Studies Online, http://www.oxfordislamicstudies.com
14 Ibid.
15 Riaz Hassan, "The Nature of Islamic Urbanization: A Historical Perspective," *Ekistics* 31, no. 182 (1971): 61-63.

Muslim peoples and introduce them to a more perfect community of disciples of Jesus. Such community is described in Acts 2:42–47 as a fellowship of believers who are devoted to the teachings of Jesus, who love Jesus and are loved by him, and who extend gracious love to one another—and even to their enemies. In addition, the church must fully grasp all the multidimensional aspects of the Islamic *ummah,* knowing how to distinguish the cultural and social from the political and religious.

CONCLUSION

Unlike their counterparts who remained at home, migrant Muslim peoples are generally more open to new ideas and tolerant of change. Robert Douglas writes,

> God, somehow in the convergence of migration, the rise of the urban world, and Islam's connection to both, is bringing together a context that can provide rich opportunities for the expansion of His kingdom. To meet the challenge of Muslim cities, God's people must find greater willingness to be cooperative, give greater attention to the range of problems associated with high density living, and discover responsive population segments in a very diverse social maze.[16]

Two thousand years ago, the Apostle Paul noticed that the Hellenized Jews in the diaspora were more receptive to the gospel than the devout orthodox Jews who remained in Palestine.[17] These Hellenized Jews who became disciples of Jesus began to reach out not only to the Jews but to the Gentiles as well (Acts 11:19–30). It was these same believers who helped Paul realize his calling to be the apostle to the Gentiles (Acts 13:1–3). Migrant Muslim peoples in Western cities today could be seen as the Hellenized Jews of the twenty-first century. The megatrends of globalization, urbanization, migration, and diversity are not problems for the church to solve but human realities that are divinely orchestrated and that provide new opportunities for the spread of the gospel in cities. May the church—national and migrant—seize the opportunity to make disciples among these new ethnic streams of the least reached who would in turn take the gospel further for the glory of God.

16 Robert Douglas, "Some Major Challenges in Missions to the Muslims," *Leaven* 7, no. 1 (1999), http://digitalcommons.pepperdine.edu/leaven/vol7/iss1/8, Accessed April 19, 2019.
17 Arthur Darby Nock, *St. Paul* (Charleston, SC: Nabu Press, 2011), 121.

DISCUSS AND APPLY

1. Have Muslims migrated to your country or city? Do you know? If not, how can you find out?

2. How have Christian communities in your area or country reacted to Muslim immigration? How have you reacted? Are these ways Christlike?

3. How could you effectively help Muslims transition to their new lives, even if you don't know them personally or if they live too far away from you to meet them yourself?

BIBLIOGRAPHY

Al-Hewar Center for Arab Culture and Dialogue. "Universal Islamic Declaration of Human Rights." http://www.alhewar.com/ISLAMDECL.html.

Bickert, Robert. "Evangelizing African Traditional Religion Migrants in Urban Contexts in West Africa: A Case Study of Freetown, Sierra Leone." *The Mediator* 8, no. 1 (2011): 51–88.

Bilal, Ahmad. "Urbanization and Urban Development in the Muslim World: From the Islamic City Model to Megacities." *GeoJournal* 37, no. 1 (1995): 113–23.

Dallal, Ahmad S., Yoginder Sikand, and Abdul Rashid Moten. "Ummah." *Oxford Islamic Studies Online*. http://www.oxfordislamicstudies.com.

Douglas, Robert. "Some Major Challenges in Missions to the Muslims." *Leaven* 7, no. 1 (1999). http://digitalcommons.pepperdine.edu/leaven/vol7/iss1/8.

Hassan, Riaz. "The Nature of Islamic Urbanization: A Historical Perspective." *Ekistics* 31, no. 182 (1971): 61–63.

International Organization for Migration. *World Migration Report 2018*. United Nations Publications.

Mortada, Hisham. *Traditional Islamic Principles of Built Environment*. London: Routledge Curson, 2003.

Muslims in Britain. "UK Mosque/Masjid Directory." http://mosques.muslimsinbritain.org/maps.php#/town/London.

Nock, Arthur Darby. *St. Paul*. Charleston, SC: Nabu Press, 2011.

United Nations. *2018 Revision of World Urbanization Prospects*. United Nations Publications.

United Nations High Commissioner for Refugees. *Statistical Yearbook 2016*. United Nations Publications.

Zaat, Kirsten. "The Protection of Forced Migrants in Islamic Law," United Nations High Commissioner for Refugees, Research Paper 146, https://www.unhcr.org/research/RESEARCH/476652cb2.pdf.

12

THE CONCEPT OF COMMUNITY AND IDENTITY AMONG MUSLIMS
A Case Study

Jonathan and Sofia Morgan worked with NGOs in South Africa and Jordan before moving to Malmö, Sweden, in 2016. Jonathan holds a master's degree in Middle Eastern studies. Sofia is a social worker with experience working with refugee families.

MAIN POINTS NOT TO MISS:

- Muslim immigrants to Europe encounter cultures that are culturally quite different and much more individualistic than the countries from which the immigrants originally came.

- These same Muslim immigrants often live in socially complex European neighborhoods that struggle with poverty, poor quality schools, and urban violence.

- These forces create both challenge and opportunity for Christians to be good neighbors to Muslim immigrants.

In recent years Europe has seen vast numbers of Middle Eastern Muslim refugees reach its shores. This trend began with the annexation of Palestine in 1948 and accelerated with the wars in Lebanon and Iraq. Even more recently there has been another acceleration of Muslims moving to Europe as a result of the Syrian uprising and civil war that began in 2011 and the ongoing conflict in Yemen. Sweden, like its neighbours, has received from these nations tens of thousands of families and individuals, all seeking to build their lives in new and unfamiliar circumstances. Between 2014 and 2017, Sweden's Office of Migration (*Migrationsverket*) received more than ninety thousand in-person asylum applications from Syrian refugees.[1] In this chapter we will look at what it means to be a Muslim in Europe; how they, as diasporic peoples, are building community; and how this poses opportunities and challenges for the church in Europe.

WHAT IS A MUSLIM?

While there are some general characteristics common to all Muslims—including a belief in the unity of God, adherence to an understanding of God revealed to the Prophet Muhammad in the Qur'an, and regular rhythms of prayer—from these starting points we find as many varieties of Islam as there are groups who call themselves Muslim. Nowhere is this more easily observed than Malmö, in southern Sweden, where most of these groups are represented and where we live and work.

Sociologists tend to look at identity formation as a process, something that individuals and groups continuously negotiate and renegotiate throughout their lives. Individuals might have periods in their lives when they are more devout than at other times, or where being Muslim deepens in its meaning. Aaron Hughes argues that this process of identity formation has been taking place within the ummah, the worldwide community of Muslims, since the religion emerged in the seventh century.[2]

Muslims in Europe, however, no longer live in a context where the entire social environment—family, school, government—is organized around developing the Muslim community. Olivier Roy describes how, because Islam has "lost its social authority," personal piety is becoming more important than religious hierarchies.[3] In Europe, being Muslim doesn't seem to be as much about nationality or family background as it is about the practices of individuals who pass on traditions between generations, as well as the new approaches to religion that come with life in a pluralist context.

1 Statistics, Swedish Migration Agency, Migrationsverket website, https://www.migrationsverket.se/English/About-the-Migration-Agency/Facts-and-statistics-/Statistics.html, accessed January 15, 2018.
2 Aaron W. Hughes, *Muslim Identities: An Introduction to Islam* (New York: Columbia University Press, 2013).
3 Olivier Roy, *Globalized Islam: The Search for a New Ummah* (New York: Columbia University Press, 2004).

DIASPORIC PEOPLES

> One of the guiding metaphors to our life as the body of Christ is that of family. We have a concept and history of living as extended family that we can draw on as we offer hospitality to those whose greatest desire is to belong.

Many of the Muslims who live in Europe belong to diasporas, communities that exist in two or more places and are connected by the same traumatic experience of displacement.[4] These communities are of great interest to researchers because, while they reflect the cultures from which they came, they develop in their own unique ways. The Palestinian diaspora is a great example of a diasporic people. While many from this community have never lived in Palestine, they have a strong sense of belonging to their ancestral homeland, they produce diasporic art and music, and communication takes place between diasporas—not just from the diaspora to the homeland.

In her research on the Lebanese diaspora, Dalia Abdelhady found that while the feelings of belonging were strong among her interviewees, they had no single understanding of Lebanese identity.[5] While all felt a strong connection to Lebanon, many did not believe they would ever return and had come to appreciate life in their new homeland.

MORE THAN JUST MUSLIM

In today's highly polarized world, many myths and stereotypes are bandied around about Muslims. At the heart of most of these arguments is the mistaken belief that Muslims are a single, monolithic group. In fact, there are as many different perspectives on what it means to be Muslim as there are people who call themselves Muslim. From place to place and subculture to subculture, there are divergent practices, beliefs, and values.

As a Christian, a helpful way to grasp this is to think about the different types of Christians in the world: what they have in common and what makes them different. For instance, Catholics in the Philippines and snake-handling Pentecostals in Appalachia call themselves Christians, but if we followed them around for a week, watched what they did, and asked what they believe, we would end up with two very different views of what it means to be a Christian.

---

4 Louise Cainkar, "Global Arab World Migrations and Diasporas," *Arab Studies Journal* 21, no. 1 (2013).
5 Dalia Abdelhady, *The Lebanese Diaspora: The Arab Immigrant Experience in Montreal, New York, and Paris*, 1st ed. (New York: New York University Press, 2011).

The same is true within Islam. A Muslim in rural Mauritania and a Muslim in inner-city Indonesia will have two very different takes on what it means to be Muslim. On top of this, some people might mistakenly assume that any single person in either of those groups represents a "typical" Muslim from that place.

An article published in *The Atlantic* highlights the great variety that exists within Islam. It tells the story of some Syrian women who found themselves in Germany and unable to find a mosque community in which they felt at home. On the one side there were the Arab mosques, which they found too conservative, and on the other the Turkish mosques, which represented a different language and culture. The refugees the author interviewed had decided that they simply did not fit in with either type of mosque.[6]

While Islam may be viewed as a holistic worldview, many have argued that religion should not be understood to be the core defining feature of the people of the Middle East.[7] In this chapter we would like to suggest taking a broader view of people from this region and point to other factors which contribute to their identity formation as they build their lives in Europe—in Sweden, in particular.

AT THE MERCY OF SOCIETY'S CATEGORIES

In many parts of Europe refugees end up living in the least desirable parts of a given city. That is true of Sweden. In Malmö, the city where we live, refugees from Syria, Iraq, Lebanon, Palestine, and other parts of North Africa and the Middle East live in apartment blocks that were hastily constructed in the 1970s to deal with the housing crisis of that era. Our neighborhood was once home to working-class Swedes and migrant workers from neighboring countries, but has since become an area notable for their absence. There is high unemployment, more gang-related and drug-related crime than in other parts of Sweden, and a tangible sense of a population living on the margins of society.

While it is true that this neighborhood is majority Muslim-background, it would be naïve to assume that all of its problems originate from this fact. It has been argued that even the most extreme examples of radicalization have more to do with marginalization than religion. Thomas Piketty, for one, has been deeply critical of the idea that ISIS recruitment is due to some kind of clash of civilizations effect, arguing that it actually has much more to do with the inequality present in so many of the nations from which ISIS recruits come.[8]

6 Alice Su, "Why Germany's New Muslims Go to Mosque Less," *The Atlantic*, July 26, 2017, https://www.theatlantic.com/international/archive/2017/07/muslim-syrian-refugees-germany/534138/, Accessed April 19, 2019.
7 Sami Zubaida, *Beyond Islam* (New York: I.B.Tauris & Co Ltd, 2011); Ahmed, *What Is Islam?*,
8 Tankersley, Jim. "'Inequality' Is Behind the Rise of Isis, Says Author Thomas Piketty." *The Independent*. November 30, 2015. https://www.independent.co.uk/news/world/middle-east/

In our neighborhood, the schools have a low success rate. Many of the children who attend these schools do not develop advanced language skills in either Swedish or their mother tongue. Although these children are born in Sweden, they are not able to compete with children born elsewhere in Sweden. When they leave school and enter the job market, they begin at a disadvantage even before they encounter structural racism in recruitment processes. Yes, these people are Muslim, but they are also poor, unemployed, stigmatized, and marginalized—and these factors shape how they see themselves and their host country.

Added to this, many of the refugees we meet report that they are unable to discuss life's challenges with their family members back home. In the eyes of their family members, these people have made it. They are living the dream! Who are they to complain about feeling lonely or isolated? Consequently, many keep their problems to themselves or look for people here in Europe to talk to.

ON NORTHERN EUROPEAN HOSPITALITY

When we lived in Jordan, we were invited every day to visit people's homes, to try their food, and to form new friendships. They were curious about people from outside and wanted to hear all about life outside of Jordan.

Here in Sweden, I (Jonathan) attend a "Swedish as a second language" class. Most of the students are from Syria. While chatting with them about their experiences of life in Sweden, I've discovered that most of them have little meaningful contact with people whose family background is Swedish. They attend classes every day, yet rarely get to speak to someone whose first language is Swedish.

Unlike Middle Easterners, Swedes do not, as a rule, invite new people into their homes on a regular basis. It's not because they are unfriendly or don't want to connect with others; it's just not part of their culture. For a Middle Easterner in Sweden, this can be experienced in a number of ways, all of which are negative. Some I have spoken to believe that Swedes are just not sociable. Others have decided it means that Swedes hate Arabs.

While this is a troubling perception of Swedish society, we see it as a great opportunity for the church. One of the guiding metaphors to our life as the body of Christ is that of family. We have a concept and history of living as extended family that we can draw on as we offer hospitality to those whose greatest desire is to belong.

> One of the challenges for the church in Europe is that people who come as refugees often spend their early years in low-income, high-unemployment neighborhoods.

Many friendships we have built so far with people from the Middle East have been the result of taking time to listen to them, to invite them into our home, and to enjoy food together. It may sound simple, but it is in these moments that it is easy to understand where those we are hosting are at in their journey with God. It is in this context that we can offer an encouraging story that, for someone who already has the desire to learn more about God's love, can lead to purposeful friendships centered on Jesus. And it is in this environment that we can offer to pray for illnesses or worries, or simply offer a prayer of blessing.

THE CHALLENGE TO LIVE INCARNATIONALLY

One of the challenges for the church in Europe is that people who come as refugees often spend their early years in low-income, high-unemployment neighborhoods. These are places where life is a little less comfortable and where life's challenges are a little more visible. As we described earlier, the neighborhood we live in is a great example of this. When Rickard Lagervall and Leif Stenberg looked into the number of mosques in Malmö in 2016, they discovered there were seventeen such communities, not counting other Muslim societies.[9] Most of these mosques are in our neighborhood. At the same time, there are no churches in this area that actively reach out to the community that lives here.

We firmly believe that those who are willing to live in less desirable neighborhoods, for the sake of sharing the love of Jesus with those who would not otherwise hear about it, will see fruit. In doing so we follow Jesus, who, rather than holding onto his rights and privileges, set them aside so that he could live among us (Phil 2:7).

THE UMMAH, AND HOW IT MIGHT INFORM OUR WORK

We have observed in Malmö a common respect shared by people who are Muslim, regardless of where they come from. This is seen in small acts of recognition, including greetings and the willingness to attend events put on by the city on behalf of Muslims.

---

9 Rickard Lagervall and Leif Stenberg, Muslimska församlingar och föreningar i Malmö och Lund–en ögonblicksbild Innehållsförteckning, Lund, 2016, http://www.cmes.lu.se/fileadmin/_migrated/content_uploads/Malmo__rapporten_20160415.pdf.

> Those who come to Europe have no choice but to ask questions about who they are in light of their new context.

In my day-to-day life, I (Sofia) have noticed that Muslim women from different backgrounds ask each other about where they buy Islamic clothing or food. I have also seen how women in the apartment blocks where we live continue a tradition that I first encountered in Jordan. When their husbands and children are at work and school, they visit each other, drink tea, and share gossip. This visiting, however, seems to take place mainly between women from the same place and religious background. In our neighborhood, that happens to be Shiites from Iraq.

This grouping together along geographic and sectarian lines is notable among the mosques as well.[10] While several large mosques claim to welcome Shiites and people from all different places, the majority of smaller communities are divided by country of origin. Our Muslim friends will refer to a mosque by the country of origin of its patrons ("Oh, you mean the Bosnian mosque?") rather than by its name. While in theory they are all part of the same ummah, in practice worship times are segregated.

For the younger generation, who have gone to school together and developed cross-cultural friendships, this segregation is less apparent. During our time living here we have noticed groups of friends from different family backgrounds who share a common inner-city culture and their own dialect of Swedish that incorporates words from their mother tongues. While these young people may be of Muslim background, they live at the intersection of Swedish and home-country cultures. Most of these young people were born in Sweden but do not feel "Swedish." At the same time, when they visit their "home countries," it is apparent that they are different. For this group, questions of identity can prove to be a particularly sensitive subject.

Here in Malmö we are often asked if we are Christians and what type of Christian we are. This question may seem simple, but it is loaded with meaning, depending on to whom we are talking. For a long time we have decided that we are more interested in representing the good news of Jesus than in defending the complex history of the church. This has led us to relating more to the idea of being "followers of Jesus" than "Christians." We have noticed that this distinction is helpful, and easy to understand, for those who have a high level of education; it can prove confusing, however, for those who do not.

---

10 Ibid.

One Syrian farmer I (Jonathan) spoke to, who left school at age eight, seemed confused when I told him I am a "follower of Jesus." "But are you a Christian?" he asked.

After a while I discovered he knew that many people in Sweden do not believe in God at all; so, in his mind, discovering that someone is a Christian is a positive thing, like finding a kindred spirit. Once I realized this, I said to him, "Yes, I am a Christian who loves Muslims"—a response that led to many Jesus-centered conversations.

The cultures of the Middle East are far less individualistic than those in Europe and North America. When building Jesus-centered friendships with Middle Easterners, it's good to bear this in mind. Many of us came to faith in churches that reflected the norms of our cultures. As a result, we view faith as something primarily personal. A strong commitment to individual liberty can tend to shape a church that doesn't really grasp what it means to be a self-sacrificial body that lays down its life for one another.

The concept of the ummah and the cultures of the Middle East lend themselves to a more communal experience of faith. Their cultures resemble the cultures of ancient Judea, where Jesus' ministry took place.[11] Our approaches to discipleship must take this into account. We should expect that whole families will journey toward Jesus together, and we must work to encourage this process from the start rather than extracting individuals from the very family units or friendship groups where they have the most influence. This doesn't mean that individual decisions to follow Jesus don't matter; it simply creates a context in which existing social structures can experience Jesus together.

BY THIS EVERYONE WILL KNOW THAT YOU ARE MY DISCIPLES

An important factor in people from a Muslim background experiencing Jesus is found in John 13:35, where Jesus tells his disciples that people will recognize them as his disciples by the way they love one another. The same applies to us today.

When we lived in Jordan, we spent time with Syrians who were encountering Jesus for the first time. Our work was connected to other believers by a church that operated as a hub of activity for those involved with food distribution and ministries of prayer, listening, and sharing. While we all celebrated the individual stories that came out of this work, I (Jonathan) think we underestimated the message that was received by the unity and love with which we worked. The people we encountered were amazed by the way the church was loving them, and this gave them an openness to receiving our message.

11 See, for example, Kenneth Bailey, *Jesus Through Middle Eastern Eyes: Cultural Studies in the Gospels* (Downers Grove, IL: InterVarsity Press, 2008).

LOOKING FOR MEANING

Those who come to Europe have no choice but to ask questions about who they are in light of their new context. While some become more conservative in the process, others are disillusioned with the institutions they have left behind.[12] They feel let down by the authority structures they lived with their whole lives and are eager to engage in conversation about what is real, to begin building a worldview of their own. What a wonderful time to encounter the life and teachings of Jesus!

CONCLUSION

In closing, the vast numbers of Muslim-background newcomers arriving in Europe offer the church very real opportunities to serve those who are in the process of making sense of who they are in an entirely new context. Through rediscovering ancient practices like hospitality, prayer, and incarnational living, we can offer hope and an ability to reconnect with what it means to be a body of people who lay down their lives for others. By embracing these people as humans first and Muslims second, we can see beyond our preconceptions, to find common ground, and to hear what God is already doing in their lives. As we do so, we will find ourselves blessed as we make new friends and begin to see Jesus "through Middle Eastern eyes."

DISCUSS AND APPLY

- What issues do immigrants face in your community? What does your community look like from their perspective?
- How can you rediscover basic Christian practices like hospitality, prayer, and incarnational living?
- What common ground (interests) do you have with non-Christians in your community?

12 Kathryn Kraft, "Religious Exploration and Conversion in Forced Displacement: A Case Study of Syrian Muslim Refugees in Lebanon Receiving Assistance from Evangelical Christians," *Journal of Contemporary Religion* 32, no. 2 (2017), doi:10.1080/13537903.2017.1298904.

BIBLIOGRAPHY

Abdelhady, Dalia. *The Lebanese Diaspora: The Arab Immigrant Experience in Montreal, New York, and Paris.* 1st ed. New York: New York University Press, 2011.

Ahmed, Shahab. *What Is Islam?* Princeton, NJ: Princeton University Press, 2016.

Bailey, Kenneth. *Jesus Through Middle Eastern Eyes: Cultural Studies in the Gospels.* Downers Grove, IL: InterVarsity Press, 2008.

Cainkar, Louise. "Global Arab World Migrations and Diasporas." *Arab Studies Journal* 21, no. 1 (2013): 126–65.

Hughes, Aaron W. *Muslim Identities: An Introduction to Islam.* New York: Columbia University Press, 2013.

Kraft, Kathryn. "Religious Exploration and Conversion in Forced Displacement: A Case Study of Syrian Muslim Refugees in Lebanon Receiving Assistance from Evangelical Christians." *Journal of Contemporary Religion* 32, no. 2 (2017): 221–35. doi:10.1080/13537903.2017 .1298904.

Lagervall, Rickard, and Leif Stenberg. *Muslimska församlingar och föreningar i Malmö och Lund—en ögonblicksbild Innehållsförteckning.* Lund, 2016. http://www.cmes.lu.se/ fileadmin/_migrated/content_uploads/Malmo__rapporten_20160415.pdf.

Migrationsverket. Statistics, Swedish Migration Agency. Migrationsverket website. https://www. migrationsverket.se/English/About-the-Migration-Agency/Facts-and-statistics-/Statistics. html.

Roy, Olivier. *Globalized Islam: The Search for a New Ummah.* New York: Columbia University Press, 2004.

Su, Alice. "Why Germany's New Muslims Go to Mosque Less." *The Atlantic,* July 26, 2017. https://www.theatlantic.com/international/archive/2017/07/muslim-syrian-refugees-germany/534138/.

Tankersley, Jim. "'Inequality' Is Behind the Rise of Isis, Says Author Thomas Piketty." *The Independent.* November 30, 2015. https://www.independent.co.uk/news/world/middle-east/inequality-is-behind-the-rise-of-isis-says-author-thomas-piketty-a6754786.html.

Zubaida, Sami. *Beyond Islam.* New York: I.B.Tauris & Co Ltd, 2011.

13 DISCIPLING THE DISPLACED IN THE GLOBAL SOUTH

John Idoko is the coordinator of CAPRO Diaspora Missions and a diaspora field leader in southern Nigeria. He and his wife, Dr. Opeyemi, previously led a multinational company while also church planting in an Arab community for more than fifteen years.

Wilson Namuwoza is the igniter of a movement of churches that has now spread to five countries and is also the Executive Director of the All Nations hub in Kampala, Uganda. In 2015 he quit his job as a bank manager to steward the growing movement of churches and missionaries in Uganda.

MAIN POINTS NOT TO MISS:

- Many Muslim refugees have recently arrived in different parts of Africa.

- In the two examples in Nigeria and Uganda, local African leaders have reached out to Muslim refugees, with great fruit resulting.

- These African leaders have insights into Muslim diaspora ministry that would be applicable to Muslim-refugee ministries anywhere.

There is a kind of social earthquake going on all over the world as wars and terrorism displace people from everywhere to everywhere. More than 65 million people have been forced from their homes by violence, war, or persecution, and approximately one-third of these have also been forced to flee their nation as refugees. In the year 2016 alone, more than 10 million people were newly displaced. Of the 22.5 million refugees worldwide, 51 percent are children under the age of eighteen.[1]

While no one wishes such suffering on anyone, this dispersion of peoples does provide one hopeful opportunity: it is bringing many Muslims into the neighborhood of the church. Consequently, the spiritual landscape and ways of doing cross-cultural mission are changing; something missiologists call "diaspora missions" is emerging.

While the refugee crisis in Europe has dominated the news cycle, a massive diaspora of refugees is moving across many areas in the Global South—places like southern Nigeria and Uganda. In Nigeria, Boko Haram's reign of terror has led to more than 2 million internally displaced persons fleeing from the Muslim north to the Christian south since 2014.[2] On the other side of the African continent, over 2.4 million South Sudanese have fled their country, nearly half into Uganda, since 2013.[3]

Many African believers are responding to this opportunity as previously distant Muslims are showing up on their doorsteps. Missiologist J. D. Payne points out, "The Sovereign Lord orchestrates the movement of peoples across the globe in order to advance his kingdom for his glory.... . Global migrations provide a Great Commission opportunity for us and our churches."[4]

GOD AT WORK IN NIGERIA

Wherever African Christians are encountering displaced Muslims—whether in Nigeria, Uganda, or elsewhere—they often find that these refugees have already supernaturally encountered Jesus. The story of a young Nigerian Muslim woman named Zahra is a case in point.

---

1 Global Trends: Forced Displacement in 2016, United Nations High Commissioner for Refugees, http://www.unhcr.org/5943e8a34.pdf
2 "Nigeria Emergency," United Nations High Commissioner for Refugees, http://www.unhcr.org/en-us/nigeria-emergency.html, accessed January 21, 2019.
3 "South Sudan Emergency," United Nations High Commissioner for Refugees http://www.unhcr.org/en-us/south-sudan-emergency.html, accessed January 21, 2019.
4 J. D. Payne, Strangers Next Door: Immigration, Migration and Mission (Downers Grove, IL: InterVarsity Press, 2012), 22, 158.

> Wherever African Christians are encountering displaced Muslims—whether in Nigeria, Uganda, or elsewhere—they often find that these refugees have already supernaturally encountered Jesus.

Zahra was born into a very committed Muslim family in a northeastern state of Nigeria that was home to Boko Haram terrorism. She attended an Islamic school and lived her life in a *hijab* (a head covering worn in public by some Muslim women). Zahra hated Christians and would have nothing to do with them, which fueled her interest in violent jihad.

Then Zahra's mother died. Because Zahra was close to her mother and loved her dearly, she began to wonder where her mother had gone: to heaven or to hell. Zahra wasn't sure. Throughout Ramadan that year, her singular prayer was that Allah would help her mother make it to heaven, not hell. During one of those nights, she had a dream. In her dream, she found herself in the women's section of the mosque. Suddenly the other women drove her away from the mosque, telling her that she was no longer part of them. As she stood crying, she saw three men in white Islamic robes under a tree close to the mosque. One of the men in the dream said, "You are now saved; you are now a Christian."

"A Christian?" she wondered. "I hate Christians—How could I become one?" Yet her journey had begun. Zahra began to inquire about how to become a Christian, as her yearning to make it to heaven became very intense. Knowing that it would never be possible for her to become a Christian in an environment controlled by Boko Haram, she ran away to the South in search of Christ. There she met Christians who helped her find Christ. Her discipleship took many detours until she stumbled into us (John and Opeyemi Idoko), as were were just beginning a diaspora ministry in that city. She was also encouraged to meet other Muslim-background believers in a diaspora church.

Today Zahra is growing in the Lord, with a passion to make it to heaven and to take others along with her! She radiates the beauty, warmth, and life of Christ within her. Zahra spreads this fragrance of Christ everywhere she goes.

DISCIPLING INTERNALLY DISPLACED PEOPLE FLEEING FROM BOKO HARAM

The combination of the Boko Haram insurgency, a spreading Sahara Desert, and other crises in northern Nigeria has greatly affected the demographics of the country and other parts of the Sahel region. Muslim peoples have been moving en masse into the seemingly peaceful and prosperous areas of southern

Nigeria. Therefore, Muslim (and non-Muslim) tribes, such as the Kanuris, Shuwa Arabs, Fulanis, Hausas, and others, are now in the neighborhood of a strong, well-established church.

While the dominant religion in the North is Islam,[5] thousands of indigenous northern Christians are affected by the crises and are also migrating to the South. This complicated situation is creating new mission approaches for the churches and mission agencies in Nigeria.

As missionaries who had themselves been displaced by the violence in the North, we (John and Opeyemi) saw new opportunities in this migration. Soon an indigenous mission agency set up a diaspora focus, made up of teams charged with the responsibility of planting new migrant churches called *Ekklisiyar Yan Arewa* (Churches of the Northern Brethren) among the northern migrant tribes who have moved to the South. This initiative is starting to ignite a church-planting movement[6] among this diaspora.

Muslims from the North are scattered across the South like "sheep without a shepherd," doing subsistence jobs like trading, digging wells, chopping firewood, and herding cattle. They are also forming their own unique settlements, called by names that reflect their homelands, such as Ama Hausa, Sabo, and Hausa Quarters. In these settlements they have established their own religious, cultural, and traditional leadership structures, some of which propagate Islam aggressively in their host communities.

Christian workers look for creative platforms to enter into these settlements in order to engage them with the gospel, following a Luke 10 model of going out into the migrant communities two by two to share the gospel. There are evangelistic outreaches showing "The Jesus Film" and *Tafiya Tare Da Ye* ("Walking with Jesus") in the Hausa language. The gospel is also broadcast on the radio in the Hausa language in addition to a distribution of tracts and other evangelistic materials.

Within these diaspora Muslim settlements, prostitution is a huge problem. Therefore female church planters go into the communities and spend time with sex workers, helping them to find the gospel and leading them to Christ. Young girls who are brought in from the North by *magajiyas*[7] are often rescued,

---

5 John Idoko, *Scattered to Be Gathered: Ministry to Migrants* (Lagos, Nigeria: CAPRO Media, 2017), xxiii.

6 A church-planting movement (also sometimes referred to as a disciple-making movement) is, according to David Garrison, a rapid multiplication of indigenous churches planting churches that sweep across a people group or population segment. David Garrison, *Church Planting Movements* (Midlothian, VA: WIGTake Resources, 2004), 21.

7 Magajiyas are madams in the migrant settlements who run eateries and hire young girls to work as waitresses and prostitutes to "service" their male customers.

rehabilitated, and empowered to live productive lives. This is just one of the many ways these displaced Muslims are being touched by the gospel and growing as disciples.

EQUIPPING DISPLACED CHRISTIAN-BACKGROUND BELIEVERS

> Since most Muslim migrants will not attend existing churches for cultural reasons, churches in the South are planting diaspora churches where migrants can be comfortable and worship in their traditional Hausa style.

Not all those displaced from the North are Muslims; some are Christians who have also fled the violence. So another strategy is to focus on these non-Muslims within the migrant communities— to disciple, empower, and envision them to reach Muslims. Because of their near-culture affinity, these northern Christians understand the language, culture, and practices of the diaspora Muslims. And therefore they are uniquely equipped to share Jesus with them. Every believer is taught that sharing the gospel and multiplying disciples is a key part of our identity in Christ. Since these CBBs (Christian-background believers) live in the same migrant communities as the diaspora Muslims, witnessing to them is natural as they do their normal daily work together.

Diaspora Muslims are now "strangers next door" to churches, ministries, and communities of faith in southern Nigeria. However, since most Muslim migrants will not attend existing churches for cultural reasons, churches in the South are planting diaspora churches where migrants can be comfortable and worship in their traditional Hausa style.

UGANDA: DISCIPLING REFUGEES OF WAR

The Idokos and their coworkers in Nigeria are not the only African Christians seeing God's kingdom advance among displaced people. Approximately three thousand miles to the southeast, in Kampala, Uganda, God is igniting a people movement of new Christ-followers among refugees of armed conflicts and failed states.

The war in South Sudan has resulted in widespread atrocities and violations of human rights. Almost 2 million people are internally displaced, and more than 2.2 million have fled to neighboring countries. Of these, almost a million have fled to Uganda since 2013, making Uganda one of the top five refugee-hosting countries in the world.[8]

---

8 "South Sudan Emergency," UNHCR.

A few years ago, I (Namuwoza Wilson) learned about church-planting movements (CPMs) and started seeing fruit in the slums of Kampala. In just a few years, the movement has grown to more than a thousand house churches. Of these, almost 20 percent are made up of Muslim-background refugees. Reaching Muslims was not the original plan, but God providentially sent Muslims to Uganda. When He did, the leaders of the movement responded.

The Muslims in Uganda include some Nubians and Somalis but are mostly Sudanese. The refugees in Uganda are distant from where the church-planting movement began, so it is difficult to get to them each week when they have their church meeting.

The core of the refugee work is a Sudanese family who were believers before the war began—"Sara" and her husband, "Munar." Sara's father was a Muslim who became a believer and was taught about Discovery Bible Studies directly from the Holy Spirit. Sara grew up watching various members of her family get arrested regularly for following Jesus.

While Uganda is a physical and emotional place of refuge for these displaced peoples, the country does not offer them legal or economic status. The refugees arrive with nothing but the clothes they are wearing, and most of them lack access to clean water. Even basic housing is in short supply. The combination of all these difficulties can be overwhelming for these displaced families. Unfortunately, most local believers aren't much better off, so it is difficult for the church to offer material aid. As a result, church members have been pushed to their knees in prayer for the refugees—for God alone can meet such overwhelming needs.

A SIMPLE CHURCH-PLANTING PROCESS

The process for planting churches and starting a church-planting movement is quite simple. All church planting starts with the *seeing* that comes from prayer. As the team goes out to meet migrants, they are always praying that they would be able to see what God wants them to see—not only people's physical needs, but their spiritual needs as well. This discernment is central to all stages of the CPM process.

Next the team *meets and connects* as much as possible with the people to whom they are reaching out. Before they share anything about Jesus they must connect on a deeper level and become friends. When they feel that they have been accepted, only then do they take the next step and *make disciples and share* about Jesus.

> Church members have been pushed to their knees in prayer for the refugees—for God alone can meet such overwhelming needs.

The church planting team seeks to share the gospel first with a "person of peace." This is drawn from Jesus' instructions in Luke 10:5–7: "When you enter a house, first say, 'Peace to this house.' If someone who promotes peace is there, your peace will rest on them; if not, it will return to you. Stay there, eating and drinking whatever they give you, for the worker deserves his wages. Do not move around from house to house."

Persons of peace are not only open to connecting with the team personally, but they are influencers who can invite their neighbors, friends, and peers to learn more about Jesus and study the Scriptures together.

After sharing Christ with them, the new friends are the ones who *gather* their peers into a group, where leaders will teach them to study Scripture using an interactive Discovery Bible Study (DBS) method. Through the DBS approach, new disciples or pre-disciples read Scripture and then, in turn, discuss what they learn about God and people, how they will obey the Scripture, and with whom they will share it.

Also, the obedience and sharing portion of the DBS model builds in the value of *multiplication* from the very beginning. The leaders give people assignments to obey, based on the Scripture they have studied together, and ask the group who they are going to share the story or spiritual truth with. There is follow-up and accountability in subsequent meetings.

Leaders in the church-planting movement believe that connecting deeply with refugees is a key to churches being planted. The more deeply one can connect, the more fruitful any future discipleship process will be. Jesus spent much time connecting with his disciples, taking them along with him, and modeling for them.

The leaders have also found that ministering to refugees flows out of their reality, which can make them more open spiritually and aware of their own need. Jesus said, "Blessed are the poor in spirit" (Matt 5:3). Poverty leads to a natural humility and availability. The leaders in the movement connect quickly with displaced people because they are accessible and have a lot of free time to spend with them. The refugees take this time to listen, to engage, and to discover Jesus. Later in the process we the refugee house churches multiply quickly because they are together most of the time, and they don't have a lot of other things to do.

> All church planting starts with the *seeing* that comes from prayer.

They have already sent out several missionaries from the movement, to five different countries. One of the sent ones from South Sudan, "Nate," is disabled. He says that his disability is the only reason he survived the war. Because he has a lame leg, none of the armies in the conflict forcibly drafted him. Nate has been able to organize and run orphanages based entirely on local monies. He buys corn when the crop comes in and then sells it for a profit and also feeds the orphans from it. He organizes the local ladies to take care of about one hundred orphans. Nate's accessibility and willingness to obey the Lord is growing the kingdom in one of the most desperate places on earth.

RETHINKING TRADITIONAL CHURCH PARADIGMS

Experience has shown the church-planting team that existing traditional churches in Uganda are not always as fruitful among diaspora people as they could be, due to their strategy of attraction and addition. The main goal of many churches near them seems to be to get more people into their buildings and meetings. Jesus didn't say to invite people to come to a meeting, but rather to go out and multiply disciples. Therefore, the team goes out to the displaced and neglected peoples of Uganda, bringing the gospel to them and empowering them to multiply house churches in their own contexts.

This multiplication pattern is the exact opposite of what some traditional churches do when they unthinkingly change the culture of the refugees they deal with. The refugees resist this attempt to strip them of their identities, and as a result they sometimes also resist the idea of following Jesus. Being a follower of Jesus does not involve someone changing their tribe or culture. These movements do not strip their Muslim-background disciples of their identities. Rather, they help these Muslim-background believers (MBBs) learn to follow and obey Jesus and then to go through a process of discerning, with the help of Holy Spirit, which parts of their culture and practices must be adapted or denied. Still, none of the believers among the refugees in this movement call themselves Muslims. It seems that when they follow Jesus, they are happy to be called Christians and change this part of their identity willingly.

Finally, the traditional approach, which places "experts" on a pedestal and reduces the congregation to passive listeners is troubling to many refugees. When refugees see passive listening happening in the church—the focus on knowledge as opposed to obedience—they interpret it as hypocrisy. Furthermore, Jesus didn't choose experts; he chose simple fishermen!

The church-planting team doesn't seek to build experts. Rather, they want simple people to obey Jesus in simple ways. This insight was foreshadowed by Phil Parshall in his book *New Paths in Muslim Evangelism:* "A laity highly motivated and enthusiastic about their faith in Jesus Christ will be key to effective outreach among Muslims. Resources should be directed towards the establishment of such a lay movement."[9]

CONCLUSION

As the Muslim diaspora swells throughout the world, many of the older, established Christian denominations would do well to learn from this move of God. These courageous African leaders have sought out the foreigners and exiles in their midst, shown them the love of Christ, and equipped them to become disciples who make disciples. In so doing, they may be igniting movements to Jesus that will shake Islam across not only the Global South but the entire world.

DISCUSS AND APPLY

- How is your local church gathering helping to grow the kingdom of God among displaced peoples?

- If you are not able to give physical assistance to refugees, what can you give to them? Is one better than the other?

- What part of the lives of believers in Nigeria and Uganda is worth emulating?

BIBLIOGRAPHY

Garrison, David. *Church Planting Movements*. Midlothian, VA: WIGTake Resources, 2004, 21.

"Global Trends: Forced Displacement in 2016," United Nations High Commissioner for Refugees, http://www.unhcr.org/5943e8a34.pdf.

Idoko, John. *Scattered to Be Gathered: Ministry to Migrants*. Lagos, Nigeria: CAPRO Media, 2017, xxiii.

"Nigeria Emergency," United Nations High Commissioner for Refugees, http://www.unhcr.org/en-us/nigeria-emergency.html.

Parshall, Phil. *New Paths in Muslim Evangelism*. Grand Rapids: Baker, 1980, 174.

Payne, J. D. *Strangers Next Door: Immigration, Migration and Mission*. Downers Grove, IL: IVP, 2012, 22, 158.

"South Sudan Emergency," United Nations High Commissioner for Refugees http://www.unhcr.org/en-us/south-sudan-emergency.html.

---

9 Phil Parshall, *New Paths in Muslim Evangelism* (Grand Rapids: Baker, 1980), 174.

14 | MINISTERING IN THE CONTEXT OF TRAUMA

Sarah G (a pseudonym) is from the UK and has been living in North Africa since 2006. She spent several years working for a humanitarian organization and now works as a supporter and advisor to local groups and partnerships within the MENA (Middle East and North Africa) region. Sarah is happily married to a man who grew up where she now lives, and together they love hosting and visiting family and friends.

MAIN POINTS NOT TO MISS:

- Although foreign workers are often in highly stressful situations, they also often have support systems to help them in the context of trauma.

- Local workers are often in the same traumatic contexts as foreign workers, but they rarely have as many support resources available to them for help.

- With a little foresight and intentionality, a web of supportive relationships can and should be put in place for local workers.

Grace[1] has spent ten years in North Africa as a development worker. She was sent by a European agency to work with an NGO as part of an international team. After the Arab Spring, the NGO decided to explore working in a nearby country, which had changed regimes and now seemed more "open."

So Grace, her husband, and a colleague made their home in the new land. Through friends of friends and networking, in six months the team had a list of likely local partners and projects. They also had lots of papers to fill out to open a branch office. Then came a period of waiting while their head office thought about whether to go ahead.

Grace found the waiting—being ready for action but unable to act—hard. Meanwhile, the better security, which had led to this new work, began to break down, with carjackings at night in quiet areas and armed fights in parts of the city. Several times in the streets around Grace's house disputes were settled with guns, and sometimes burning tires held up traffic on the main road. There were also stories of taxis driving their clients to lonely side streets and robbing them.

One night, Grace was woken by a friend phoning to make sure they stayed away from the windows. There was a battle on the street and an RPG (rocket propelled grenade launcher) on a truck outside their bedroom. The caller was shocked that Grace and her husband had slept through two hours of fighting; but, sadly, gunfire was a sound they had gotten used to.

Days later, Grace was in a street close to home when a man tried to molest her. She escaped and ran for home. The next month, Grace's husband called to say that he had been held up at gunpoint while driving in the town center at lunchtime. His car was one of 150 cars stolen just that morning.

Shortly after that, there was another gunfight outside the house; and Grace and her husband decided it was time to return to their previous location. At the same time, the NGO also decided they could not go ahead with work in the country.

During this time, Grace felt supported in many ways. The team of three chose to live near one another so that they could see each other easily; they met often for prayer and study and had fun with other foreigners with a similar calling. As the security situation got worse, they began to check on one another daily and share news updates. The NGO staff in the original country were a great support and kept in regular contact. They ensured that there were up-to-date security and escape plans, but they also listened to the local team's take on the situation.

---

1 Name changed for security reasons.

Part of their member-care plan involved letting the team leave the country every few weeks to release the pressure. Grace's sending group also kept in regular contact and found funds to buy a car so that Grace and her colleague could travel more safely. They made sure of medical checks and a debrief during a break in Grace's home country. Counseling was available if needed. The company offered staff regular spiritual retreats. When Grace returned "home" to the neighboring country, she was able to have debrief sessions, in her mother tongue, with a member-care team that was working in the region.

A CONTEXT OF ONGOING TRAUMA

During her time of service, Grace experienced many traumatic things. Trauma is defined as "severe emotional shock and pain caused by an extremely upsetting experience."[2] Diane Langberg reminds us that trauma is not just war, natural disaster, or extreme abuse: it's also children going missing, murder, car accidents, and infidelity. "A crisis is literally 'a separating' ... something that becomes a marker. You think of life before and after a crisis."[3]

But as we listen to the voices of local workers, it would be good to ask ourselves what systems are in place to support those who are called but not "sent," self-supporting and doing ministry in their "spare" time, dealing with hostility from family and community, and living in fragile nations.

Research by Frauke Schaeffer says that stress, for many cross-cultural workers, is a routine part of their lives, and they often learn to treat this as normal. She records that they may suffer from many traumas over the course of their ministry. Her key finding was that missionaries are resilient, have a higher exposure to trauma than many others, and that their resilience increases as they are exposed to more trauma.[4]

In recent years there has been an increase in people offering member care to humanitarian workers and missionaries, together with a growth in the number of mental health professionals who understand Christian ministry and its pressures. Manuals like *Doing Member Care Well* look at the care of cross-cultural workers from a variety of views, such as where workers are sent out from, which region they work in, and whether they are single, married, and/or parents. Other books and articles deal with issues of being raised in a culture different

---

2 *Cambridge Dictionary Online*, s.v. "trauma," accessed October 22, 2018, https://dictionary.cambridge.org/us/dictionary/english/trauma.

3 Diane Langberg, *Suffering and the Heart of God: How Trauma Destroys and Christ Restores* (Greensboro, NC: New Growth Press, 2015), 107.

4 Frauke Schaefer and Charles Schaefer, eds., *Trauma and Resilience*, Kindle ed. (Condeo Press, 2012), Preface.

from a parents' home culture, how to stay on the field, how to work in or lead multicultural teams, how to support cross-cultural workers, and how to leave the field well at the end of a term of service and settle back into a home country.

Common themes are found in these works about how cross-cultural workers can be resilient during their service, continue to be able to minister, and cope well with the trauma that will come.

They need:
- a good orientation ahead of arrival
- a deep personal relationship with God
- a clear sense of call
- a local team or community that offers support
- regular breaks/time away
- good communication to, and from, their sending organization
- good health helped by proper food, exercise, sleep, relaxation, and fun
- debriefing
- an understanding of trauma and self-care
- preparation for spiritual warfare
- security procedures
- to know when it is time to leave and when it is right to continue

As well as support for those on the field, these works also provide advice for leaders and sending groups—for example, advice on staff policies, debriefing methods, and organizations that can help during and after times of crisis.

For many people, trauma isn't a one-off event. There are many ministry situations around the world where trauma is constant—for example, where there is war or hostility to the Christian faith. In a safe, post-trauma context, people may be able to work toward recovery with a mix of talking and counseling, tears and time. However, this is not the case in situations where trauma is ongoing. At such times, Langberg advises:

> When trauma is continuous [talking, tears, and time] are still needed for healing, but ... the focus is not so much on recovery or healing as it is on managing, containing, working together, surviving with dignity, and protecting those things which are valued and can be protected (such as pouring into the next generation). That means the talking and tears are far less, and expression alone is not the goal, but rather that expression is done so as to build and protect and nurture life in the midst of the things of death that are all around. That process is not linear ... but has all the factors simultaneously woven together and strengthened.[5]

---

5 Langberg, *Suffering and the Heart of God*, 170–71.

Support and advice is available for workers like Grace who need to minister in the context of trauma, and a growing number of specialists are able to advise them and the organizations they work with. However, many other workers who are involved in Christian ministry do not have easy access to resources that can help them be resilient. Let's look at another case.

THE LOCAL WORKER

Leila[6] is a North African with a heart for outreach and working with vulnerable women. She is active in her local church, makes the most of every opportunity to share her faith, encourages others, and seeks to learn more of God and his Word.

When Leila first came to faith ten years ago, she decided to share the good news with her family. They were horrified and tried to get her to change her mind by beating her and locking her in a room until she "came to her senses." Eventually they threw her out, and she left home with only the clothes on her back and a few coins. Leila was taken in by Christian friends, and for the next eight years she had little contact with her family; most contacts ended in tears.

Along with having a full-time job, Leila was one of the leaders of a local house church. After two years in this work, there was a nasty church split, and some gossiped lies that Leila was being paid by a Western group and using the house group as a project. A year later, she suddenly lost her job when her firm closed. Meanwhile, after years of dictatorship, a revolution in her country started a period of turmoil as the nation worked out what democracy meant for them. Two years ago, Leila felt like quitting. She couldn't make ends meet. She was frustrated that in her contacts with her family their main aim was to make her give up her faith. She was worn down by again feeling betrayed by fellow believers.

Leila's resources are very different than Grace's. Since she came to faith in Christ, much of her moral support has come from foreign workers serving in her country. At present there are no qualified, local-language speaking Christian counselors or mental health practitioners in her nation, although some could be paid to come from further away in the region. Leila is from the same country where she ministers and does not have a sending group; therefore she doesn't enjoy regular, paid-for medicals, debriefs, or retreats, and she has no personnel department keeping an eye on how much rest time she takes or how she is managing her workload and stresses.

---

6 Leila's story is a composite account of real events.

THE CHALLENGE

In 2017, Vision 5:9 held its "Abide, Bear Fruit" conference. The purpose was to listen to God's heart, to better understand the Muslim world, and to hear from believers from Muslim backgrounds (MBBs) about how to reach their people groups for Christ. The goal was to gather 1,200 leaders, including 50 percent from the Majority World, 25 percent MBBs, 25 percent young workers, and 25 percent women. Other conferences and consultations also seek to ensure that discussions on ministry in the Muslim world include those who are from that world: nationals, MBBs, those living in the region, etc. But as we listen to the voices of local workers, it would be good to ask ourselves what systems are in place to support those who are called but not "sent," self-supporting and doing ministry in their "spare" time, dealing with hostility from family and community, and living in fragile nations.

Many locals involved in ministry in the Muslim world realize the scale and urgency of the task; they are aware that they are a precious but scarce resource in building the church. This can result in them taking on many and varied responsibilities and feeling that they can't say no, take breaks, or give time to recovery after setbacks and traumatic events.

As Naji Abi-Hashem and Anneke Companjen point out,

> To be effective, Christian workers need sound training and continuing education, as well as skills in problem solving, crisis intervention and basic counselling. They also have needs for belonging and for true camaraderie, needs for personal and intellectual growth, and a need for someone to check on them, stand by them and encourage them.[7]

Fortunately, some resources are available: experienced, thoughtful foreigners who speak the local language and understand context can stand alongside nationals; member-care teams which offer their services to locals as well, although these are not always available in local dialects; and the Trauma Healing Institute (THI), which provides training to start and run healing groups.[8] THI teaching material is adapted and translated for non-English speakers. There is room, however, for more professional resources, retreats, debriefing, and medical screening, as well as the equivalent of pre-field training and orientation for nationals.

---

7 Naji Abi-Hashem and Anneke Companjen, "Ministering Wisely in the Middle East: Christian Service Under Pressure," in *Doing Member Care Well*, ed. Kelly O'Donnell (Pasadena, CA: William Carey Library, 2002), 184–85.
8 Trauma Healing Institute is facilitated by American Bible Society, http://thi.americanbible.org.

Internationals can assist locals by modeling good rhythms of work and rest, facilitating local networks for sharing and support, advising on self-care and setting limits, and talking through stress and recovery. They can also encourage visits from specialized teams and point locals to resources available in their own language.

In a chapter focused on local staff in *Doing Member Care Well,* John Fawcett advises humanitarian organizations that recruit locals to ensure that their policies include:

- similar employment practices for nationals and internationals.
- attention to the physical and mental health of local staff.
- attention to skill building and career planning.[9]

ANOTHER ENDING

Leila's story could turn out differently. Although her circumstances might not change, how she journeyed through them could. Let's retell her story, with additional help in italics.

Leila is a North African with a heart for outreach and working with vulnerable women. She is active in her local church, makes the most of every opportunity to share her faith, encourages others, and seeks to learn more of God and his Word.

When Leila first came to faith ten years ago, she decided to share the good news with her family. They were horrified and tried to get her to change her mind by beating her and locking her in a room until she "came to her senses." Eventually they threw her out, and she left home with only the clothes on her back and a few coins. Leila was taken in by Christian friends, *who treated her like their own daughter;* and for the next eight years *they cried with her when contact with her family ended in tears. They also found a long-distance counselor who spoke her language and was willing to talk through issues of loss using the Internet.*

Along with having a full-time job, Leila was one of the leaders of a local house church. After two years in this work, there was a nasty church split, and some gossiped lies that Leila was being paid by a Western group and using the house group as a project. *During this time Leila was able to meet often with a group of local leaders. This had been set up a few years earlier by a foreign worker keen to see locals giving each other mutual support.*

9 John Fawcett, "Care and Support of Local Staff in Christian Humanitarian Ministry," in *Doing Member Care Well*, ed. Kelly O'Donnell (Pasadena, CA: William Carey Library, 2002).

A year later, Leila suddenly lost her job when her firm closed. Meanwhile, after years of dictatorship, a revolution in her country started a period of turmoil as the nation worked out what democracy meant for them. *Although Leila's surrogate family had left the country two years earlier, they made sure she was settled into a house-share with another local Christian woman, and they kept up regular contact by phone and Skype. On a recent visit, they spent time with Leila and paid for a brief retreat for her and other local workers.*

Although Leila found ministry tough at times, her conversations with her flatmate, her surrogate family, her counselor, and the group of local leaders were an encouragement and helped her feel that she wasn't alone. An international conference, which included MBBs from other countries, helped Leila understand that what she was experiencing wasn't unusual. In fact, it helped her feel part of a larger movement! This gave her strength and purpose and confidence that God would help her. A distance-learning course from an Arab Bible college was helping her grow and giving her insight into her local context.

DISCUSS AND APPLY

1. If you are an international cross-cultural worker, what can you do to support and encourage locals ministering in traumatic circumstances?

2. If you are a local worker, what can you do to strengthen yourself and other nationals involved in ministry?

BIBLIOGRAPHY

Abi-Hashem, Naji, and Anneke Companjen, "Ministering Wisely in the Middle East: Christian Service Under Pressure," in *Doing Member Care Well*, ed. Kelly O'Donnell. Pasadena, CA: William Carey Library, 2002, 184–85.

Cambridge Dictionary Online, s.v. "trauma," https://dictionary.cambridge.org/us/dictionary/english/trauma.

Fawcett, John. "Care and Support of Local Staff in Christian Humanitarian Ministry." In *Doing Member Care Well*, ed. Kelly O'Donnell. Pasadena, CA: William Carey Library, 2002.

Langberg, Diane. *Suffering and the Heart of God: How Trauma Destroys and Christ Restores.* Greensboro, NC: New Growth Press, 2015, 107 and 170–71.

Schaefer, Frauke, and Charles Schaefer, eds., *Trauma and Resilience*, Kindle ed. Condeo Press, 2012, Preface.

USEFUL RESOURCES FOR NATIONAL WORKERS

Barnabas International, Care for Global Workers, https://www.barnabas.org/member-care/care-for-global-workers

Cornerstone Counseling in Chiang Mai, Thailand, for Christian workers in Asia (ccfthailand.org)

Olive Tree Counseling Center (olivetreecounseling.org), Antalya, Turkey; can help national workers, but currently only in English

Globalmembercare.org gmcn.globalmembercare.com—links to some resources in languages other than English

https://sites.google.com/site/arabicmembercare/—translation of Doing Member Care Well

Sharpening Your Interpersonal Skills courses—material and facilitators possible in several languages—e.g., www.itpartners.org

Trauma Healing Institute http://thi.americanbible.org resources, training, and setting up of healing groups

15 SHEEP IN NEED OF A SHEPHERD

Caleb Rome (a pseudonym) currently leads workers in North Africa after serving in church formation among nomads in the Horn of Africa for twelve years.

MAIN POINTS NOT TO MISS:

- Nomads are not poor-quality farmers or ranchers, but have a unique lifestyle that makes them survivors.

- Nomads are overwhelmingly Muslim and have even less access to the good news of Jesus than other Muslim peoples.

- Engaging nomadic Muslims is not impossible, but missionaries will have to change underlying assumptions and practices of how to serve and honor them.

In 1916, Rowland Bingham observed Fulani nomads in northern Nigeria for the first time. He wrote, "They are worse off than their cattle. The cattle have a guiding voice and a protecting care but the Fulani has no herdman to guard or guide."

"The missionary to this tribe," Bingham continued, "has no easy task before him.... . He will need [to] … make his headquarters in one of their few towns, and then … spend half of his time in the saddle following his flock, who are wandering sheep, having no shepherd."[1]

The task of this chapter is to humbly represent the deep and continuing need of Christ among more than three hundred nomadic peoples still moving today.[2] While workers make inroads into the most resistant of settled people groups, nomads are being left behind. Not nearly enough workers are being sent to them, and those who do go face great challenges—just as Bingham pointed out over a century ago.

WHAT IS A NOMAD?

Nomads are survivalists. They can live and flourish where sedentary peoples are not able to because they use mobility to survive.

People typically confuse nomads with migrants. In the mission world this error sometimes reflects people's understanding of Abraham. One might conclude that Abraham was a nomad because he traveled from Ur to Haran and on to Canaan, but that only shows that he was a migrant. Abraham was a nomad—not because he traveled long distances—but because he moved seasonally with his animals to keep them well fed. He was a nomad in Ur, then in Haran, and then in Canaan.

There are three types of nomads. Most are nomadic pastoralists like the Fulani, sustaining herds of cows, sheep, goats, and camels by moving their animals to prescribed pasturelands on an annual cycle, following water and rain. Many pastoralists range great distances in the desert, while others are vertical nomads—grazing goats, horses, and yaks from valleys in the winter to high-mountain pastures in the summer.

---

1 *The Evangelical Christian*, vol. XII, no. 5, May 1916, Toronto, 145.
2 See "List of Nomadic Peoples," Wikipedia, last modified January 14, 2019, https://en.wikipedia.org/wiki/List_of_nomadic_peoples. An accurate compilation of nomadic peoples is difficult to find. The Nomadic Peoples Network is currently working with the International Missions Board to identify all nomadic groups. With work still to do, they have already identified over 250 groups.

Others are service-trade nomads, like the Romany (Gypsy) peoples around the world. These may move on an annual cycle or they may just keep traveling, seeking cities where they see opportunities to trade, entertain, or provide simple services.

The vast majority of nomads in centuries past were hunter-gatherers, living in forests and jungles or ranging across great arable plains. With centuries of colonization, population growth, and development, only a few groups survive today where sedentary people (like you and me) have not yet penetrated their lands.

All nomads share the following four characteristics, which conveniently form the acronym **NOMAD**:

1. **Not Individualistic**—Nomads' identity, security, allegiance, and moral codes are found in the clan or tribe. Nomads do not stand in this world as individuals.

2. **Mobility as a Resource**—Nomads survive in an environment that is insufficient to support them unless they move. Some members of the group may be mobile, while others settle in order to benefit the group. The key is not that they are currently mobile, but that their ancestors were, and that they continue to believe in mobility as a resource for survival as a people.

3. **Autonomous**—Nomads value their ability to make their own decisions vis-à-vis the nation state and other communities around which they live. They have little loyalty to the nation state they live in. This can bring tension with farming communities for pastoralists and with town communities for service nomads. Some nomads choose to continue a mobile lifestyle in order to maintain their autonomy.

4. **Distinct Identity**—Nomads self-identify as different from non-nomads or sedentary peoples. They see themselves as standing outside of sedentary systems, hierarchy, or class, even when they are living in the midst of them[3]

NOMADS AS SURVIVALISTS

Nomads are survivalists. They can live and flourish where sedentary peoples are not able to because they use mobility to survive. By moving with their animals, they increase their herds and live where others wouldn't even try to live. Perhaps it was this reality that caused Bingham to conclude that workers have no easy task when they try to reach nomads.

---

3 James Morris, "What Is a Nomad?," *Mission Frontiers*, January-February 2017, http://www.missionfrontiers.org/issue/article/what-is-a-nomad, Accessed April 19, 2019.

During the last century the population of the earth quadrupled. This put great stress on nomadic territories. When government officials set their sights on nomadic lands for economic growth, they offer money in exchange for land use rights. If nomads refuse, force is employed. The end is always the same. Nomads get pushed off good land and either make due with poorer land or are herded into settlement schemes. Land, once available to nomads, now teems with urban dwellers, forcing the nomads into the harshest of landscapes—the only places left where they have the freedom to be mobile and autonomous—and they survive.

WHY DID GOD CHOOSE NOMADS?

After Adam and Eve were sent out of the garden, nomadic pastoralism and farming emerged as ways of life. As societies developed, many farmers opted to come under the protection of local city-states who could guarantee their security and a market for their products. Nomads chose to remain as outliers. Rather than grow crops, nomads traded their animals for supplies found in the cities; but they remained distinct and autonomous, at times defending themselves from cities.[4]

God might have selected a notable city-state as his chosen people if power was what he was after. Instead he picked Abraham, one man in a small group of nomads migrating from Mesopotamia to be the father of his chosen people. Some 250 years later, Jacob's family still only totaled about seventy-five people.[5] Their autonomy, survival instincts, and distinct identity were perfect for God's plan to establish his people in a land he was still preparing them to live in.

Even when Jacob arrived in Egypt, Joseph encouraged him to settle in Goshen, where other shepherds lived. It was important that they remain shepherds, even if every shepherd was detestable to the Egyptians.[6] God knew his people would need to leave Egypt en masse four hundred years later. Only people with a nomadic history and a continuing value for mobility could entertain such an outrageous idea.

David Phillips writes, "It is clear that nomadic pastoralism was God's way of preserving the patriarchs' independence from the neighboring pagan powers of their day so that he could fulfill his purpose."[7] Who better than nomads to obey God's directives to refrain from mixing and intermarrying with other peoples? They already had a strong tendency toward independence, distinct identity, and self-sufficiency.

---

4 See Abram's rescue of Lot in Genesis 14:8-24.
5 Genesis 46:26; Acts 7:14.
6 Genesis 46:34
7 David J. Phillips, *Peoples on the Move* (Carlisle, UK: Piquant, 2001), 57.

Also consider Abraham's understanding of God. He experienced God as the one whom he could trust to lead him to a place that he himself did not know.[8] In Abraham, God had a nomad with a worldview that was amenable to a covenant of following. By faith, he obediently walked. God justified him for that faith.[9] One can hardly imagine a settled person of some aristocratic background and power being as open to God's leading as Abraham was.

Jacob referred to God as the God before whom his fathers Abraham and Isaac had walked and as the God who had been a shepherd to him.[10] Long before God was known as King of kings and Lord of lords, he was known as the Good Shepherd to a small group of nomads. Both ideas are needed to best comprehend Jesus. If God chose to reveal himself to nomads because they could more readily follow him, why is the settled church so unable to reach nomads for his glory?

A LOOK AT NOMAD MISSION STATISTICS

Although nomads account for less than 2.5 percent of all the people groups (less than three hundred), only 7 percent of those are reached. Compare this to the more than 40 percent of the sedentary people groups who have been reached.[11]

When we turn our attention to the Muslim world, we encounter more than half the world's nomads: 147 million people in 161 groups.[12] Nearly 7 percent of Muslim people groups are nomadic, which is almost three times the concentration in the rest of the world. Over half of these groups number more than 100,000 people. Let's look at their spiritual status:

- 85 percent of all unengaged nomadic people groups are Muslim (95 percent by population).
- There are 77 unengaged Muslim nomadic groups, but because these groups average more than 350,000 people, 1 in 5 people in Muslim unengaged groups are nomads (28.4 million).
- 95 percent of nomadic Muslim groups are under-engaged (not enough resident workers). By comparison, 87 percent of sedentary Muslim people groups are under-engaged.
- By population, 74 percent of nomadic Muslims are under-engaged. By comparison, 60 percent of sedentary Muslims are under-engaged.
- 0.6 percent of nomadic Muslim people groups are reached. By comparison, 9.4 percent of sedentary Muslim people groups are reached.

8 Hebrews 11:8.
9 Genesis 15:6.
10 Genesis 48:15
11 Listing of People Groups, published by International Mission Board at http://grd.imb.org/research-data/.
12 Ibid.

Although sedentary Muslims are being reached with the gospel at an unprecedented rate, nomadic Muslims are not. Currently, sedentary Muslim people groups are fifteen times more likely to be reached than nomadic groups.

WHY AREN'T NOMADS BEING REACHED WITH THE REST OF THE HARVEST?

1. Nomads live where sedentary people cannot live.

Rowland Bingham identified the great challenge of where and how to live among nomads. When people think of nomads, they think of godforsaken places where no person would ever choose to live. Churches cannot envision sending and people cannot envision going.

When people do follow the Holy Spirit into a nomadic region, they can become burdened by the mission maxim that they somehow find a way to live among people who are constantly moving. This feels impossible and *is* impossible for just about everyone called to nomads. As a result, few stick with nomadic ministry for very long.

2. Nomads are distinctly different than sedentary people.

Most believers who have a desire to reach nomads fail to recognize them as distinct from sedentary peoples. Nomadic pastoralists are not a type of farmer or rancher. They have a distinctly different understanding of land, ownership, wealth, family, blessing, curses, etc. Consider some values shared by most nomadic pastoralists:

- Land is their chief resource to be managed.
- Animals, rather than money and property, are their primary security.
- Animals are cared for and owned by clans.
- With survival as every day's chief priority, primary health care is vital.
- Justice is pragmatic, forgiveness is speedy, and reparation is paid by the clan rather than the individual.
- For clan security, they depend on reliable news and abhor gossip.
- Mobile housing is their most useful structure.
- The clan is family, while others are outsiders or even enemies.

If we fail to understand nomads as a distinctive set of peoples, we risk treating them as the most unfortunate and least successful of the earth's farmers—those to be pitied. This will lead to misdirected, ineffective work that will prohibit deep relationships with nomads. The truth is that these people are some of the most successful and resilient people on earth. We need to see them as Jesus sees them.[13]

---

13 From Caleb Rome, "Why Focus on Nomads?," *Mission Frontiers*, January-February 2017, http://www.missionfrontiers.org/issue/article/why-focus-on-nomads.

> Once we see nomads as magnificent survivalists, doors will begin to open.

I have met Ibrahim, who owns one thousand yaks, serves as a university professor, and imports cars. I know Mohammed, who has hundreds of head of livestock and has personally lived through eight to ten famines. But my favorites are three women in the desert who had an idea. They took a $300 loan, parleyed it into a thriving cooperative storehouse, and used the profits to fund a health-care scheme for all those in the cooperative. Once we see nomads as magnificent survivalists, doors will begin to open.[14]

If we conclude that in order for nomads to come to Jesus they need to be rescued from the suffering they experience as nomads, we belittle their identity and offend their hearts. Jesus calls us to engage, love, and respect the nomads exactly as they are. This is how God encountered and blessed Abraham.

3. Published methodologies are written for sedentary peoples.

Very little has been written about mission to nomads. Nomad workers are faced with the daunting task of trying to create and adapt strategies on their own because everything published is written for ministry among sedentary peoples.

Not long ago I watched as several nomads attending a disciple-making movement (DMM) seminar asked a well-known presenter how this might work among their people. How could they disciple groups weekly if people were scattered over the countryside from week to week? The presenter had to admit that he had never considered how DMM might be applied to their setting.

ADAPTATION NEEDED TO REACH NOMADS

Millions of nomads will be gathered around the throne of God one day. We know that breakthroughs with nomads are coming. The Lord is faithful. One way he will bring fruitfulness among nomads is by teaching us to become adept at adapting. We need to learn from nomads and listen to how God wants us to engage them.

1. Do We Really Need to Live with Nomads to Reach Them?

We insist that all workers live among the people they are trying to reach. What if we adapted that obligation for nomads? Is it not viable to visit the people regularly instead of live with them? A century ago, Bingham thought so. It turns out that scores of workers have proven him correct. Workers have found success with vertical nomads by basing their home in a valley settlement or partway up the mountains.

---

14 Ibid.

We took our cue from a family that had tried to move with desert nomads. One day they needed to return to the city to pick up school supplies for their children. When they returned, they found their square stick house standing alone in a deserted camp. The people had moved on to new pastures. The elders had waited to move until the family left, delaying the normal schedule. After some thought and prayer, they realized that they could never fit in with the nomadic lifestyle. So, they moved back to the city and still interacted with the nomadic peoples as they could and have had a fruitful ministry among nomads ever since.

Think about this from the perspective of nomads. They know that sedentary people find it impossible to become nomads.[15] We can make a nuisance of ourselves by insisting on staying with them. By visiting them regularly we are not so different than herders returning to the camp after a couple of weeks away. In both cases the worker and the herder are greeted with the same question: "What's the news out there?" It is like we are nomads of a different sort intersecting with their clan.

2. A High Value for Nomads Will Motivate Strategic Adaptation

When we work hard to learn about nomads and value the godly bits of their worldview, we will tend to reject pressures to settle nomads when they don't want to be settled. We will learn to examine Scripture with an eye on how God encountered nomads, and we will adapt known strategies and methodologies as best practice.

I will accept your faith if you can put it on the back of my camel.

On advice from a nomad, we decided not to ask them what their needs were, but engaged the people by asking them what their challenges were. We adapted the felt-needs approach. Because nomads are survivors, highly self-sufficient, and proud, they can be trusted to respond well to a felt-needs approach. By offering to work with them on their challenges, a partnership is created where we are the learners and they are the advisors.

Illiteracy among the nomads we were working with was almost 100 percent. The people told us they wanted their children to learn how to read and write. Workers immediately had the green light to work on the situation. There were schools in the area, but they were failing because they operated as schools for sedentary children. This called for adaptation. The workers determined to form a committee of nomads to design a school that worked for their children.

---

15 Recall the story of Exodus and how much complaining the Israelites did in the desert. They had become settled in Goshen over four hundred years.

They took into account the best times of day to have classes and then invented a mobile school with two identical campuses. Today that school has graduated half its students and has a few young people entering university, just as the people desired, and the other schools have opened their doors to nomadic training.

What will the church look like among nomads? It will almost certainly be an adaptation of what sedentary peoples already know, but nomads themselves will work out those adaptations, guided by workers whose task is to impart the whole Word of Truth. One Somali is reported to have told Dr. Malcolm Hunter, the founder of the Nomadic Peoples Network, "I will accept your faith if you can put it on the back of my camel."

God once walked with Abraham and his family in the same manner, leading Abraham as his shepherd from place to place, blessing him and multiplying his offspring. There God met him and, through him, blessed all peoples just as he promised. Now it is time to bless the nomads with the gospel of Jesus, the Good Shepherd.

DISCUSS AND APPLY

- Are you or your group engaging nomads? What would it look like for you to begin effective engagement among nomads?

- What attitudes or thoughts toward nomads need to be adjusted?

- What will it take to reach nomadic Muslims for Jesus? What barriers can you help remove?

BIBLIOGRAPHY

Listing of People Groups, published by International Mission Board, http://grd.imb.org/research-data/.

Morris, James. "What Is a Nomad?" *Mission Frontiers*, January–February 2017, http://www.missionfrontiers.org/issue/article/what-is-a-nomad,

Phillips, David J. *Peoples on the Move.* Carlisle, UK: Piquant, 2001, 57.

The Evangelical Christian, vol. XII, no. 5, May 1916, Toronto, 145.

16 | LIVING WATER FOR MUSLIM WOMEN

Moyra Dale spent over two decades in the Middle East. During that time she conducted ethnographic research on adult literacy, and the women's mosque movement. She now writes and teaches on Islam and cultural anthropology. She holds doctorates in education and psychology.

Cathy Hine spent nearly three decades in South Asia and the Middle East, working in education, community development, and the church. She was part of Interserve's international leadership for nine years. Her PhD explored women's activism in Pakistan.

Hasinoro Raja has worked among Muslims in South Africa for more than three decades. She currently researches Islam, evangelism, and the equipping and training of Christians for ministry with Muslims. She has a Master of Theology.

MAIN POINTS NOT TO MISS:

- Muslim women are very diverse and come from a variety of cultural and social backgrounds.

- Muslims women's approach to their place in society, their families, and Islam differ dramatically across the world but can still be helpfully understood within a few broad categories.

- Christ has hope for each Muslim woman, no matter where she is currently in relation to him.

According to the Pew Research Center, Muslim women made up about 12 percent of the world population in 2009.[1] They can be found throughout a whole range of different geographic and cultural contexts: speaking various languages, wearing divergent clothes. When so much of what is written about Islam is written by men, how can we learn to answer the questions and hear the longings of Muslim women?[2]

Across these regions around the world we find different expressions of Islam, along with different faces of Muslim women. Like all women, Muslim women are beautifully diverse. As such, these categories are not designed to pigeonhole Muslim women into small and confined categories. Each woman is to be celebrated for the unique individual she is. Nevertheless, it is still useful to see both the differences *and* the similarities of Muslim women.

In this chapter we look at "five plus one" faces of Muslim women. This reflects the "five plus one" pillars[3] and classic beliefs of Islam.[4] We have redrawn John Azumah's helpful essay, "Five Faces of Islam," to categories that fit Muslim women.[5] Corresponding to Azumah's categories, the faces we describe for Muslim women around the world are missionary (*da'wa*) Muslims; experiential, or folk, Muslims; militant Muslims; modernist Muslims; and nonreligious, or secular, Muslims. Refugees and displaced peoples are the "plus one" category we examine here. As we encounter Muslim women in these pages, we also make suggestions on how to meet them where they are and love them in the name of Jesus.

MISSIONARY / DA'WA MUSLIMS

The level of education of women around the world has increased dramatically in recent years;[6] and this has coincided with the growth of Islamism, which both feeds and is fed by growing accessibility to materials that teach on Islam—in communications forms ranging from pamphlets to satellite stations. This has enabled many more women to be involved in the *da'wa* movement, which calls Muslims to the proper practice of Islam and calls non-Muslims to Islam.

1 Pew Research Center, The Future of the Global Muslim Population, January 2011, available at http://www.pewforum.org/2011/01/27/the-future-of-the-global-muslim-population/, Accessed April 19, 2019.
2 It is encouraging to see more women's voices emerging, such as Evelyne Reisacher's recent award-winning book, *Joyful Witness in the Muslim World*, and through the When Women Speak network (www.whenwomenspeak.net).
3 1. Saying the creed. 2. Praying five times a day. 3. Fasting during Ramadan. 4. Giving alms. 5. Pilgrimage to Mecca. Plus one: Jihad—holy struggle.
4 Belief in: 1. one God. 2. His angels. 3. His books of revelation. 4. His prophets. 5. The day of judgment. Plus one: Belief in predestination, or fate.
5 John Azumah, "Five Faces of Islam," 2016, available at http://www.scholarleaders.org/insights-essay-archives/five-faces-islam/, accessed May 1, 2018.
6 United Nations Statistics Division, *The World's Women* 2015, https://unstats.un.org/unsd/gender/chapter3/chapter3.html, Accessed April 19, 2019.

> *Da'wa*, or missionary, Muslim women are in some ways closest to evangelical Christian women: seeking to find honor in every aspect of their lives and family interactions according to their faith, and sharing it with others.

More women are enrolling in classes to memorize the Qur'an and to learn its interpretation, both in mosque classes and in homes all around the Muslim world. Perhaps the fastest-growing contemporary movement among women in Islam, it links with such diverse contexts as Indonesian *pesantren* (boarding schools), women's mosques among the Hui in China,[7] and the *Tablighi Jama'at* (a popular Islamic renewal movement), which has spread from its home in Bangladesh to become a worldwide movement.

The *da'wa* movement is characterized by organized classes to learn the Qur'an and its interpretation, with a focus on questions relating to women's daily lives. Women are trained to use rites of passage such as birthdays, weddings, and funerals as an opportunity to urge their peers and families in more rigorous observation of Islam.

In these movements, women are encouraged to give primary allegiance to the mosque culture and to Islam rather than to family.[8] They conform to conservative religious practices of dress and general behavior. By becoming increasingly educated in the Qur'an and Islamic traditions, they are able to challenge family norms and legal and cultural practices. They do this by drawing on Islamic writings that carry a higher moral imperative than other aspects of society. Through their focus on questions relating to women, they are reforming the role of women within Islam.

Da'wa, or missionary, Muslim women are in some ways closest to evangelical Christian women: seeking to find honor in every aspect of their lives and family interactions according to their faith, and sharing it with others. We share with these women a common commitment to our faith in God and its implications for our lives. If we help them discover this, they may realize that they can find honor through Christ. We need to know our faith well, and we also need to know some apologetics to help respond to objections they've learned. We pray that their quest to lead lives of honor to God will draw them to his heart of faithfulness through Jesus Messiah reaching out to us all.

7 Maria Jaschok and Shui Jingjun, *The History of Women's Mosques in Chinese Islam* (Richmond, UK: Curzon Press, 2000).

8 Moyra Dale, *Shifting Allegiances: Networks of Kinship and of Faith: The Women's Program in a Syrian Mosque* (Eugene, OR: Wipf and Stock, 2016).

EXPERIENTIAL, OR FOLK, MUSLIMS

In a formal sense, Islam is about submission to Allah. In actual reality, however, ordinary Muslims spend hours of the day and night, as well as a significant portion of their income, seeking to deal with different areas of human concern to change their destiny. Folk, or popular, Islam is a mixture of Muslim and animistic practices. Bill Musk notes that it "betrays a hunger of the heart" of its adherents and reveals "their felt needs," which the rules of faith and ritual performances of formal Islam fail to fulfill.[9]

According to Phil Parshall, perhaps 70 percent of all Muslims are folk, or popular, Muslims.[10] Dudley Woodberry agrees with that figure, but Rick Love's estimates are even higher, suggesting that 75 percent of the Muslim world is influenced by folk Islam.[11] Nevertheless, missiologists agree that women make up the vast majority of folk Muslims. Since they don't have direct access to the divine, they need and seek help to be able to experience spiritual powers, please their husbands, solve everyday human problems, and earn merit for the hereafter.[12]

> Like all women, Muslim women are beautifully diverse.

While these women are found within the context of Islam, their actual experiences and practices are varied, depending on their given sociocultural milieu.[13] For them, Islam is not just about belief and ideology, but is essentially about practices and discourses embedded in their societal relations, their cultures, and their environments. The issue of power, a concern for equilibrium, and supernatural beings are strong components of their cosmological understanding, and they function from within an experience-oriented view of reality.

In encountering these women, we point to the power in Jesus, as he healed, cast out demons, calmed storms, fed thousands, raised people to life, overcame death and sin—opening the way to freedom for us all. We can give them hope by letting them know that Jesus is the one who walks beside us all, is concerned for every detail of our lives, and has ultimate victory over all powers and shame.

---

9   Bill A. Musk, "Popular Islam: The Hunger of the Heart," in *The Gospel and Islam: A 1978 Compendium*, ed. Don McCurry (Monrovia, CA: MARC, 1979), 213.

10 Phil Parshall, *Bridges to Islam: A Christian Perspective on Folk Islam* (Grand Rapids: Baker, 1983), 16.

11 Rick Love, *Muslims, Magic and the Kingdom of God* (Pasadena, CA: William Carey Library, 2000), 2.

12 Musk, *Popular Islam*, 223-24.

13 Baudouin Dupret, Thomas Pierret, Paulo G. Pinto, and Kathryn Spellman-Poots, eds., *Ethnographies of Islam: Ritual Performances and Everyday Practices* (Edinburgh: Edinburgh University Press, 2013), 2.

MILITANT MUSLIMS

It has been surprising, perhaps, to see that a number of Muslim women have readily embraced the use of violence and warfare for political ends. Equally surprising is that they have done this as a free choice, joining militant groups in acceptance of their radical ideologies. Estimates suggest that about 10 percent of foreign recruits to ISIS-related movements—those from places like Europe, the US, and Australia—are women.[14] The appeal to women is summed up by female ISIS blogger Umm Layth:

> The imperative to respond with love rather than fear is never more important than in relation to militant Muslims.

Our role is even more important as women in Islam, since if we don't have sisters with the correct *Aqeedah* [conviction] and understanding who are willing to sacrifice all their desires and give up their families and lives in the west in order to make *Hijrah* [migration] and please Allah, then who will raise the next generation of Lions?[15]

Engaging with a militant vision for life, women are encouraged to participate in jihad. Women-only brigades have been working in a number of areas, including Kurdish regions, Raqqa in Syria, and many other places. This allows women's participation in the higher cause while maintaining strict segregation.

Women who practice militant expressions of Islam are engaging a utopian vision of a world that they dream to return to, the Golden Age of Islam. They too are seeking for faithfulness to truth as they have understood or been taught it, desiring a better world that they are willing to pursue at all costs. They are reacting to the brokenness of a world in which they have felt marginalized and excluded and experienced oppression in some form. Their future is bound up in creating a new order of life that they believe is expressed in the dogmatic enforcement of their vision of religious utopia.

While militant Muslims are not the largest group in Islam, this group tends to dominate the media headlines. The imperative to respond with love rather than fear is never more important than in relation to militant Muslims. We recognize their search for honor in a world that can marginalize them—and the anger they feel at injustice between nations. We can affirm their feelings of injustice in the world, and even agree with them. The solution in Christ, however, is different and hope-filled. However, the solution, in Christ is different and hope

14 Rafia Zakaria, "Women and Islamic Militancy," *Dissent*, Winter 2015, https://www.dissentmagazine. org/article/why-women-choose-isis-islamic-militancy, Accessed April 19, 2019.
15 Ibid.

filled. Jesus came from a small and peripheral nation, but changed the course of the occupying empire and world history through his self-sacrifice—not human war.

MODERNIST / PROGRESSIVE MUSLIMS

Modernist, or progressive, Muslim women are openly challenging the orthodox Islamic understanding as the only appropriate interpretation of Islam. Writer and gender justice activist Ayaan Hirsi Ali points out that "no human culture compromises the rights of women more than Islam."[16] Women like Zainah Anwar seek to end discrimination against women in the name of religion. She explains: "Today's women are challenging the values of patriarchal society where power and authority reside exclusively with the husband, father and brother, to whom the wife, daughter and sister owe obedience."[17]

Since the second half of the twentieth century, debates grappling with the women's question within Islam have been generated by progressive scholars and jurists such as Amina Wadud-Mushin, Asma Barlas, Kecia Ali, Khaled Abou El Fadl, and Omid Safi. These scholars reject the heavy patriarchal legacy of Islamic orthodoxy and provide new interpretations of the scriptural message, making distinctions between its universal and context-specific parts. For example, Wadud-Mushin is a pioneer of feminist Qur'anic exegesis and a leader in what is now known as the "gender jihad." She engages the sacred Qur'anic text in a way that its emancipatory potential for women is released.[18] Likewise, Barlas' approach to the Qur'an argues that "men cannot claim the Qur'an as their own, because the Qur'an has been opened to women for all times and only women can answer for their understanding of it on the Day of Din."[19]

Anwar expresses the aspirations of women who wish to live in modernity, while remaining Muslims, when she writes,

> For most Muslim women, rejecting religion is not an option. We are believers: as believers we want to find liberation, truth and justice within our own faith. We strongly feel we have a right to reclaim our religion, to redefine it, to participate in it and to contribute to an understanding of what Islam is and how it is codified and implemented—in ways that take into consideration the realities and experience of women's lives today.[20]

16 Phyllis Chesler, *Islamic Gender Apartheid: Exposing a Veiled War against Women* (Nashville and London: New English Review Press, 2017), 6.
17 Kari Vogt, Lena Larsen, and Christian Moe, eds., *New Directions in Islamic Thought* (London and New York: I.B.Tauris, 2009) 176.
18 Wadud-Mushin, *Qur'an and Woman* (Kuala Lumpur, Malaysia: Penerbit Fajar Bakati Sdn. Bhd, 1992).
19 Vogt, Larsen, and Moe, *New Directions*, 21.
20 Ibid., 176.

Modernist Muslims are ready to engage in dialogue in which both sides seek to listen to each other. Their pluralism makes them ready to listen, but it also makes it harder to hear the exclusive claims of Jesus Messiah. We appreciate their commitment to oppressed people, and we may share the struggles that we have faced as women also seeking honor and dignity in our own contexts.

NONRELIGIOUS, OR SECULAR, MUSLIMS (SOCIAL ACTIVISTS)

> Since they don't have direct access to the divine, they need and seek help to be able to experience spiritual powers, please their husbands, solve everyday human problems, and earn merit for the hereafter.

The discourses of rights and equality are a force in shaping the way Muslim women negotiate their place in the world. This has resulted in an increase of Muslim women activists, as evident in major international networks such as Women Living Under Muslim Law (WLUML), Sisters in Islam in Malaysia, Women's Action Forum in Pakistan, and the Revolutionary Association of Women in Afghanistan (RAWA). There are also many grassroots projects, such as the Association for the Protection of the Environment (APE) in Cairo and Rahima in Indonesia. Additionally, many individual women are also activists, such as Hina Jilani and Farida Shaheed in Pakistan, Tawakkol Karmen in Yemen, Razan Ghazzawi from Syria, and Manal al-Sharif in Saudi Arabia, just to name a few.

There are emerging groups of women who live under Islam for whom secularism means a total rejection of religious belief. The majority of such women, however, must negotiate the tensions between a religion that they feel has failed to address the glaring inequalities in society—usually in issues particularly affecting women—and their personal visions for women's place and role in society. They must do this in a community in which religion shapes the fabric of society and government. So they variously use discourses of feminism, human rights, international conventions and law, and religious ideology.

As these women engage the discourses of religious ideology for change, they are also reframing what it means to be Muslim. Nonreligious, or secular, Muslim women are challenging Islam in both its beliefs and practices. Many of the women who are labeled nonreligious or secular are impacting the world through their participation in women's movements and the recognition they are afforded on the international stage.

When "Muslim" is a statement of ethnicity, we cannot assume religious beliefs or practices. We can honor the culture and history that these women bring, even as they look beyond traditional religious allegiance. We affirm and work with them in their commitment to bring change in their own societies and communities. Some of these women may be slow to trust in Jesus, but Jesus is deeply attractive as we look at his life, work, and teachings. He is able to establish the honor and dignity of these women, and also the women to whom they seek to bring human rights and the rule of law.

REFUGEES AND DISPLACED PEOPLES

Global forced displacement continues at record-high levels, surpassing even the numbers of displaced peoples after World War II.[21] Among both source and host countries for refugees, Muslim countries and communities are highly represented. Current major hosting countries include Turkey, Pakistan, Lebanon, Iran, Ethiopia, Jordan, and Chad. Source countries include Syria, Afghanistan, Iraq, Libya, Somalia, Sudan, Yemen, and Myanmar (the Rohingya).[22]

To relate to Muslim women in different parts of the world is increasingly to meet displaced women and girls who carry the impact of the trauma and displacement they have experienced. This includes the loss of family and home, with the community and history that have defined them. They are seeking to make new lives and care for their families, without their traditional support networks and relationships. Sometimes they also encounter hostility or discrimination in their host community. Resources such as counseling, health services, legal advice, and vocational training can help women who are resilient survivors of trauma.

These women should not be viewed only as victims, of recipients of pity or help, but rather as agents of change—as women who, even in the face of alienation and struggle, respond with initiative and creativity. The place of a new community is important in helping them negotiate the challenges and responsibilities they face. In many places around the world we find displaced and refugee people looking for hope, honor, and a new identity beyond the contexts from which they came. Where they encounter the love and care of Christian people and the Word of God, they may discover a hope and new identity in Jesus Messiah and his people. These communities are where we are seeing some of the greatest response to Christ today.

---

21 United Nations High Commissioner for Refugees, "Data," available at http://www.unhcr.org/en-us/data.html, accessed October 23, 2018.
22 Ibid.

CONCLUSION

None of these "faces" of Muslim women are sealed categories; rather, they overlap and influence one another. As we meet Muslim women, we seek to understand each one where they are—in the challenges they face and the longings of their hearts. We seek to share with them how Jesus can help restore their honor and dignity and finally fulfill the longing of their hearts.

Although each woman is unique, all of them were created to be in relationship with Jesus and to worship him. By understanding some of their background and perspective, perhaps we can introduce them to Jesus in a meaningful and powerful way. Together, we can introduce them to the living water of Jesus Christ. In many communities in which we have a chance to encounter Muslim women, they feel on the outskirts of society—like our Samaritan sister who met Jesus at the well long ago (John 4). We can help these women, like her, to find dignity, honor, liberation, and living water in Jesus Christ. To do so, however, we might have to travel an unusual path (as Jesus did that day) or even go out of our way to be with them. This living water is powerful for all women everywhere. We pray it may be offered to them in a way in which they can receive it.

DISCUSS AND APPLY

- How have you viewed Muslim women? What parts of that view might need to change?
- How can you pray for, meet with, and minister to Muslim women?
- How can you process the news from the Muslim world differently, knowing the true diversity of the world of Muslim women?

BIBLIOGRAPHY

Azumah, John. "Five Faces of Islam." 2016. Available at http://www.scholarleaders.org/wp-content/uploads/2016/10/Five-Faces-of-Islam-Azumah.pdf.

Chesler, Phyllis. *Islamic Gender Apartheid: Exposing a Veiled War against Women.* Nashville and London: New English Review Press, 2017.

Dale, Moyra. *Shifting Allegiances: Networks of Kinship and of Faith: The Women's Program in a Syrian Mosque.* Eugene, OR: Wipf and Stock, 2016.

Dupret, Baudouin, Thomas Pierret, Paulo G. Pinto, and Kathryn Spellman-Poots, eds. *Ethnographies of Islam: Ritual Performances and Everyday Practices.* Edinburgh: Edinburgh University Press, 2013.

Jaschok, Maria, and Shui Jingjun. *The History of Women's Mosques in Chinese Islam.* Richmond, UK: Curzon Press, 2000.

Love, Rick. *Muslims, Magic and the Kingdom of God*. Pasadena, CA: William Carey Library, 2000.

Musk, Bill A. "Popular Islam: The Hunger of the Heart." In *The Gospel and Islam: A 1978 Compendium*, edited by Don McCurry. Monrovia, CA: MARC, 1979.

Parshall, Phil. *Bridges to Islam: A Christian Perspective on Folk Islam*. Grand Rapids: Baker, 1983.

Pew Research Center. *The Future of the Global Muslim Population*. January 2011. Available at http://www.pewforum.org/2011/01/27/the-future-of-the-global-muslim-population/.

United Nations High Commissioner for Refugees. "Data." Available at http://www.unhcr.org/en-us/data.html.

United Nations Statistics Division. *The World's Women 2015*. https://unstats.un.org/unsd/gender/chapter3/chapter3.html.

Vogt, Kari, Lena Larsen, and Christian Moe, eds. *New Directions in Islamic Thought*. London and New York: I.B.Tauris, 2009.

Wadud-Mushin, Amina. *Qur'an and Woman*. Kuala Lumpur, Malaysia: Penerbit Fajar Bakati Sdn. Bhd, 1992.

Zakaria, Rafia. "Women and Islamic Militancy." *Dissent*, Winter 2015. https://www.dissentmagazine.org/article/why-women-choose-isis-islamic-militancy.

17 | UNDERSTANDING THE ROLE OF HONOR IN MUSLIM SOCIETY

Audrey Frank is the author of *Covered Glory: The Face of Honor and Shame in the Muslim World* (Harvest House, 2019). Audrey and her husband have shared the good news of the gospel with Muslims across the globe for over twenty years.

Jairo de Oliveira was born in Brazil and serves among Muslim peoples with PMI (Pueblos Musulmanes Internacional). He is a PhD candidate in Intercultural Studies at Columbia International University and a contributing author of *Where There Is Now a Church*.

MAIN POINTS NOT TO MISS:

- The central role of honor in the Bible is often missed or overlooked, but it is prevalent throughout the Bible.

- Understanding honor is critical to understanding the hearts and minds of our Muslim friends.

- Learn a new way to discover the themes of shame and honor in the Bible so that those who are not used to reading the Bible in this way can retrain their eyes and empower their ability to share Jesus with Muslims.

Mohammad knocked on the massive red wooden door of his American friend's house. He needed business advice today, and Samuel had vast experience as a successful business owner in the city. Their families had enjoyed many meals together and occasionally spent a day in the local mountains picnicking and roasting lamb while their children played together. Samuel had stood by him the past year when his father passed away, praying for him and comforting him. Samuel was a man of the Book, a follower of Jesus. His prayers brought peace to Mohammad's heart. Samuel was indeed a good friend. He would surely help Mohammad.

The door opened and Samuel greeted Mohammad with a wide grin and kisses on both cheeks. Ushering him into the guest salon, Samuel asked his wife to make some tea for his dear friend.

Over the next hour, Mohammad explained that his father had left him a large sum of money. Mohammad wanted to open a business, and he was brimming with ideas. Could Samuel help him with a business plan? Perhaps with Samuel's connections, Mohammad could tap into the tourism business. He had dreamed of owning a fleet of motorcycles ever since he was a boy and he and his cousins took turns riding a dilapidated motorcycle on his uncle's farm. Sometimes he saw foreigners passing through the city on their way to the desert, colorful motorcycles loaded on four-wheel-drive trucks. What if he rented cycles to tourists for desert adventures? The idea had merit and a ready market.

Together Samuel and Mohammad carefully drew up a business plan. For several weeks, over cups of strong coffee, they planned and revised until they were satisfied. In the end they produced a solid business model with a strong chance of success. Now all Mohammad had to do was meet with the right officials to begin the licensure process. In the meantime, Samuel and his family were heading back to the United States for two weeks to attend his sister's wedding. Mohammad was all set to complete the final steps to make his business official. By the time Samuel got back, he should be ready to shop for motorcycles.

With everything in place, Samuel and Mohammad said their goodbyes, each looking forward to the fulfillment of Mohammad's dream.

When Samuel returned three weeks later, he couldn't wait to see his friend. As they pulled up chairs at their favorite café, he asked, "So how did it go? Did you get the permissions you need? Are we ready to look at motorcycles?"

He fought to keep his jaw from dropping in astonishment at Mohammad's reply. "I bought a fruit orchard instead."

Struggling to understand, Samuel tried to think of what to say. Silently he thought to himself, "We developed an impressive plan with great potential! What about all those long hours spent preparing? What about the excitement you had about your childhood dream?"

Samuel suspected there was something cultural here that he was missing. A blank space loomed in his mind, a disconnect between his culture and Mohammad's.

As if sensing his friend's confusion, Mohammad offered, "If the motorcycle business fails, only I fail. But if the fruit orchard fails due to the weather conditions, everyone fails."

Understanding dawned on Samuel with a jolt. Mohammad was doing what all Muslim men do. He was thinking about how to avoid shame. No shame would be attached to his family if he suffered a loss shared by other farmers due to circumstances beyond his control. If Mohammad invested in the motorcycle venture and failed, however, he alone would bear the shame.

THE ROLE OF HONOR IN WORLDVIEW

In Samuel's worldview, a solid, well-developed plan made sense because it had been done carefully, thoughtfully, right. Western culture is largely individualistic, placing focus on the rights of the individual above the group. The individual, not the group, bears responsibility for success. According to the Western worldview, if Mohammad worked hard enough and did things right, he would be successful. To abandon a well-laid plan for the sake of one's position of honor in the group was literally a foreign concept to Samuel.

Indeed, this is the key to understanding the role of honor in Muslim society: *honor is a position to be maintained at all costs.* In contrast to individualist societies like Samuel's, Muslim cultures are collectivist. For those from collectivist societies, where emphasis is placed upon the group rather than the individual, honor is an actual position. Honor and shame are always attached to a group. The group might be one's family, tribe, community, or nation. One with an honor-shame worldview always considers his behavior within the context of the group. Consequently, behavior outside prescribed group rules and conventions could result in loss of one's status. The result is shame. Shame expels one outside the group, and therefore is to be avoided.

> Indeed, this is the key to understanding the role of honor in Muslim society: *honor is a position to be maintained at all costs.*

Much misunderstanding occurs between Muslims and those who minister to them because of differences in worldview. For the Westerner, choosing the group over the individual doesn't always make sense. For the one from an honor-shame background, the Westerner's individualism might appear selfish and rude. Too often relationships stagnate at this impasse between worldviews.

UNDERSTANDING THE GOSPEL THROUGH THE LENSES OF HONOR AND SHAME

It does not have to be this way. The junction of misunderstanding can instead become a portal to greater effectiveness and friendship. We can begin by asking the following questions: What is the role of honor in Muslim evangelism? How do the lenses of honor and shame impact the Muslim view of the gospel?

The good news is that God, through Jesus Christ, not only provides forgiveness of sin but also the removal of shame and power over fear. To understand the element of shame in the gospel message, it is helpful to consider its beginning, together alongside that of fear and guilt. Shame, fear, and guilt were all responses to original sin in the garden of Eden, and all are addressed by the gospel.

In the fresh days of Creation, man and woman stood in perfect relationship with God. They walked with him, talked with him, and enjoyed undivided communion with him. Adam and Eve, the masterpieces of God's creation, belonged to God and God belonged to them. Shame did not exist, fear did not exist, and guilt did not exist. The biblical narrative assures that Adam and Eve walked in purity and had no concerns related to shame: "Adam and his wife were both naked, and they felt no shame" (Gen 2:25) Theirs was the model of relationship as it was intended.

What happened next changed the course of human history. The serpent, God's great enemy, whispered his lie into the hearts of man and woman, and the result was devastating. With their belief in the first lie, Adam and Eve were sent out of God's presence, away from the comfort and constancy of communion with him.

After they sinned, Adam and Eve tried to cover up the shame of nakedness, hid in fear, and passed the guilt to one another, according to the biblical account.

- Attempting to cover the shame of nakedness: "Then the man and his wife heard the sound of the Lord God as he was walking in the garden in the cool of the day, and they hid from the Lord God among the trees of the garden" (Gen 3:8);

- Struggling to deal effectively with fear: "I heard you in the garden, and I was afraid because I was naked; so I hid" (Gen 3:10); and

- Striving to pass forth the guilt: "The man said, 'The woman you put here with me—she gave me some fruit from the tree, and I ate it.' ... The woman said, 'The serpent deceived me, and I ate'" (Gen 3:12–13).

Guilt, shame, and fear crept over Adam and Eve's souls like dark, menacing clouds, forecasting the storm to come. Brand-new feelings like loneliness, hunger, and pain marked this new existence. The unblemished relationship with God they had once enjoyed was now marred by sin. The generations after them would toil under its burden. Humanity would inherit a predisposition to sin and a fallen nature. Shame, fear, and guilt would be the signature of this new human nature.

MAKING SENSE

In the Western world, this pivotal moment is primarily viewed through the framework of guilt and innocence. Adam and Eve were guilty of sin and disobedience. In parts of the majority world, the same event is perceived as the moment fear entered the heart of humanity. People began seeking power to overcome it, engaging in appeasement of evil spirits and appeasement of God. Fear drove humanity further away from God, and animism was born.

For others in the majority world, Adam and Eve's choice to eat the forbidden fruit symbolizes humanity's first encounter with shame. The separation from God that resulted was man and woman's first loss of position and belonging. They no longer belonged to God. The honor of belonging to God had been lost. They were outsiders and felt ashamed.

Roland Muller states that guilt, fear, and shame became the building blocks of worldview.[1] Every culture has elements of all three, but one is predominant at any given time in history.[2] Scholars have agreed that although the influences of guilt, fear, and shame are existent in all cultures, one of them is usually primary in every cultural setting.

Historically, due to the impact of Roman law on the early church and the influence of early theologians, Christians developed a tendency to explain sin exclusively from a guilt perspective. Emphasis was placed on the sinner's guilt and need for forgiveness and justification through the work of Christ. As a result of this tendency, the realities of shame and fear have been forgotten,

---

1 Roland Muller, *Honor and Shame: Unlocking the Door* (Los Gatos, CA: Smashwords Edition, 2013), 13.
2 Moyra Dale, *Shifting Allegiances: Networks of Kinship and of Faith: The Women's Program in a Syrian Mosque* (Eugene, OR: Wipf and Stock, 2016).

ignored, and, overlooked, as Robin Stockitt states in his book *Restoring the Shamed: Towards a Theology of Shame.*[3]

An approach that considers only one of these realities is limited and risks inadequately communicating the full extent of Christ's work. Conversely, focusing on guilt alone, for example, may not make sense in cultural contexts where it is believed that God's sovereignty excludes any necessity to forgive. As Moyra Dale explains in her book *Shifting Allegiances,*

> It is easy for an omnipotent God to forgive: because he has not been sinned against (for sin hurts the sinner rather than God), there is no cost involved for Him. In this understanding of the transaction between forgiver and the forgiven, there is no obligation to forgive, and neither any cost.[4]

A gospel appeal along the lines of one's guilt toward God can fall on deaf ears to the one who believes he has not sinned against him in the first place. From a theological and missiological point of view, the threefold reality composed of shame, fear, and guilt needs proper consideration in our biblical approach to sin. For those working among Muslims, understanding how the gospel addresses shame is paramount to making the gospel message understood.

THE ROLE OF HONOR IN SHARING THE GOSPEL

Samuel smiled and greeted his friends at the lamp shop as he climbed the winding cobbled street to the Al Nour Café. He was meeting Mohammad this afternoon to discuss the fruit orchard, but Samuel had more than lemons and oranges on his mind. Since their last conversation, he had been thinking deeply about Mohammad's surprising decision, reading all he could about honor and shame. He and his wife prayed God would show him how to address Mohammad's desire for honor with the honor-giving gospel of Christ.

Mohammad, on the other hand, was relieved his American friend had so easily accepted his decision. Americans could be so rigid with their elaborate plans and hyperfocus. Maybe Samuel was becoming more Middle-Eastern in his thinking. He had understood Mohammad's need to avoid the potential shame that could come if his motorcycle business failed. Now they were meeting for coffee, and Mohammad was looking forward to their rich conversation. Maybe over the weekend their families could drive to the orchard and have a picnic.

---

3 Robin Stockitt, *Restoring the Shamed: Towards a Theology of Shame* (Eugene, OR: Cascade Books, 2012), 23.
4 Dale, *Shifting Allegiances,* 187.

It would be an honor to show his friend the beautiful property with its proud rows of strong young fruit trees.

In the weeks that followed, Samuel shared stories from the Bible with Mohammad to illustrate God's keen interest in honor and shame. Mohammad was surprised to learn that the book Christians revered was so full of honor and shame themes. The stories read like his own culture more than the Western culture as he understood it. More and more, his interest grew. Occasional conversations evolved into regular Bible study together. As Mohammad learned about the power of the gospel to remove shame and give honor, Samuel learned to see his own Book through the marvelous eyes of the honor-shame worldview of his friend. Both were blessed, and both were changed.

On the day Mohammad made the message his own, Samuel knew the bridge between their worldviews had truly been built. Lounging back on brightly colored couches at Mohammad's house after a filling meal of lamb, rice, and vegetables, Mohammad grew animated as he explained Christianity to their friend Sayed.

"The Messiah Jesus has brought man to God again. We no longer have to hide our faces. We can look at God, and he looks at us. There is no more shame!"

Samuel looked away, afraid his friend would see the hot tears of joy that sprang unbidden to his eyes. Could it be that in the quiet place of faith Mohammad had taken Jesus' hand?

IDENTIFYING HONOR AND SHAME IN THE BIBLE

After gaining a basic understanding of the honor and shame worldview, learning to read the Bible through that framework is one of the most practical things workers can do to share the gospel with Muslims effectively. Interestingly, the Bible was recorded by people from an honor-shame worldview for people from an honor-shame worldview. It does not need contextualization. Learning to recognize honor and shame in the Bible opens a whole new understanding of the glory and gospel of God.

There are some questions you can ask yourself to help you recognize honor and shame in Scripture. The keys below have been taken from the book *Covered Glory* where they are discussed at greater length.

> After gaining a basic understanding of the honor and shame worldview, learning to read the Bible through that framework is one of the most practical things workers can do to share the gospel with Muslims effectively.

Shame Conceals

It is shame's nature to conceal the truth. From the beginning, shame forced its bearers into hiding. Adam and Eve hid because they were ashamed. In the fascinating narratives of the Bible, we often find men and women burdened with shame, the truth about their value and identity hidden. Our first step in identifying honor and shame in the Bible is to ask, *What does shame conceal?*

An example is found in Mark 5:24–34, where we read of a woman with an issue of blood. If we apply the question to this passage, we find that shame hid from the woman her value to God. It hid hope. Shame concealed the pride of the onlookers, who had rejected her for a problem over which she had no control.

Honor Reveals

Contrary to the hiding nature of shame, it is the character of honor to reveal and expose. Honor shines light on what is true about a person. Our second step is to ask, *What does honor reveal?*

In the Mark 5 story, we find that Jesus' honoring of the sick woman reveals her value. It proclaims the veracity of the very thing hidden only moments before. Honor reveals hope, healing, and a future. Honor restores the woman's position to one worthy of the Teacher's time and ministry. It restores her position from outsider to insider. She belongs again. She is made clean.

The Gospel Appeal

Once we have examined what shame conceals and what honor reveals, we are ready to ask, What is the gospel appeal? For the woman who touched Jesus' garment in Mark 5, the good news was that she could, indeed, be made clean again. In an ironic, magnificent twist, the blood of the Savior would cleanse her of the shame her physical issue of blood had brought. She was restored physically, mentally, emotionally, and spiritually. Jesus' closing words to her in verse 34 were "Daughter, your faith has healed you. Go in peace and be freed from your suffering."

The message that restored honor to this woman is a relevant and powerful message for Muslim women today.

CONCLUSION

The good news for Muslims is this: The Messiah Jesus has abolished shame, and through him honor has been restored to humanity. No longer is our relationship with God broken. We are insiders once again, our place of honor in God's sight made secure by Jesus Christ.

For Samuel's friend Mohammad, everything in life was viewed through the framework of honor and shame. His perceptions about the world around him and the decisions he faced were all weighed within the context of his family and community. The maintaining of his honor in the group was paramount.

The Old and New Testaments are teeming with rich and beautiful illustrations of the loving, compassionate Creator God removing the shame of his people and honoring them instead. This message of redemption is one our Muslim friends are eager to hear. The role of honor in Muslim societies, in the end, a gateway to the gospel of Christ.

DISCUSS AND APPLY

- Have you noticed the theme of shame and honor in the Bible? Reread a favorite portion of the Bible and look for the theme of honor in that passage.

- Have you had any confusing interactions with Muslims? Think through the interaction in light of honor. Does the new lens of honor shed any insight on the interaction?

- In light of honor, what sorts of expectations of behavior might be involved in friendships with Muslims? Do you need to change how you relate to anyone?

BIBLIOGRAPHY

Dale, Moyra. *Shifting Allegiances: Networks of Kinship and of Faith: The Women's Program in a Syrian Mosque.* Eugene, OR: Wipf and Stock, 2016.

Frank, Audrey. *Covered Glory: The Face of Honor and Shame in the Muslim World.* 1st ed. Eugene, OR: Harvest House Publishers, 2019.

Muller, Roland. *Honor and Shame: Unlocking the Door.* Los Gatos, CA: Smashwords Edition, 2013.

Stockitt, Robin. *Restoring the Shamed: Towards a Theology of Shame.* Eugene, OR: Cascade Books, 2012.

HONOR-SHAME RESOURCES FOR FURTHER READING

Books:

Honor and Shame: Unlocking the Door, by Roland Muller (Xlibris, 2001)

The 3D Gospel: Ministry in Guilt, Shame, and Fear Cultures, by Jayson Georges (Tim& 275; Press, 2014)

Ministering in Honor-Shame Cultures, by Jayson Georges and Mark Baker (InterVarsity, 2016)

The Global Gospel, by Werner Mischke (Misson ONE, 2015)

Shame and Honor in the Book of Esther, by Timothy Laniak (Society of Biblical Literature, 1998)

Honor, Patronage, Kinship and Purity, by David deSilva (InterVarsity, 2000)

Restoring the Shamed: Towards a Theology of Shame, by Robin Stockitt (Cascade Books, 2012)

Shame and Grace: Healing the Shame We Don't Deserve, by Lewis Smedes (HarperOne, 2009)

Shame Interrupted: How God Lifts the Pain of Worthlessness and Rejection, by Edward T. Welch (New Growth Press, 2012)

Without Shame or Fear: From Adam to Christ, by A. Robert Hirschfeld (Church Publishing, 2017)

Misreading Scripture with Western Eyes: Removing Cultural Blinders to Better Understand the Bible, by E. Randolph Richards and Brandon J. O'Brien (InterVarsity, 2012)

Saving God's Face: A Chinese Contextualization of Salvation through Honor and Shame, by Jackson Wu (William Carey International University Press, 2012)

Covered Glory: The Face of Honor and Shame in the Muslim World, by Audrey Frank (Harvest House Publishers, 2019)

Articles:

"Disgraced Yet Graced: The Gospel According to 1 Peter in the Key of Honor and Shame," by John Elliott, in *Journal of Bible and Culture,* November 1995

"Does the 'Plan of Salvation' Make Disciples? Why Honor and Shame Are Essential for Christian Ministry," by Jackson Wu, in *Leadership Development for the 21st Century Asian Mission*

"From Shame to Honor: A Theological Reading of Romans for Honor-Shame Contexts," by Jayson Georges

"Honor and Shame in God's Mission," by Jayson Georges

"Human Identity in Shame-Based Cultures of the Far East," by Timothy Tennent

"The Eight Guidelines for Relationships in Honor-Shame Cultures," by Jayson Georges and Mark Baker

"The Saving Significance of the Cross in a Honduran Barrio," by Mark Baker

Websites:

HonorShame.com

JacksonWu.org

18 HOW WOULD JESUS SHEPHERD AN MBB'S HEART?

David Faouzi Arzouni is a Lebanese Muslim-background believer (MBB) from Senegal. He and his wife, Linda, have served for forty-two years in Africa. David holds an MA in Biblical Studies and is a doctoral student in Biblical Counseling.

MAIN POINTS NOT TO MISS:

- To truly shepherd the heart of an MBB we must first understand how Jesus shepherded the heart of his disciples.

- Jesus addressed the issues of importance to MBBs, but Westerners often fail to miss the implications for Jesus' teachings and too quickly turn to other discipleship methods—methods that are ultimately less effective.

- MBBs expect those shepherding them to walk with them and guide them in all aspects of life, something a typical Westerner might not feel comfortable doing.

"*Above all else,* guard your heart, for *everything* you do flows from it" (Prov 4:23, emphasis added). *The term everything* is quite an expansive arena, and many volumes have been written about guarding and shaping those things that exist in the recesses of the human heart. So let us consider for a moment a young Muslim-background believer (MBB) named "Ali." What goes on in Ali's heart? Is it different than in the heart of any other disciple?

Like many things in life, the answer is both yes and no. In general, an MBB has many of the same spiritual needs as anyone else. But an MBB's life experiences are *very* different than those of people who grew up in, for example, a "Christian" culture. And even more importantly, I believe there is a biblical basis for saying that Ali's heart is particularly vulnerable to certain tendencies— tendencies to which someone discipling him needs to pay particular attention. This is the concern of this chapter.

Five important premises guide this discussion. Although it isn't possible to completely unpack them in a primer such as this, you (dear reader) must at least be aware of them, since they permeate everything that follows.

Premise 1

Jesus came into the world at a time when the system of the Jewish Pharisees bore a striking resemblance to the religious culture and society later structured by Muhammad. In the past few decades various scholars, such as Harland, Neusner, and Sonn, have picked up on the emphasis on rituals, law, purity, and honor codes shared by both the Pharisees and Muhammad. So dare I suggest we might say, in some ways, that Jesus was essentially ministering to a first-century version of Muslims?

Scripture says that "when the set time had fully come, God sent his Son, born of a woman, born under the law, to redeem those under the law, that we might receive adoption to sonship" (Gal 4:4–5) This is but one of many passages from which I understand that God was deliberate in the timing of Christ's advent. Those of us working among Muslims can be confident that one aspect of that timing was that God anticipated Islam and sent his Son into a relevant context with a similar mind-set. The theological evidence for this is ample both in the Old Testament and in early rabbinic literature.[1]

---

1 In fact, God anticipated all of the religious, cultural, and philosophical categories that were ever to reappear in the world by sending Jesus when they all had already manifested themselves. But here we focus on and proceed from the notion that by the first century Israel had all the earmarks of what was essentially Islam. For the biblical and theological basis of this premise and the others presented here, a copyrighted paper will be made available by sending a request to the author at dlarzouni@gmail.com.

Premise 2

When we look at Jesus' interaction with the Judaism of his day, we can glean very specific ideas about how to interact with those coming to him out of Islamic theology and culture. Understood in this way, Christ's ministry offers us specific insights into the deeper parts of the Muslim's heart and a demonstration of how to shepherd modern MBBs.

Premise 3

Discipleship is understood as something that usually begins before full identification with all that Christ is. During the first year or so of MBBs' spiritual journeys, they are often like the disciples of Jesus, who were "Christians-in-the-making." I see Jesus' disciples much like the Muslims I disciple: needing to be challenged and changed, empowered and sent—all while they are led out of most of the things they knew in their religious life before.

Premise 4

Although the New Testament presents us with one single gospel for both Jews and Gentiles, that doesn't mean the best approach to discipleship will be the same for both. True, there is only one outcome to discipleship—that is, to be like Jesus. But I propose that there is more than one approach to achieving this. In his early ministry, Jesus was focused on twelve Jewish men who lived in a context bearing a great deal of resemblance to that of Muslim life today. Therefore I believe we need to pattern our ways of shepherding and discipling MBBs very directly on the way Jesus cared for the Twelve.

Premise 5

If a practitioner is shepherding MBBs, I assume they have already covered some significant ground with them—that is, the MBBs have assimilated some important biblical truths. Specifically, I assume they already understand that Jesus is more than a prophet: that he is the Redeemer in whose name God graciously grants us the forgiveness of our sins and that he is the Lord we are called to follow.

BUT HOW DOES THIS IMPACT SHEPHERDING ALI'S HEART?

What would a "shepherding curriculum" suited specifically for people who are coming out of Islam look like if it were based on Jesus' handling of his disciples? We could undertake the kind of extensive research that some have done to answer our question, and much can indeed be learned from their research.[2] However, I believe it is important to remember that Jesus, in dealing with his disciples, was dealing with people whose worldview was very similar to that of Muslims.

If this point is missed, the common outcome is a rush to develop shepherding/discipling models that are more focused on the Pauline literature, and thus more focused on the people who were the center of his calling: the Gentiles (see Galatians 2:8). Although all discipleship models will eventually merge and embrace Paul's teaching, I believe it is wiser to limit oneself initially to Jesus' approach when working with MBBs.

> But the key element is for us to see the importance of *demonstrating* for MBBs how to follow Christ—not just informing them about it.

Therefore, shepherding our friend Ali's heart should be primarily informed by what Jesus did. With this in mind, we must ask ourselves what did our Lord focus upon and addressed, perhaps even consider what he left out while shepherding his disciples. Hence, our first task in discipling MBBs is to carefully study and discern any features of Christ's ministry that might be "Muslim-specific." The second task would be to glean from Paul what addresses Judaic (thus Islamic) issues specifically. I repeat, although *both* Jesus' and Paul's teachings are necessary when shepherding MBBs, the more appropriate way is to begin with Jesus' teachings and then gradually introduce them to Paul's teachings.

My perspective is that of an MBB who has struggled to shepherd other MBBs for over four decades. Based on that, and from my studies of Christ's interaction with the Judaism of his day, what follows are some of the more salient matters upon which we need to focus.

DEMONSTRATION-BASED SHEPHERDING

In John 21, when Jesus asked Peter three times if Peter loved him, and then three times mandated Peter to feed his sheep, Peter was distressed by the question being repeated—not by the call to shepherd. And notice there was no follow-up question from Peter about how he would do this or what that should look like. Indeed, he already knew because he just experienced three years of such a ministry modeled for him by Christ.

---

2 Don Little offers an excellent and succinct treatment of these issues in *Effective Discipling in Muslim Communities: Scripture, History and Seasoned Practices* (Downers Grove, IL: InterVarsity, 2015). This book is a must-read for those who would shepherd MBBs.

Similarly, we can learn by what Jesus demonstrated, along with what Peter emphasized in his shepherding themes in 1 and 2 Peter. But the key element is for us to see the importance of *demonstrating* for MBBs how to follow Christ—not just informing them about it.

Demonstration-based shepherding/discipleship is very demanding in any context, but particularly so in a Muslim context. It requires a substantial investment of the practitioner's time at every stage of ministry to Muslims: pre-conversion and post-conversion. Some call this *with*ness.[3] This is where we need to graduate from the idea that evangelism and/or discipleship is something "relational" and move to the notion that it is at every step "pastoral." Spiritual sheep-tending was at the heart of everything Jesus did, both with his disciples and with the crowds (Matt 9:36; 18:12–14; John 10:16), and that is the model he gave us to follow.

Demonstration-based shepherding/discipleship is time-consuming. Therefore, no matter how many MBBs might be in your circle of influence, take a clue from the Master and limit yourself to a select few. Though Jesus interacted with at least seventy followers, he shepherded the Twelve. A team is a good way to approach this so that no one person is constrained to care for all the MBBs and shepherding becomes a shared responsibility.[4]

ADDRESSING ISLAMIC BAGGAGE

Every convert, from any background, brings cultural baggage into his/her walk with Christ; and our friend Ali will be no different. Yet we know that the Holy Spirit penetrates and transforms all cultures, while preserving any godly traits that are part of their unique identities. Ali's cultural baggage will have to undergo the same process. What is different about Muslim culture is that, like its Jewish counterpart, it ascribes a religious dimension to traditions and values for which it demands varying degrees of allegiance. MBBs will hear echoes of the accusation thrown at Jesus and his disciples: "Why do your disciples break the tradition of the elders?" (Matt 15:2).

Ali is very likely to bring into his Christian life a perspective in which all actions take shape in a religio-cultural matrix. MBBs are often unaware that a lot of the Sharia still permeates their life. This is true even in instances where MBBs are celebrating their deliverance from the more obvious legalistic aspects

---

3 This concept has guided our work among Muslims for decades, but the expression has been disseminated in recent years by Joel Butz in his book, *Bent but Not Broken: A Journal of Devotional Theology* (CreateSpace: Amazon Digital Services, 2014), and by David E. Fitch, *Faithful Presence: Seven Disciplines That Shape the Church for Mission* (Downers Grove, IL: InterVarsity, 2016).
4 See Greg Livingstone's seminal work, *Planting Churches in Muslim Cities: A Team Approach* (Grand Rapids: Baker, 1993).

of Islam. In altogether too many instances, I have observed that an MBB's spiritual growth is hampered by still trying to live according to what Sharia says is *mafrud* (obligatory) in order to be blessed by God.[5] This easily leads to Pharisaism. Biblical instructions are often understood through the prism of what is either *mustahabb* (preferred and loved) or *makruh* (hated by God), and especially what is *halal* (virtuous and allowed) or *haram* (shameful and forbidden). The problem here is that Islamic Sharia is still influencing, if not defining, these matters in the life of the MBB. Thus a redefinition of these issues, as Jesus did in his Jewish context, becomes a key concern in shepherding the hearts of MBBs.

Note particularly how Matthew structures the message of Jesus to address these very issues right after the Sermon on the Mount. He touches a leper, then considered both *makruh* and *haram* (Matt 8:1–4). He helps a Roman centurion, one who is both a *kafir* (blasphemer) and *haram* (Matt 8:5–13). He touches a sick woman who is not a blood relative, a type of *haram* (Matt 8:14–15). He even calls Levi/Matthew, a *makruh* (traitor) working for the Roman enemy, to be his disciple. Jesus makes them all *halal* and *mustahabb.* Paying close attention to such Muslim-relevant issues in the ministry of Christ can help us know how to better shepherd MBBs.

MUSLIM-SPECIFIC VULNERABILITIES

I am always a bit surprised that seasoned practitioners neglect to highlight, in their lists of obstacles to an MBB's spiritual growth, sexual issues, marital tensions, the intimacy with God possible through Christ, the love of money (and its contingent root problems), religious ideology and legalism, lack of integrity, anger and vindictiveness, and ongoing demonic influence.[6] These points are, in fact, the very matters Jesus focused upon, especially in the Sermon on the Mount.

In contrast, the issues most often mentioned to explain an MBB's lack of growth are family pressures and persecution. But a careful look at Christ's teaching about persecution indicates that spiritual immaturity due to worldly cares is most likely the reason for returning to Islam. It would seem that Jesus pointed to the problems of shallow ground, surface roots, and thorn-infested soil as the primary reasons for falling away (Matt 13:5–7, 20–22).

---

5 For an excellent summary of how Sharia affects all of a Muslim's life, see Alexander Pierce's *Facing Islam, Engaging Muslims* (Enumclaw, WA: Redemption Press, 2012), Kindle edition, chap. 5, location 1024.
6 See Little's table of such obstacles, *Effective Discipling in Muslim Communities*, 172-73.

CONSTRUCTIVE DECONSTRUCTION

An integral part of Jesus' ministry in his particular context had to do with the task of defeating Pharisaism.[7] He was not focused on defeating Jews per se (as is claimed by some of my Muslim friends), but he did make a point to address the fallacies of the Pharisees' teachings. Similarly, we should recognize that shepherding Ali will necessarily involve a wise deconstruction of Islamic ideals and unbiblical cultural values that most likely linger in his heart. For example, the person of Muhammad has been revered for so long, and so deeply, that it is hard for most MBBs to dethrone him from their lives. It is our task to help them discover for themselves who and what Muhammad really was and to deconstruct his place in their lives.

In this process, we should not shy away from being somewhat prescriptive in our biblical counseling and/or our spiritual mentorship. The process that leads to maturity for Ali may be somewhat different because of so many years of having every detail of life—even the most mundane task of going to the bathroom—decided for him by tradition! For Ali, the concept that religion should encompass every aspect of living and offer detailed guidance for every action is immensely cherished. Consequently, many MBBs will expect their shepherd to be much more forthcoming, detailed, and outright prescriptive than we are used to with Western models of discipleship.

As much as you want your MBBs to take up personal reading of the Bible for guidance, don't assume that this will occur quickly. In fact, many MBBs are no more prone to reading the Bible now than they were to reading the Qur'an before. The initial, even avid, interest in reading the Bible that MBBs often have is short-lived simply because they have a deeply ingrained reliance on tradition, rather than on an actual text, for guidance. Therefore, being prescriptive in dealing with this issue may take the form of structuring daily Bible reading tasks for Ali.

However, as you study Jesus' method of dealing with *doctrine* (less than 10 percent of his oral teaching), you will see that a prescriptive approach is not the best way to go. For example, Ali will want *you* to define biblical words, events, concepts, and doctrines. We need to study carefully how Jesus responded to such matters, how he asked questions and guided the discussion so that the disciples would arrive at the right conclusion. Consider how the use of parables astutely confronts the listeners by having them try to figure out what is being communicated. Grasp the huge importance of allowing the listener to discover this and respond without losing face in a culture steeped in the values of honor and shame.

---

7 See Gary Tyra, *Defeating Pharisaism: Recovering Jesus' Disciple-Making Method* (Downers Grove, IL: InterVarsity, 2009). Although written for churches in a Western setting, this work sheds much light on an aspect of Jesus' ministry that is essential but often overlooked.

> We should recognize that shepherding Ali will necessarily involve a wise deconstruction of Islamic ideals and unbiblical cultural values that most likely linger in his heart.

Shepherding MBBs requires that rather than answering every question, we patiently lead our converts through the same journey the disciples experienced. Allow MBBs to wrestle with questions, and be patient if they sometimes miss the mark. For example, it is a mistake to assume that an MBB will automatically have a clear understanding of what "Son of God" means, or its implications about Christ's divinity. Think of how long it took the Twelve to come to grips with these issues. Many are surprised when they see an MBB who is genuinely born again and growing spiritually yet struggling with doubts about the divine nature of Christ—as if any of us were saved by right theology.

CONCLUSION

An African proverb says that the final shape of a straw mat will always reflect how its first corner was woven together. Starting points are crucial. It is crucial—from the start—that we see how the Father, through Christ, graciously provided a shepherding model perfectly suited for the Islamic mind-set. If we build our shepherding approach on the way Jesus dealt with first-century Jews, we will more easily sort out which issues are more relevant to meeting the needs of present-day MBBs.

This has just been a primer to these issues, however, as we have only scratched the surface of what is involved in shepherding Ali's MBB heart. We couldn't possibly address every issue, and the few topics mentioned were necessarily covered briefly. It wasn't possible to elaborate on other important Muslim-specific vulnerabilities, such as the felt needs that often drive even the most orthodox Muslims to resort to folk Islamic practices. But what is crucial to grasp is that our task is to understand these vulnerabilities, and to proactively meet the challenges they represent. It is my hope that these thoughts and suggestions will challenge you to rediscover powerful and relevant shepherding principles from the examples given by our Great Shepherd himself—in a manner long neglected by the church. We need to reread Islam, as well as the Gospel accounts, in light of the Judaism of Jesus' day. I believe this process will give us fresh, new, and even more effective approaches to our pastoral care of our MBB friends like Ali.

DISCUSS AND APPLY

- Looking again at the Gospel of Matthew in particular, find how Jesus addresses issues of cleanness/uncleanness and how he challenges those notions within the Jewish paradigm. Do you see any insights for how to shepherd MBBs, who are concerned with similar issues?

- Does your method for discipling MBBs take into account the issues of the law, cleanness, the role of Sharia, etc.? Thinking about Muslims you know, do you recognize those issues in your conversations with them? Based on Jesus' approach, how could you help them?

- Do you spend time with Muslim friends? Do you need to be spending more time modeling and demonstrating how to live a Christ-like life before them?

BIBLIOGRAPHY

Butz, Joel. *Bent but Not Broken: A Journal of Devotional Theology*. CreateSpace: Amazon Digital Services, 2014.

Fitch, David E. *Faithful Presence: Seven Disciplines That Shape the Church for Mission*. Downers Grove, IL: InterVarsity, 2016.

Little, Don. *Effective Discipling in Muslim Communities: Scripture, History and Seasoned Practices*. Downers Grove, IL: InterVarsity, 2015.

Livingstone, Greg. *Planting Churches in Muslim Cities: A Team Approach*. Grand Rapids: Baker, 1993.

Neusner, Jacob, and Tamara Sonn. *Comparing Religions through Law: Judaism and Islam*. New York: Routledge, 1999.

Pierce, Alexander. *Facing Islam, Engaging Muslims*. Enumclaw, WA: Redemption Press, 2012.

Tyra, Gary. *Defeating Pharisaism: Recovering Jesus' Disciple-Making Method*. Downers Grove, IL: InterVarsity, 2009.

SERMON № 3

ROYA AND JAVED

Scripture Reading: Luke 9:23

I (Roya) was born in a Muslim country. My father was a great man who used to work for the government. He was my hero. Before I finished high school, the mujahideen came to my house, took my father, and after torturing him and breaking his arms, they killed him. In just one night everything changed in my life. I lost my hero.

Years later, I had another life-changing experience after I was married. One day my husband beat me severely. As a result, I started fighting with God. I went to my room and asked him harsh questions: "What kind of God are you? Do you really exist? If you are there, show yourself to me. Why are you are hiding? Where are you?"

During the night, I had a dream. I saw angels taking me to heaven. I entered a big room that seemed extremely beautiful. At the center of the room was placed a chair with a man sitting on it. I could not see his face clearly because it was shining brightly. I found myself walking around and asking, "Why I am here?" I looked at an angel who was standing beside me, and I recognized that it was Gabriel. He turned to me and said, "This is the Living God—worship him." So I bowed down and I started worshiping the one sitting on the throne.

I woke up in the morning and I went to talk to my husband. I was so excited about the dream that I even forgot he had beaten me the night before. So I told him, "I saw God. I am special because God showed himself to me."

I remembered that I had a Christian in my extended family. So I decided to go to her house and ask if she would take me to church. After we talked, she gave me a positive answer. I asked her to come to my house for a cup of tea and then I would make the same request in front of my husband. In this way, I could ask his permission.

She came to my house, and while we were in my husband's presence, we started talking about a possible visit to the church. Then I looked at him and asked if I could go to church. Because our culture is oriented by honor and shame, my husband felt he could not say no, and gave his permission for me to go. I was so happy.

The next day we went to church. The first thing I noticed was that people were singing worship songs in my native language, and it was beautiful. Next we had a Bible study, and we were asked to memorize a verse. It was from John 14:6, where Jesus said, "I am the truth, the way, and the life. And nobody will go to heaven except through me." I just loved and memorized it.

Then we went to the main church. It was a big room with about three hundred people, mostly Iranians. They welcomed and hugged me. The preaching was about God's love, based in John 3:16. I said I wanted to accept God's love because he loves me unconditionally and he loves every person in this world. On that day and I gave my life to Christ, knowing that my husband might want to kill me. But I was ready for that.

When I returned home, I found my husband was really mad. He was pacing the floor and seemed ready to beat me. So I looked at him and I said, "I found God. Today I accepted Jesus Christ. Do you want to leave me alive or do you want to kill me? I am a Christian; I have accepted Jesus."

Because he did not kill me, I knew that my life was in God's hands, and I was not afraid. So I shared the gospel with everyone: my uncles, my mother, my sister, all my relatives, and everyone who lived in Pakistan at that time. They were all shocked and said, "You are crazy."

At some point, my husband went to church with me. He also heard God's voice and gave his life to Jesus. His life was transformed, and today we proclaim the gospel together. We have been to places where we know people were trying to kill us, but they couldn't because it wasn't our time to die. Our lives are in God's hands.

We have to share the gospel boldly with Muslims, because when they see people who are bold, then they know that people filled with boldness are doing the right thing. Don't be afraid. The coward will die every day, but the bold man will only die once.

At the turn of the millennium, prior to widespread Internet availability and mobile phone usage, Muslims rarely decided to change their allegiance to Jesus. Most workers in Muslim lands accepted that there would likely be little or no fruit to show for a lifetime of commitment. Yet, in 2007, a Vision 5:9 consultation was able to identify and unleash some fruitful practices from those few who were making a kingdom impact. After circulating and applying those insights for the past ten years, the reality has changed. Where before, most cross-cultural workers had never met a Muslim-background believer in Jesus, now we frequently work alongside them. Happily, over two hundred Muslim-background believers (MBBs) participated in the "Abide, Bear Fruit" consultation.

Throughout the history of Jesus' disciples making disciples, the mission field has always transformed into the mission force. A new day has now dawned in missions. Many Muslim-background believers have matured and developed their own schools of missiological thought. The chapter titled "The Current Shift in Leadership from Expatriate to Local Workers" explores how the sea change to Global South missions leadership is well underway.

Now three communities are learning to dance and coexist in the family of God, and perhaps even to merge: the Western church, the national, persecuted church, and the growing clusters of Muslim-background believers. There is a God-ordained balance to be sought between careful preservation of orthodox expressions of the faith and seeking to win lost sheep with reckless abandon.

In the chapter titled "The Joy of the Harvest," we are reminded of the courageously inclusive Jerusalem Council from Acts 15, as similar struggles for integration and unity are facing the global church. In the chapter "Suffering as A Blessing," Jesus-followers receive a firsthand glimpse of the trials we face amid opposition from surrounding Islamic strongholds. Some are accepting higher risk as they are sent. In addition, the migration of servant-class Christians from countries with disadvantaged economies is quietly causing a kingdom groundswell, as introduced in the chapter "House Lights: Slaves Who Bring Freedom."

—Nate Scholtz, section editor

SECTION 3: Harvest Force

Nate Scholtz, section editor

19

THE CURRENT SHIFT IN LEADERSHIP FROM EXPATRIATE TO LOCAL WORKERS

Gene Daniels (a pseudonym) is a missionary, researcher, and writer. He is the director of Fruitful Practice Research, a part of Vision 5:9. He has been involved in ministry to Muslims since 1997 and has a doctorate in religious studies.

MAIN POINTS NOT TO MISS:

- Many who were very recently part of the *mission field* have now become a powerful *mission force* in global leadership.

- Western workers must respectfully make space for strategic adaptations as local leaders conceive culturally innovative ideas.

- Different aspects of the gospel represent "better" news than others, depending on the perspective of the cross-cultural receiver of the message.

My friends Jonas and Sofia (not their actual names) are a multinational couple. He's from Central Europe and she's from northern Africa. They were raised in a global economy and are very aware of what's going on in the world. They are comfortable with "virtual" friendships and speak "technology" like it's their mother tongue. They share many common characteristics with other Christian-background believers in Canada, Singapore, India, and elsewhere. They and many other millennials have been deeply touched by images of 9/11, the Syrian refugee crisis, and other events involving Islam. They have a strong sense of calling on their lives. They're moved to tears every time they think about millions of Muslims dying without Christ. They long to see more Muslims know the blessedness of God's forgiveness and experience that reality in a community of people like themselves.

> 74 percent of the MBBs in attendance were themselves successful church planters.

In other words, Jonas and Sofia represent part of the next generation of church planters in the Muslim world. As I think of them, I see a bit of myself thirty years ago. The world has changed dramatically since then, but the ache of the missionary call has not. One dimension of that dramatic change was on display at the "Abide, Bear Fruit" consultation. Ten years before, in 2007, Vision 5:9 hosted the consultation that produced the book *Seed to Fruit*. We had the general sense coming out of that meeting that church planting in the Muslim world had reached an exciting stage, but primarily was the work of a select few, especially blessed, expatriate missionaries. When we convened in Thailand this time the river's course had obviously changed, and the sheer number of Muslim-background church and mission leaders present helped many to see the new channel God is creating—the other part of the next generation of church planters.

Today, not only can we be excited that churches are being established in virtually all parts of the Muslim world, but more importantly a large percentage of these new churches are being started by Muslim-background believers (MBBs). While we did not even try to quantify the church-planting picture at "Abide, Bear Fruit," one piece of demographic data self-reported during that meeting offers an interesting insight: 74 percent of the MBBs in attendance were themselves successful church planters, whereas only 33 percent of the rest were. We haven't yet learned precisely how many churches are being planted by MBBs, but it does illustrate the trend.

GROWING BEYOND OUR CONTROL

There are many reasons for this shift, but the primary one is both simple and logical. As the number of MBBs has slowly yet steadily grown, the number of mature, gifted leaders among them has too. Thus the pool of potential church planters among them is continually increasing as time goes on. When this is combined with the increasing use of mission strategies that focus on multiplication, we have a ripe environment for a rapid expansion of churches planted by those from a Muslim background.

In the past, churches in the Muslim world were like singular dots on a map: one here, another there. Connections between them were rare because there were few, if any, connections between those who planted them. Rather than a single tree bearing fruit in this capital city or another, now the fruit of those trees planted earlier are becoming orchards—thanks to multiplication.

> Little birds have carried the seed we sowed to places far away. We can't see them now, but we can hear the tweeting of the birds in the distance.

In South Central Asia, a young Muslim man named Mahmud came to Christ while in jail. Upon his release, he was discipled by foreign missionaries living in the capital city. Eventually a few other young village men who were displaced to the city also came to believe. They formed a small group for Bible study, worship, and prayer. Little by little, they began to reach out to relatives back in their home district and then to villages in other districts. As the ministry grew, these men grew—in knowledge of the Word and in leadership abilities. The push further into rural areas also placed both geographic and emotional distance between Mahmud's team and their missionary friends. Eventually they parted ways, but the ministry continues. In the decade since that simple start, these same brothers have seen Muslims joyfully respond to the gospel in many remote villages. Not long ago Mahmud said, "Little birds have carried the seed we sowed to places far away. We can't see them now, but we can hear the tweeting of the birds in the distance."

This new reality of MBBs moving into the driver's seat of church planting should be a point of great rejoicing. Over the last few decades countless Christians from around the world have been praying that the Lord would send more workers into the field of the Muslim world. These MBB church planters are his answer. Beyond thanking God, however, we also need to recognize that this trend will have a huge influence on the entire mission enterprise in the

> As there are more
> and more MBB-led
> churches, the future
> will require expatriate
> missionaries to not
> only partner as equals
> but to participate as
> subordinates.

coming years. Going back to my friends Jonas and Sofia, we can confidently say that they are entering a different field than my generation of church planters experienced, one in which they must learn to share the mission with Muslim-background believers.

I reflected long and hard in the weeks and months after "Abide, Bear Fruit." Eventually a series of related questions began forming in my mind—questions like:

- exactly does this mean to Jonas and Sofia and others of their generation?
- How will this trend impact their ministry?
- How will their relationship with MBBs be different from my own?

To follow this line of reasoning, let's unpack some of the implications this shift will have on the next generation of missionaries—men and women who will come from places as diverse as Korea, Mexico, and Kenya.

SHIFT TO SERVE UNDER MBB LEADERSHIP

One of the reasons we have reached this wonderful moment in mission history is that mission agencies have given great effort to partnering together, and the Vision 5:9 network is a good example. Today many expatriate missionaries are taking the logical next step and partnering with local leaders from Muslim background in relief, in training, and in church planting. As there are more and more MBB-led churches, the future will require expatriate missionaries to not only partner as equals but to participate as subordinates.

Several Muslim-background church planters at "Abide, Bear Fruit" spoke of this kind of shift from partnering with Westerners to driving their own mission plans and strategies. One MBB from Central Asia explained it this way:

> In the beginning, we worked with a group from Europe. Then there were Koreans that came and helped us. Over time, we saw that foreign methods of church planting did not work well in our culture. So we began to study and look at many different sources. Over the years, we have developed our own way of church planting here in Central Asia. Now the only groups we partner with are local MBB churches in our country. Some church leaders from a Christian people group in a neighboring country help us, but they help us enact *our* plans.

Notice that MBB leaders are directing the mission. Outsiders are sometimes participants in their plans, but not even necessarily as coequals. In some places, Muslim background church planters are still following a more "equal partnership" model with foreigners; but even then the projects they partner on are conceptualized, designed, and driven by local leaders.

The journey to moving beyond equal partnership will also expose the biases that some expatriate missionaries bring to the field. For example, one MBB in Central Asia expressed frustration about double bias she faces as a local and as a woman leader:

> I have been in the ministry among my own people for over fifteen years. But still, whenever a young American or Australian shows up on the field, they assume they know more about church planting than I do, particularly if that person is a man.

This kind of attitude has been far too common in the past. I pray that Jonas and Sofia's generation of church planters will have more humility than past generations of missionaries.

OTHER WAYS OF UNDERSTANDING THE TASK

> Those who want to participate with local MBBs in church planting may have to rethink some of their deeply held mission logic.

As the leadership and direction for church planting in the Muslim world slowly shifts to those from Muslim backgrounds, the way such mission is perceived and expressed will change. When foreigners observe a country or people, they do so with an *etic* perspective—meaning the viewpoint of an external observer. They describe, organize, and classify what they see by applying forms of reason and logic that make sense to them. This is not necessarily wrong, but it can be quite different from the way internal participants see the very same things—something we call the *emic* perspective. This potentially large difference can have a significant effect on the conduct of mission, especially when that mission is directed by local perceptions. Let's look at a few examples.

In the Middle East, a cohort of solely MBB leaders direct a network of house churches. When they describe the scope and limits of their ministry, they don't speak in terms of ethnic or linguistic boundaries; they frame their "people group" in terms of which sect of Islam they are part of. In their world, the lines drawn by Islamic religious discourse are much more rigid than those of language or dialect. Therefore it seems quite strange to them to shape church-planting strategies around ethnolinguistic categories. In other words, the MBB church planter may rightly perceive the scope and dimensions of the unengaged or unreached peoples around him differently than our current lists of country location, ethnicity, and spoken dialect. Given the potential differences in understanding of the task remaining between the outsider and the MBB, those who want to participate with local MBBs in church planting may have to rethink some of their deeply held mission logic.

Another example has to do with the structure of many "churches" being planted in the Muslim world. Today most expatriate missionaries have at least heard of several different models of church, such as congregational-church, cell-church, and house-church, to name only a few. But what about new ways of being the church—that is, "the called-out ones"—that missionaries have never really thought about? In some contexts the emic—that is, native—perspective has very little in common with the way expatriates understand church, and MBB leaders don't speak of gatherings but rather of *communities*—such as the "Umah of Isa." The emphasis is on shared faith and a common way of life, not on ideas of membership and meetings, which dominate Western church thought.

Of course, it is only right that those who do the heavy lifting of mission should be the ones who define its terms. Yet this may be an uncomfortable role reversal for many foreign missionaries who are not used to having the emic, or insider, perspective take precedence over their own.

GLOCAL WORSHIP IS BECOMING INDIGENOUS WORSHIP

The online Oxford English Dictionary defines *glocal* as "that which reflects or is characterized by both local and global considerations." In many MBB contexts, we are hearing new expressions of worship that reflect the era of cross-cultural exchange in which we live. As globalization makes the mission world smaller, local MBB leaders are emerging who have exposure to a wide menu of musical culture from YouTube and other forms of the global music phenomena.

For example, one local leader explained how the globalization of music was affecting the small MBB movement he leads in a harsh South Asian context:

> [Due to security issues] most of our groups sing songs without any musical instruments at all. However, there is also Western-style music among our believers, especially those who have now moved abroad. Worship is one of the ways that TV and radio programs influence the believers, even those in the country.

However, that does not mean their worship is simply mimicking Hillsong or Matt Redman. Just as the "Asian Fusion" restaurant has become a very real (and delicious) dining option in many cities, fusions of traditional music and global Christian worship are finding their way into many parts of the mission field, sometimes even in the most remote places. For example, one MBB church in Central Asia, in a celebration of pastoral succession, fused traditional nomadic song style with the use of beautiful silk flags in dance worship—and they topped it off with the trumpeting sound of a Jewish ram's horn! It was a truly glocal blend of elements that were meaningful for that congregation.

For the purists, this move toward glocal can be frustrating because we often believe that indigenous means "traditional." But indigenous is better thought of as that "which belongs in a place," so if local people are already synthesizing musical styles, perhaps the most indigenous thing do to is to encourage them to do the same with worship. Jonas and Sofia might struggle with this—as I did. Then again, they might take the opposite tack and unthinkingly encourage worship that simply mimics styles from home. In both cases, MBBs leading the church-planting effort means foreign missionaries must learn to refrain from imposing their opinions.

CONCESSIONS, OR CONTENTIONS, ON THEOLOGY

As more and more church planters in the Muslim world are first-generation followers of Christ, they will rethink how the Bible relates and applies to the believers' lives. The process of interpreting Scripture, then applying it, is practical theology. Those who engage in practical theology are shaping their own spiritual, intellectual, and cultural heritage as they go. A Muslim-background leader in East Africa explains it this way:

> Most theologies we see in the evangelical church today come down to us from the early, Greek-speaking church fathers. They thought and wrote in their own categories of thought, shaped by their culture. My people are Semitic peoples. We speak, think, and do theology in different categories. It's not that the older theologies are wrong, but that they were developed for believers very different from my people.

> Those who engage in practical theology are shaping their own spiritual, intellectual, and cultural heritage as they go.

For Jonas and Sofia and others like them, this will be hard because, as evangelicals, their theology is substantially rooted in their home-church environment. Like all the expatriate missionaries who have gone before them, Jonas and Sofia will inevitably start out with theology encased in their mental luggage when they arrive. But if God so blesses them to serve alongside MBB church planters, they may wrestle with when to stand their theological ground and when to relax and trust the Holy Spirit to lead them to different positions—even on key issues.

Doing practical theology is hard in any cross-cultural environment, but working it out in a frontier mission setting is even more demanding. On the one hand, Jonas and Sofia will often appreciate the "fresh eyes" these MBB leaders bring to the text, yet at some points they will struggle and question if their ideas are syncretistic. To make matters worse, when supporters back home don't understand the complexity of the issues or know and trust the local MBB leaders the way Jonas and Sofia have learned to, they may accuse Jonas and Sofia of becoming "too Muslim-friendly."

For example, evangelicals in the West tend to paint pictures of Jesus as a wise teacher or the suffering Savior. Children are often in the picture or somewhere nearby. What if, instead, our MBB friends chose to emphasize some of the more intense images of Jesus, such as the angry prophet driving sellers out of the temple courts (Matt 21:12–13), or the blood-soaked king returning in the book of Revelation (19:11–16)? The practical outworking of this shift in imagery would probably carry a more austere flavor than we are used to. It might even cause Jonas and Sofia to revolt because it "feels" too much like Muhammad's militancy. At the very least, it would make many evangelicals uncomfortable— but would that make it wrong?

CONCLUSION

"Look at the nations and watch—and be utterly amazed. For I am going to do something in your days that you would not believe, even if you were told" (Hab 1:5).

God often does things that are truly amazing. No matter how wise or learned we are, the Lord of the Harvest seems to surprise us whenever we take the time to really look at what he is doing among the nations. This is certainly true today when we look at changes taking place in the part of his harvest field we call the Muslim world. Since the whole reason for the existence of the Vision 5:9 network is to see effective church-planting efforts among all Muslim peoples, one change that is of particular interest is that more and more churches are being planted by first-generation MBBs. Therefore it is vital that we not only know this fact but carefully consider the implications of this shift in church-planting agency.

First, expatriate missionaries need to stretch themselves beyond the "partnership" paradigm. In a context where more and more churches are started by MBBs themselves, expatriate missionaries will have to learn not only to partner as equals but to participate as subordinates. This will force expatriate missionaries to confront the assumptions we sometimes make about our superior enlightenment.

Second, we must recognize that church planters who are from a Muslim background will see and shape the task differently. It may be in the way they understand "people groups"; it might be in the structure and nature of the church they plant.

Third, globalization is making the mission world smaller, and in doing so it is impacting the meaning of "indigenous" worship. Foreign missionaries must step back and allow—and even encourage—this process as local MBB leaders help their people find ways to express devotion to Christ from their hearts.

And finally, strong, truly indigenous churches require theology that is rooted to questions and concerns of the local people. This will be very challenging, since theology is one of the most contentious issues in the church world.

In this chapter, I have tried to reflect on what that means to the next wave of expatriate church planters like my friends Jonas and Sofia and the many others like them throughout the world. I tried to think of their faces as I wrote this. I wanted this to be like a heartfelt letter to a dear friend, because I do care deeply about the next generation of church planters in the Muslim world and want them to be as fruitful as possible.

DISCUSS AND APPLY

- Do you find the prospect of independent missions-sending from the Global South exciting or worrisome? Discuss the benefits and risks that you can foresee.
- What do you think of the idea that the one gospel can have interpretive cultural nuances that are more relevant to different cultures?

FOR FURTHER READING

Sanneh, Lamin. *Whose Religion Is Christianity?* Eerdmans, 2003.

Walls, Andrew F. *The Cross-Cultural Process in Christian History.* Orbis, 2015.

20 | THE JOY OF THE HARVEST

Leina E. (a pseudonym) is an Arab follower of Christ who is passionate about reaching and empowering believers from the Arabian Peninsula to impact their own communities for Christ. She has over twenty years of experience in TV, film, and radio production.

MAIN POINTS NOT TO MISS:

- We pursue a God-ordained balance between careful preservation of orthodox expressions of the faith and seeking to win lost sheep with reckless abandon.

- In many locations around the globe there are ancient expressions of the church which have withstood the test of time amid much persecution from the surrounding Muslim community.

- Integrating new Muslim-background believers into the existing faith community is both challenging and deeply joyful.

> God was inviting us to walk with him on the water amid the mighty storms that arise in reaching Muslims—risking it all.

Khalda spoke, with tearful eyes: "I have been searching for the last two years. I rejected the old but realized I can't live without a religion. I considered Christianity and visited a church, but I was told no one could help me. I understand there are security problems, but I need help."

This is not uncommon. As a Middle Eastern Christian, I can say that many churches are so fearful about security that they will not help Muslims who are searching for Christ.

I came face-to-face with this fear one morning when my husband called and said, "Would you please cancel all my appointments? I will be very late today. Actually, I'm not sure when or if I will return home." He hung up and turned his phone off.

I didn't know anything about his appointments, so why was he asking me to cancel them? What was he really trying to tell me? Since I couldn't reach him to clarify, I just prayed, prayed, and prayed more.

At ten o'clock that night he finally returned home and explained, "I received a phone call from a Muslim who is seeking. He asked to meet me. I didn't know if it was real or a trap. So I needed to tell you just in case, but I couldn't say it over the phone."

That day brought my husband and me to our knees, asking God to show us his will about our involvement with Muslims. Even though we live in the heart of the Muslim world, our ministry had always been with believers from a Christian background (BCBs). But it was now clear that he was asking us to jump out of the security of that boat. As Jesus called Peter to "Take courage! It is I. Don't be afraid" (Matt 14:27), God was inviting us to walk with him on the water amid the mighty storms that arise in reaching Muslims—risking it all. We are learning that we can trust our omniscient and omnipotent God to know the whole story and have it all in his control.

The joys and challenges of ministry go hand in hand. We believe the harvest is plentiful in our region, but it is waiting for more harvesters who are willing to pay the cost. Ministry and prayer have been focused on this area for more than sixty years, but the fruit experienced by those first missionaries was quite limited. Joyfully, God is allowing us now to witness multiplying fruit which is due to the prayers, hard work, and seed sown by those who preceded us. We are blessed to reap what others have sown.

THE JOY OF TOUCHING MUSLIMS' LIVES

The journey starts as we are simply God's light to Muslims. My friend Fatima loves to get hugs from me. Like the woman who touched Jesus' hem, she wants to be touched by the Master, and he does touch her through a pure hug from us, his vessels. It is a privilege when women like her feel safe to share their deepest heartaches with us because they trust us. It is an honor to realize we have been welcomed into their closed community—one that rarely opens up to anyone different, especially a Christian.

There are wonderful joys in the ministry of just loving Muslims, as we watch them being drawn to Christ though us. It is an honor when we are asked to pray for them. Our prayer life is such a contrast to their experience of God as someone distant; they come to trust that our God does indeed answer prayer.

It is also reassuring to realize that their salvation is not up to us. We must always remember that the incarnated Christ loved, taught, healed, and delivered, yet he never forced anyone to follow him. This is what we are called to do, present Jesus to them and release them to make their own free choice.

We can truly say to them, "I love you as one created by God and paid for by Christ's blood. I pray you will receive eternal life. Just as I was given the opportunity to choose Christ, you too deserve that same freedom. But I will keep loving you whatever choice you make." This type of approach opens doors, whereas hidden agendas close them. They can sense who genuinely loves them, in comparison to those who want something from them—even if it is for their eternal good.

It is very challenging to break the stereotypes presented in Muslim media about Christians: alcohol drinkers, pork eaters, and adulterers. But God always opens a door. They watch how we live and start silently questioning the false image of Christians they grew up with. We do not need to defend God; he can defend himself.

It is amazing to see new believers from a Muslim background (BMBs): transparent and innocent, realizing God's love, seeing his grace sweep away past insignificance, loneliness, distress, and fear of punishment. And one cannot help but feel encouraged to see their hunger for God's Word when they turn from Islam to Christ. Their sense of longing and their eagerness to ask questions reveal a desire to know the Lord and his ways.

Many times, I feel jealous of the way BMBs interact with God with a fresh understanding. They challenge what we take for granted and help us see God and his Word in a completely different light. I often wish I would have the same attitude as they do toward my loving Lord and his Word.

BECOMING A COMMUNITY

Furthermore, I love the look on Muslim-background believers' faces when they meet others who have preceded them in following Christ. They suddenly know they are not alone. It brings so much comfort, knowing how much they also suffer for him. And as they fellowship with others, they start living like the church in Acts; and we are so blessed that they accept us to be part of such a pure and genuine church.

It is an even greater joy to see the passion of new BMBs as they reach out to their own community. Their appreciation for what God has done for them shines, and they never take grace for granted. They pray for each other and for their unsaved family members. Their hearts burn for their own people, as they pray with tears. And as a new community, they seek safe and creative ways to get the message to their own people—sometimes doing things we have never thought as Christian-background believers.

> Their hearts burn for their own people, as they pray with tears.

While there are a multitude of joys, there are also challenges. It is heartbreaking to walk alongside these new believers, eager to see their own people reached and yet being held back for the sake of security. We struggle with them to discern if it is the right time to take a certain risk or if they should hold back. They need to mature in their faith and develop a solid biblical foundation, sharing via their conduct before their words. But we must help them be careful. Sometimes their hearts, aching for their families, drive them to share their new faith prematurely, which might even result in the loss of their lives.

Our friends struggle with the reality of living a hybrid identity—Muslims overtly and Christians at heart. How can they keep going to the mosque, for the sake of security, yet find their identity in Christ? How can they move away from past values and live the new? How can they pray the five daily Islamic prayers? Does that not betray their new faith? These and many more heartbreaking issues challenge us as much as they do the new believers.

DIFFICULT REALITIES

If, by the grace of God, the BMBs' families allow the BMBs to keep living with them, they treat them as if they are dirty. They are considered unworthy to eat at the same table or to play with any of the children in the family. It is worse yet if the family sees them as a disgrace. Some parents will throw their children into mental institutions or jail. Others will kick them out of their home without their identity papers and educational certificates, in which case they cannot earn money. BMBs have been forced, by their families or by their in-laws, to divorce their spouse and be deprived of their children.

When things like this happen, they pass through long periods of depression and won't even answer our calls. This is so hard, because we know this may lead to them abandoning their faith or even taking their own lives. Situations like this bring us to our knees, standing in the gap for them. And when they restart communication with us they need to hear our hearts and not merely our mouths telling them, "You are not alone."

It is very important to realize that the BMBs' families don't treat them harshly because they hate them. On the contrary, they treat them that way because they love them and want them to return to Islam, which they believe to be the straight path. They are trying to sanctify them in the slight hope that they might still go to paradise before their full conversion away from Islam.

Death is a penalty that the BMB may be required to pay. This is very hard for new believers who know in their hearts that this could be their destiny. We weep with them, yet we need to help them see that there is a better life after death. This is a horribly painful process, yet a very challenging fact.

> Unfortunately, methods and therapies developed in the West do not translate well into this honor/shame culture.

Many believers come with backgrounds in witchcraft and the related psychological problems. Unfortunately, methods and therapies developed in the West do not translate well into this honor/shame culture. Counseling is in its infancy here. Counselors from the same background are few, and those with a deep understanding of BMBs are nearly nonexistent. This is very challenging. If BMBs can't get the core sickness treated, they are trapped in a vicious cycle. This is an urgent need.

As we know, the old self continues to resurface in the lives of believers, regardless of how long they have been Christians. The former ways and previous attitudes toward marriage and divorce seem to bring many marriages to the brink of divorce. Discipleship can teach about the biblical covenant of marriage, but it is a struggle to help BMBs work through such a deep paradigm shift. Laying a completely new foundation is easier than plucking out the rotten roots, clearing the land, and then planting new seeds of that which never existed before.

How can we quiet our worry when we know BMBs marry a Muslim because they can't find a Christian to marry them? How can we protect them from trying to discover every single denomination and redefine biblical truths according to what suits them? When BMBs say, "We came out of a religion that suppressed us, and we want our freedom," how do we find the balance between grace and discipline? They do pass through intervals of questioning and even rebellion sometimes. It is hard to receive them back with open arms when they return. We want to accept them without judging them or saying "We told you so." We simply need to be available, looking forward with excitement to the rest of their journey with God. It is a very humbling experience.

We worry when BMBs stop communicating with us. Maybe it has become too much, or their family members are watching them, or they feel the need to hide something from us. We often wonder if they are in jail, if they are being held captive in their home, or if they have even been killed. If we doubt for a second that God is in control, none of us would be able to handle any of these situations.

RESPECTING BMBS

If all these challenges aren't enough, we believers from a Christian background sometimes add to them. Those of us from a Christian background sometimes see BMBs as second-class believers with no right to be a part of us until they meet our stereotype of a Christian. Or we more easily cater to those who have learned to act like us. Also, many churches don't welcome BMBs because they fear being closed by the government. Oftentimes BMBs aren't even welcome in home gatherings for the same reason. As a result, these believers are denied being a part of the body. It sometimes makes me wonder who we think protects the church—God or us?

When we accept BMBs, they are expected to know everything we know and speak the Christianized language we speak. If they dare say a word from the past, we judge them to be unbelievers. If we do accept BMBs, we don't allow even the mature among them to teach, disciple, or take leadership positions. We are threatened by their deep questions about the Christian faith, since we as believers are often lacking in biblical knowledge and spiritual depth.

Many times, an BMB feels like only a number on someone's list. "Have you prayed and asked for salvation? Have you been baptized? Great—my work is done. Now, as a missionary, I need to move on." The BMB is left behind to wonder, "Has this missionary ever loved me? Does God really love me? If he does, why am I left behind as if I was a commodity? They tell me God sees me as being as precious as the blood of Christ, so why do they treat me so cheaply?"

Even worse, sometimes we showcase BMBs as prized trophies, taking them from place to place. They never grow, but instead become prideful in their hearts and come to think that others should be their servants. They want to be spoon-fed. And when money runs out from one missionary, they know tricks by which they can approach another. I don't blame those who reach this point, because that is the culture we teach them. We need to learn to treat them as equals, not as the ones *we* brought to faith.

A BMB once said, "What will happen after that?" It is painful.

Coming out of a judgmental religion, BMBs can naively expect the beauty of Christianity to radiate throughout the church—that is, until they meet BCBs and get hit by the harsh truth. Too often we are not good ambassadors for our loving God and Lord. How do we explain to our BMB brothers and sisters that traditional Christians don't always accept them? How can we help them fight with love for their right to be part of Christ's body? How can we help them to lift up their eyes and look to God (Ps 121:1–2) rather than to have unrealistic expectations of mere fellow-redeemed humans? We need to trust BMBs and equip them to reach out to their own people. Expecting conformity to the existing church can harm their ability to be salt and light in their own contexts.

What a joy to have partners in ministry when we can serve alongside each other, knowing God is the boss. This partnership binds us together in his love as we pray for his vision collectively listen to his voice, and obey his direction. By supporting each other through everyday frustrations and lifting up each other's arms in the battle, we find satisfaction in deepening fellowship. We experience the interdependence of the body of Christ as we take diverse roles that build on one another. We celebrate the rich mix of nationality, age, background, and language and the unique gifts God gives to each of us. With the Lord Jesus as our common bond, such diversity can bring much joy.

On this side of eternity, however, our sinful imperfections are still present. We struggle to achieve unity when each believer has a personal agenda. We are too easily sidetracked from larger, divinely set goals to concentrate instead on personal or organizational aims. Rather than being learners, we might think we know it all. A multinational ministry context can sometimes cause us to look down on other nationalities. Regular self-examination in God's light, and obedience to his corrections, ensures that we start and end well in this ministry.

A ministry culture that releases new believers for the work brings joy. A culture that constrains ministry brings struggles. A culture of release emerges when we realize that it is God who brings the fruit, not us. When we lead individuals to Christ, we don't own them. If they find the fulfillment of their discipleship needs with another group, we bless them and release them. There is only one body—Christ's body.

The desire for control is tempting and may emerge from good intentions to care for new believers. Yet whether they are humanly seen as good or bad does not matter. We need to make a conscious choice about which culture we will adopt: the release-based culture or the control-based culture. Our choice will affect the maturity of BMBs—either positively or negatively.

CONCLUSION

God is at work, and the harvest is plentiful. He merely asks, "Do you love me? Then take care of my sheep." Let us love him and each other as he loves us. I pray that we may see our BMB brothers and sisters as equals, equipping them and supporting them so that they can take the good news to their own people.

I remember the time I had the privilege of overhearing a conversation between a Muslim seeker and an BMB. I was amazed as they went from point A to point B in seconds. The same would have taken me forever. Not only were they speaking the same language, but they were speaking from the same deep places in the heart. I look forward to that most joyful day when we have BMB pastors, leaders, and counselors here in this very country, ministering to their own people. This may be a scene yet unseen, but our confidence is in the God who is able. Such confidence brings joy and peace. God strengthens our eyes by allowing us to view challenges as bricks that can build bridges rather than walls. The more a situation seems impossible, the more we know it is a situation for God. So we soak in his presence, expecting him as who he is. What a joy!

DISCUSS AND APPLY

- How might concerns about security be negatively shaping the way you do ministry?

- Is anything you are currently doing in ministry sending a message of disrespect to the BMBs you know?

- If your BMB friends are persecuted, it will impact you emotionally. How will you deal with that?

FOR FURTHER READING

Reisacher, Evelyne A. *Joyful Witness in the Muslim World: Sharing the Gospel in Everyday Encounters*. Baker Academic, 2016.

21 | SUFFERING AS A BLESSING!

B. Osman (a pseudonym) is a Muslim-background believer from
Central Asia who is a veteran church planter and evangelist. He and his
family have served the Lord for over twenty years in several Muslim-
majority countries in Asia.

MAIN POINTS NOT TO MISS:

- The source and cause of suffering is often hard to
  discern, leading to doubt and isolation.
- Counseling others on the path of suffering demands
  careful discernment and prayer.
- The testing of our faith provides powerful identification
  with the suffering Savior.

> During my time of persecution, when my life was in danger, I felt God's love and power stronger than I had ever experienced.

As is true of every Muslim who has come to faith in Jesus Christ, my life demonstrates a unique experience in walking with Jesus. When I became a believer in Jesus, all my relatives turned away from me. I wanted to keep my normal relationship with them, but I also clung to hope that this resistance would stop one day and I would see God's grace upon me, and his victory.

It is hard to be rejected by your own family and your own people. It is difficult to understand how God will turn this situation in a good way. It may be that over time our hope and expectation for our relatives to know him goes away. Eventually you have many questions about your circumstances and even about God. To not give up, you have to understand that everything is in God's control. Learning comes slowly; you must lean on God daily.

During my time of persecution, when my life was in danger, I felt God's love and power stronger than I had ever experienced. My relationship with our heavenly Father developed step by step; I became able to hear his voice clearly. I was able to understand that he has a plan for me, and that his plan was for good. From that experience and from reflecting on God's Word, I have learned principles that help me encourage others going through a similar experience.

HELPING THOSE WHO SUFFER

Perhaps we can bring the most benefit to believers by preparing them (and ourselves too) for suffering, explaining its inevitability and usefulness. The apostle Paul perfectly understood the importance of such preparation (1 Thess 3:3–4). Sometimes these sorrows are planned as part of God's providence, but very often we suffer because of wrong actions and decisions. Such suffering could be avoided. People find it easier to bear the second kind of suffering because it can be explained; in the first kind of suffering, it is harder to trust God no matter what happens.

The degree and duration of our suffering are influenced by various factors. I will mention three factors that are useful to recognize, both for preparation and to help those who already suffer.

We expect ease. Often, Faithful people generally consider suffering to be unlikely. When suffering is unexpected, we experience its maximum severity at 100 percent strength.

We have unrealistically high expectations. The higher my expectations of myself, of other believers, and even of God, the more frustrating and painful it is when those expectations are not met.

The role of suffering is misunderstood. The better we understand the causes of suffering, the easier it is to deal with. Inept attempts to "explain everything" only aggravate the sufferings of the sufferer. They reveal the inconsistency of the comforter and the superficiality of his judgments.

SUFFERING CHANGES, CHANGING RESPONSES

> Outwardly we may pretend we are OK and wear a mask of humility and submission to the will of God, while inwardly we are experiencing a secret rebellion.

Suffering is dynamic, not static; it changes and is not always the same. Misunderstanding this is one of the reasons for failure in helping people who suffer. It seems to us that if the sufferer expresses doubts about God's love today, those doubts will last both tomorrow and the day after tomorrow. But suffering is dynamic; it involves a certain process, which often can be described as a gradual overcoming of the crisis of faith. Such dynamics can be observed frequently in the book of Psalms. A typical psalm of this type is Psalm 42. It contains a clear transition from doubt, even despair, to hope.

The dynamics of suffering involve the stages of experiencing suffering. There are various descriptions of these stages. They are not always indisputable and universal, but the principle guiding a counselor's response remains unchanged: give the right medicine to achieve its intended purpose. Sometimes you just need to be quiet and listen; sometimes you need to give advice. There is a time for admonition and even for the invasion of another's life—for direct confrontation. Here God's power and wisdom and spiritual insight are important.

SUFFERING AND CRISES OF FAITH

Suffering can lead to a crisis of faith, a crisis that is like a disease. Treatment of the disease takes time. The disease develops; it grows, and its conclusion can be fatal to the spiritual life of the believer. It can also safely end in the recovery and renewal of faith. Unfortunately, most believers who are trying to help a person in such a crisis demand that the sufferer "repent and cease to be 'sick'" rather than wisely and patiently listening and encouraging.

What happens to a person during a crisis of faith? Let us answer this question in the following three planes.

Relating to God

In times when our faith is challenged, we feel angry toward God and doubt his love. We may try to suppress negative emotions aimed at him but fall into deep depression because of our confused status. We cry out before God with voices of indignation, pain, disappointment, and even resentment.

Relating to Self

Another response is to blame ourselves and perhaps imagine that we have earned these hardships through past failures. It is hard to escape being immersed in low self-esteem when we think that God has abandoned us.

Relating to Others

It's common to avoid contact with other people while in a season of suffering. We become highly self-conscious and fear condemnation from others or having our vulnerabilities exposed in public. This leads to isolation. We may even feel irritated by the attempts of friends and family members to comfort us. Their explanations for what has happened are rarely satisfying to us in the moment of suffering. Outwardly we may pretend we are OK and wear a mask of humility and submission to the will of God, while inwardly we are experiencing a secret rebellion.

It is necessary to take into account the state of the sufferer who is experiencing a crisis of faith. If, for example, he or she feels humiliated by God, words about God's love are unlikely to be accepted. Think about Job's condition, as he exclaimed, "The arrows of the Almighty are in me, my spirit drinks in their poison; God's terrors are marshaled against me." (Job 6:4). It is also important to remember that because of our propensity to "attack" the sufferer, the one suffering, like Job, has to "fight on two fronts"—with God and with us.

SUFFERING: A SIGN OF SIN?

It often seems like Christians have placed a ban on the experiencing of suffering, as if suffering is a sign of sin or of a weak spiritual life. We must reject this idea for a number of reasons. First of all, Scripture contains many examples of how the strongest people in the faith sometimes experienced suffering. At times they complained about God and even rebuked him. Second, many great missionaries and preachers have experienced a "dark night of the soul" when they have felt a deep loss of self-worth, experienced a crisis of faith, and poured out their disappointment before God, who often seems distant and unwilling to answer or show his love in the midst of these situations. And lastly, Jesus Christ himself persevered through suffering." His prayer in the garden that the Father would "let this cup pass" shows the depth of his suffering.

Some may argue that the experience of suffering is permitted only in the Old Testament, while the New Testament commands us to "rejoice always." But Paul wrote:

> "Not only so, but we also glory in our sufferings, because we know that suffering produces perseverance; perseverance, character; and character, hope. And hope does not put us to shame, because God's love has been poured out into our hearts through the Holy Spirit, who has been given to us."
>
> —Rom 5:3-5

In this he was not describing the experience of suffering, but the retrospective reaction to it; when the believer has passed the crisis of faith (when doubts and complaints are possible) and thus it strengthens our faith so that we can boast of this experience.

However, in the first case described by Chrysostom, Scripture is not describing the experience of suffering, but a retrospective reaction to it; having passed the crisis of faith (when doubts and complaints are possible) and thus strengthening our faith, we can boast of this experience. Chrysostom's second Scripture concerns suffering for Christ. Few have been disappointed in God while undergoing such suffering.

CONCLUSION

Most Muslims come from societies that place a high value on community. Many who have become followers of Jesus Christ have found themselves cut off from this community—accused of bringing shame on the family, or worse. At the same time, fear and other barriers may leave them only superficially accepted by the Christian community. One South Asian follower of Jesus described himself and several friends as longing for community but caught between the ummah and the church, not truly welcome in either.

When we walk the path of suffering, we can teach others that it is a blessing and that God will never leave us in that situation. He is faithful; he knows what is going on in our lives. Sharing deep fellowship and loving with understanding may help ease the burden of shame that accompanies suffering by Muslims who have become followers of Jesus Christ.

ILLUSTRATION

My name is "Andri." I am from Southeast Asia. I was Muslim, but now I am an evangelist. Some time ago, I was imprisoned for three years for the gospel of Jesus. During that time, God gave me the opportunity to reach other prisoners for Jesus from my father's Muslim people group. I experienced extraordinary persecution while in prison because they knew I was an evangelist for Jesus Christ. I give thanks, because God gave me the opportunity to share the good news of salvation with some of those who tortured me. Also, during that time thirty-six of the other prisoners responded to receive Jesus and to be baptized.

After three years I got out of jail. I felt burdened to find the other prisoners who had believed before they were released from jail. I prayed, and our awesome God directed me to them. I tried to disciple them, but many of them left me; and I cried over them, longing for them to please God. After five years, only three remained with me. But these three had a heart to love others and truly wanted to help those who had not yet believed in Jesus.

I prayed to God, asking him how I could aid these three men. God answered— they found some of the others who had turned away, and they decided to rejoin us. Twelve of these have returned to Christ and are now being used by God greatly as leaders and teachers of others. Each of them now serves between one hundred and two hundred believers, and Muslims on other unreached islands have been responding to the good news.

DISCUSS AND APPLY

- When you have undergone suffering, what were your methods for discerning whether it was from God for the sake of the gospel, a result of the need for personal correction in the flesh, or an attack from the enemy?

- What are the best ways to approach counseling a fellow believer who is undergoing suffering that will help them avoid the spiritually deadly isolation of which the author speaks?

- We commonly pray for healing and safety as if these are God's highest priorities for our lives. Is there biblical support for this?

FOR FURTHER READING

Harrigan, John. *The Gospel of Christ Crucified: A Theology of Suffering before Glory.* Paroikos, 2016.

Ripken, Nik. *The Insanity of God: A True Story of Faith Resurrected.* B&H Publishing Group, 2013.

22 | HOUSE LIGHTS:
Slaves Who Bring Freedom

Gene Daniels (a pseudonym) is a missionary, researcher, and writer. He is the director of Fruitful Practice Research, a part of Vision 5:9. He has been involved in ministry to Muslims since 1997 and has a doctorate in religious studies.

Brother Barnabas (a pseudonym) is from East Africa. Besides his personal ministry to Muslims, for the past ten years he has been equipping and mentoring other Africans for reaching Muslims in the Middle East.

MAIN POINTS NOT TO MISS:

- The gospel is being spread in creative, grassroots ways that defy our typical developed-to-underdeveloped directional expectations.

- Christian house helpers, working cross-culturally in nonbelieving homes, face different obstacles in sharing their faith.

- New sustainable strategies for financing global missions-sending are being employed in parts of the world where patron/worker partnership is not feasible due to economic limitations.

One of the familiar stories of the Old Testament is that of the Syrian military commander Naaman in 2 Kings 5. But sometimes we forget that this incredible story of God's power was set in motion by a young servant girl: "Now bands of raiders from Aram had gone out and had taken captive a young girl from Israel, and she served Naaman's wife." (2 Kgs 5:2).

We kind of ignore this little household servant, and we certainly don't often think about the painful backstory of this girl's life, which is alluded to in verse 2. The most literal translation should be "slave," but most Bible translations refer to her as a "servant" because translators often cater to our frail sensibilities. The reality is that the difference between the two is hard to clearly discern. Nevertheless, what is clear is that the witness of this simple household worker was the catalyst for the conversion of a powerful Syrian military commander.

And this should not surprise us since the harsh institution of servitude has a long history as a conduit of gospel transmission. Take, for example, the story of how the harsh barbarians of Scandinavia were won to Christ. When Viking raiders plundered the towns and monasteries in places like the Scottish coast, one of the valuables they carried away were slaves. Among them were monks who were plucked from a life of contemplation and prayer and then cast into hard labor for Norsemen masters. In time, many pagan Viking raiders were converted by the steadfast witness of these household servants.

Therefore it should not surprise us when we see God using domestic workers (modern-day housemaids) to spread the gospel. Globalization is opening job opportunities in many places for these economic migrants, many of whom are Christians, and the Middle East is one of the primary destinations. They come from diverse places: some from as close as Ethiopia, others from as distant as the islands of the Philippines. The backgrounds of the Christians who take these jobs varies—some are highly educated, others are not—but the lack of economic opportunity in their homeland has driven them to look for work elsewhere. Something else they have in common, and which makes them attractive to potential Muslim household employers, is their honesty and their honorable work ethic.

It may be hard for us in the West to imagine God working this way because we typically associate mission with Christians going to relatively poorer, less-developed peoples of the world. This has been the general shape of mission ever since William Carey sailed for the Indian subcontinent about 250 years ago. But times have changed! The church's center of gravity has moved, and with it, her mission force—something on clear display at the "Abide, Bear Fruit" consultation, where over 50 percent of those attending were from the Global South.

> We typically associate mission with Christians going to relatively poorer, less-developed peoples of the world.

This massive change in the makeup of the church means that more and more people from relatively lesser conditions are being called by God to reach Muslims, some of whom are far more affluent. This is a huge overturning of the mission tables. Can the weak reach the powerful? What does Scripture say?

> For consider your calling, brothers: not many of you were wise according to worldly standards, not many were powerful, not many were of noble birth... . God chose what is weak in the world to shame the strong. —1 Cor 1:26–27 (ESV)

It would seem that God delights in using the very people whom no one expects him to use, just to show that all the glory belongs to him alone. Given what we see in both Scripture and history, it shouldn't be hard for us to believe that God would gift, call, and send humble Christians to reach Muslims—even very affluent ones. Therefore it only makes sense that it would be people who are themselves from the Global South who are training, equipping, and mentoring the modern versions of Naaman's little servant girl. That is exactly what we see when we meet an unassuming brother from East Africa who has a passion for the gospel to shine through the lives of some of the "least in the kingdom."

GOD'S HOUSELIGHTS

I (Barnabas) first started ministry among unreached Muslim peoples in my own country, but soon drew the ire of local authorities and was forced to move to a nearby country and start over. There I again faced persecution when the ministry became fruitful, but this time I landed in jail. So, the cost of obedience to God's call is very clear.

Upon release, I moved to the Middle East. Being an expatriate from an underprivileged African community, I soon became acquainted with other East African Christians from several nations w.ho were resident guest workers in that country. It was during that time that the idea of the "house light" ministry was birthed. It became clear that the goal was not to see how much one person could do to reach Muslims, but rather how to see the most Muslims encounter the living Lord of the Bible. And the Scripture that inspired the ministry was the one mentioned at the beginning of this chapter: the story in 2 Kings 5 about the little servant girl in the house of Naaman the Syrian.

Since God orders the steps of those who love him, he was the one who placed these Christians as domestic workers in Muslim households. And if God was *sending* them to these families, they weren't different, in principle, than other missionaries. They needed encouragement and training to thrive and be fruitful. Thus a vision was birthed to equip domestic workers as tentmaker missionaries among the Muslim peoples they serve.

In this particular country, there was enough freedom to experiment. And soon there was evidence of God's blessing: this little house light ministry began to multiply house churches. Some of these churches were among the domestic workers themselves; others sprang up within the Muslim households. After seven fruitful years, the movement was significant enough to draw government attention. Consequently, I and other fellow workers were imprisoned and then deported.

With this experience, the ministry was enabled to move to another part of the Muslim world to start again. And once again the ministry of house lights is growing. I focus on Africans like myself; the vast majority are household domestics such as maids, nannies, drivers, gardeners, etc. But some of these bivocational missionaries are professionals in their own right: private nurses, private doctors, and children's tutors. The key commonality is quite similar to the first-century Roman world—that is, as household servants, they become a member of their employer's *oikos,* or household; and thus they are uniquely positioned to minister to the Muslim families they serve.

When possible, these workers are trained in their home countries, before they come to the Middle East. However, most of the training is "on the job" in the most literal sense. To do this, our ministry has had to be very creative. Ideally, the trainers spend time with the workers face-to-face—Barnabas with the men and his wife with the women. Each worker is part of a small cell group that meets on his or her day off. The life of a house servant is often difficult. Sometimes we are able to pass along CDs or books to them, and then later follow up. In other cases, the only contact we can have with one of the house lights is by telephone, which we have learned how to use to train and teach, even though it is in a less-than-optimal way.

This entrance strategy is very different from that of most expat professionals, who come to the Muslim world in high-status positions, such as college professors and engineers, and speak to Muslims as equals.[1] For these house lights, the situation is the complete opposite and raises the question of how someone of lower socioeconomic status can make their faith attractive to a Muslim who is "above" them. Because they cannot use the eloquence of speech and human wisdom as many so often do, these houselights must have a completely different "apologetic."

THE POWER OF PRAYER

One of the primary ways that house lights go about their ministry is through the supernatural power of prayer ministry. They are taught to pray constantly for their employers as they go about their daily tasks. The worker may be the only Christian who has ever prayed for the salvation of that family. Also, because of their close proximity to household members, the house lights are often able to pray for the sick, rebuke the activities of witchcraft, and cast out demons in Jesus' name.

One sister had worked for a Muslim family for nine years when a baby daughter suddenly became very ill and was taken to the hospital. The mother came home crying because the doctors said the girl was going to die. It was the maid's day off, but she came when she found out and told the mother, "Don't worry, my God will heal her." The mother thought she was talking about some kind of magic. But the maid replied, "I don't have any ability, but I know my God." The maid then fasted and prayed for seven days, only drinking water. She also asked others to pray. She anointed the baby with oil and prayed over her every day as she gave her a bottle. After seven days the parents took the baby back to the hospital and discovered that she was completely healed. They wanted to learn more about the maid's faith.

It's easy to see how this kind of spiritual authority opens many doors, and these house lights then use a variety of ways to follow up on answered prayers: verbal witness, Scripture portions, giving *The Jesus Film*—to name only a few. While these seem like fairly common mission activities, there are a multitude of complications due to the very uneven power dynamics involved. This is where Brother Barnabas' ministry exerts its spiritual leverage. By spending time training and encouraging these servants of Christ, he is spiritually investing at the exact point of maximum impact.

---

1 The truth is that many Muslims do not consider Christians their "equals." Furthermore, expat professionals, in some parts of the Muslim world, are indeed not on the same socioeconomic level as many of their host-nation neighbors, friends, and employers.

Another important approach of the house light ministry involves the children of these wealthy Muslim homes. Sometimes interaction is part of a domestic's responsibilities; other times a dedicated nanny will be hired. Either way, this interaction offers many opportunities for house lights to plant and water seeds that will bear fruit in the next generation of the Muslim world.

In one example, a nanny was hired to care for a very young Muslim boy. It soon became apparent that something was wrong; he was not learning to walk or talk at the normal ages. The nanny began to fast and pray for the little boy. Suddenly he was healed and reached normal developmental goals. The Muslim father was so overjoyed that he immediately believed in Christ and started watching Christian television on a satellite channel.

In another case, the twelve-year-old son of an important sheikh was demon-possessed. The family's maid recognized the problem and told the father. The parents tried various Islamic remedies, but after six months nothing had changed. They remembered what the maid had said, so they called her in to ask what could be done. She wanted to call for help from the ministry, but she couldn't refer to someone as her "pastor," so she asked if her "sheikh" could come and pray for the boy. When we came and prayed, and the boy was immediately delivered. After an explanation, the parents understood that his power came not from magic but from faith in the name of Isa.

With a multitude of similar stories, there is much cause for rejoicing in the ministries of these house lights. We must remember, however, that these dear servants of Christ are essentially slaves to the Muslims who hire them. As such they face dangers and difficulties that are almost unthinkable to expat professionals. They often are overworked or beaten. Like guest workers the world over, their employers can easily cheat them, yet they have no legal recourse. Sometimes their passports are taken away so they cannot even return home. Many times their employers try to force them to become Muslims. Young women are particularly vulnerable in such situations, with some being sexually assaulted. And sadly a few of these house lights have paid the ultimate price for their faith—receiving the martyr's crown in return.

CONCLUSION

One of the great forces at work in Christian mission today is that more and more gifted and anointed people *from* the Global South are entering into the Lord's harvest fields. And an increasing number of them are from lower socioeconomic backgrounds. The story of the house lights from Africa is only one example of this new paradigm in mission, where brothers and sisters from lower socioeconomic backgrounds are going to affluent parts of the Muslim world.

We started out by considering the impact of one young girl who was carried away to a foreign land to work in the house of a powerful man. Her simple testimony, when paired with a supernatural healing, brought truth into a lost household in the Middle East. While the story in 2 Kings 5 is thousands of years old, it seems that God is recycling the story line.

ILLUSTRATION

Lola found a job as a nanny for a wealthy Muslim family in the Middle East. She spent twelve to fourteen hours a day with the five children in the family as their primary caregiver. Along the way, as Lola fed, bathed, and played with the children, she also taught them the stories and songs she heard learned as a child.

One night the children's private school had a talent program. In an impromptu moment, one of the youngest was asked to sing his favorite song. The little Muslim boy proudly began, "Jesus loves me this I know, for the Bible tells me so."

The next morning Lola was harshly reprimanded by the father and immediately dismissed from employment and escorted to the airport for deportation. The parents tried to explain to their children what happened to their beloved Lola, but they refused to listen. They wanted Lola and went on a "strike." They refused to do their school work or bathe or do many other things that she had previously done with them. The father hired another nanny, but the children still refused. Finally, out of utter desperation, the father sent a cousin to the Philippines to find Lola and ask her to come back, because "the children are sick and need the care only Lola can give."

DISCUSS AND APPLY

- How would you imagine shifting your strategy for sharing the gospel in an environment of power dynamics in which you had "taken on the nature of a servant"?

- How does this chapter impact your moral sensitivities regarding the safety of workers from the perspective of a sending structure?

- Can you think of any ways that expat professionals and their servant-class counterparts could partner with each other in creative kingdom-oriented ways in a given country?

FOR FURTHER READING

Adeney, Miriam, and Sadiri Joy Tira. *Wealth, Women and God: How to Flourish Spiritually and Economically in Tough Places*. William Carey, 2016.

Pantoja, Luis L., Jr., Sadiri Joy Tira, and Enoch Wan, eds. *Scattered: The Filipino Global Presence*. LifeChange, 2004.

Thomas, T. V. "South Asian Diaspora Christianity in the Persian Gulf." In *Global Diasporas and Mission*, edited by Chandler H. Im and Amos Yong, Regnum Edinburgh Centenary Series, Vol. 23, 2014.

SERMON №4

YASSIR ERIC

Scripture Reading: 2 Timothy 4:1-5

In this biblical passage, the apostle Paul opens the curtains and allows us to take a glimpse of events related to his life and ministry. We need to keep in mind that these were the last words that Paul wrote to his son in the faith. Paul writes the letter with the aim to send pastoral advice to Timothy. The experienced apostle tells the young minister to follow his example. Paul sends a clear message to Timothy, highlighting that he had fulfilled his ministry, fought the good fight, and was finishing well. So follow my steps, don't give up, and fulfill your ministry as a preacher. These were the words of Paul.

Along the passage, Paul refers to Jesus Christ as the one who will judge the living and the dead. Of the hundred things he could say about Jesus, Paul describes him as the one who is to judge. The fact is that when it comes to preaching the gospel, the consequences are related to death and life. The proclamation of the gospel has eternal implications. This explains the language Paul used when he said, "by his appearing and his kingdom" (2 Tim 4:1 ESV).

We preach the Word, we preach the gospel, we preach Christ crucified. That is our message, and it is described in the Scripture as "a stumbling block to Jews and foolishness to Gentiles (1 Cor 1:23). "But to us who are being saved it is the power of God" (1 Cor 1:18).

The fact is that the cross of Christ will always upset people, because it is offensive. The message of the Cross implies that humankind is lost because no one has merits to be saved. Salvation can only be attained by faith in the works of Jesus Christ. Even though the Cross makes people uncomfortable, we cannot minimize it. We have to follow Paul's example, who would embrace every opportunity to preach Christ crucified.

We need to keep in mind that the authority and the power we have come from the Word of God. Our most important evangelistic tool is not the dream we had, but the Word of God. It is not the stories we tell, but the gospel of Jesus Christ. As born-again Christians, we are often invited to tell our testimonies. But we have to remember that salvation doesn't come through the power of our testimonies, but from the Word of God. So when we tell our testimony, the message of the Cross needs to be at the center of it.

Concerning the gospel, Paul told Timothy to proclaim it. To proclaim a message is to declare it loud and clear to as many people as possible. Paul was telling Timothy to proclaim the Word so loud that everybody would be able to hear it.

Thus we should not be ashamed of the gospel, but whenever possible proclaim grace and mercy in every opportunity God gives us. The text teaches us that we have to speak about Jesus Christ "in season and out of season" (2 Tim 4:2).

Paul teaches us to preach the Word, but what does this mean? Do we focus on a specific aspect of the message and forget the rest? Paul made it very clear that our commitment is with the proclamation of the whole Word of God: "All Scripture is breathed out by God and profitable for teaching, for reproof, for correction, and for training in righteousness, that the man of God may be complete, equipped for every good work" (2 Tim 3:16-17 ESV).

It is such a serious task to preach the Word of God that Paul referred to the presence of God as he commanded Timothy to be a preacher. So we must preach all the Scripture, as we cannot be selective.

Moreover, we are commanded to persevere preaching the Word even if people turn away from the truth and start searching for false teaching. "For the time will come when people will not put up with sound doctrine. Instead, to suit their own desires, they will gather around them a great number of teachers to say what their itching ears want to hear. They will turn their ears away from the truth and turn aside to myths" (2 Tim 4:3-4).

Let us submit ourselves to the same instructions Paul wrote to Timothy. Let us press on. "Preach the word; be prepared in season and out of season; correct, rebuke and encourage—with great patience and careful instruction" (2 Tim 4:2).

Maybe you have been hurt by so many people, or labored for years without seeing any fruit, or served friends who have betrayed you. Please do not lose heart. Keep going, and do not give up. "Preach the word.... Do the work of an evangelist" (2 Tim 4:2,5).

I n the past, the pathway that workers followed to the harvest of the Muslim world was difficult but fairly constant. Expatriates from the West used their relatively greater wealth and political power to gain residence and access to the people to whom God had called them. But as we have seen in earlier chapters, both the workers and the fields have changed, thus generating a need for new pathways between the two.

In this section you will encounter some of the creative new ways that workers in the Vision 5:9 Network are engaging the Muslim world. Through prayer and innovation, the writers in this section are opening new possibilities for other workers to follow. Come explore with them some of these new pathways.

—Gene Daniels, section editor

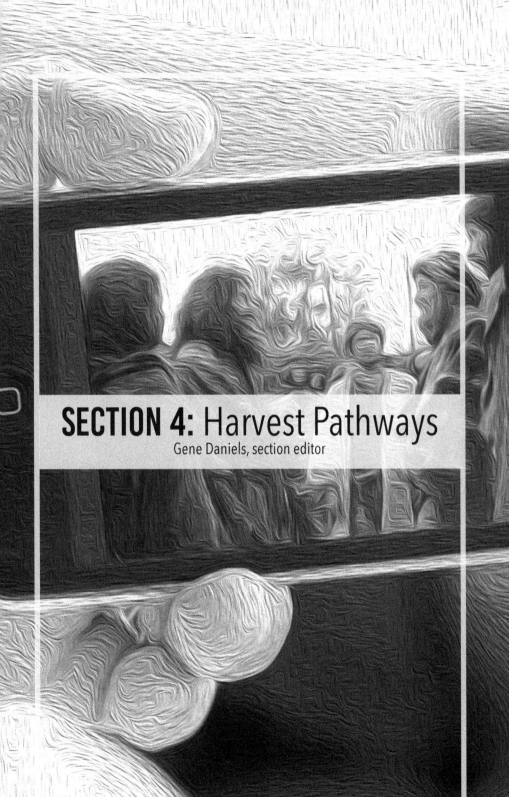

SECTION 4: Harvest Pathways

Gene Daniels, section editor

23 | SENDING STRUCTURES THAT WORK:
Unleashing the Global South

FD has served among Muslims for more than twenty years. A native of the Philippines, he has lived in three countries, reaching Muslims and catalyzing Global South sending structures. He currently lives in Europe with his wife and two children.

JS has served in North Africa for nineteen years, where he runs a B4T ("business for transformation") and partners in the creation of sending structures for the Global South. His passion is to see the whole church participate in reaching the unengaged, unreached peoples of the world. He continues to live in North Africa with his wife and four children.

MAIN POINTS NOT TO MISS:

- Emerging missions in the Global South need sending structures that fit their context.
- The first steps in cross-cultural mission are often close-proximity sending.
- Global labor migration means bivocational models are a key part of the future of missions.

For many years the church in the Global South has been the recipient of Christian missionaries. Now, as churches are multiplying in countries once cut off from the Gospel, there are increasing numbers of workers from the Global South. A number of challenges face these new workers as they seek to join God's global mission, two of the most significant being the lack of appropriate sending structures and the lack of financial resources. This chapter explores some of the ways believers from the Global South are overcoming these challenges.

> Adel and Niveen are North Africans who felt a clear call of God on their lives to go to the hardest places. But in the absence of a sending structure they struggled to find their way. Eventually they moved to an unreached area and established a small business as their reason to be in the country and to provide for their family. During the Arab Spring their business was forcibly closed, but they chose to stay. Without financial resources, their utilities were shut off. Although hungry and thirsty, they persevered. Eventually they found jobs to become self-supporting, yet they were largely isolated and alone.

Traditional sending structures can hinder Global South participation in the Great Commission. Simpler, more appropriate structures need to emerge.

Believers from the Global South have a unique opportunity to reach Muslims. Like Adel and Niveen, the majority of these believers will follow a nontraditional route to reaching the field. How much easier would their journey have been if there was an established structure to work through? When David fought Goliath, Saul wanted to send him with his armor, but it didn't fit (1 Sam 17:38–40). It would have hindered him, not helped. In a similar way, traditional sending structures can hinder Global South participation in the Great Commission. Simpler, more appropriate structures need to emerge.

Global South mission usually begins by releasing workers where they already are, then moves toward sending them within their own geographic or political boundaries. They find that the farther they go, the more challenges they face. Thus international sending can be an insurmountable challenge. Sending Global South workers to distant lands requires a more capable sending structure than is usually available.

> We need to create sending structures that intentionally recruit and care for such bivocational workers.

SENDING TO CULTURALLY PROXIMATE PEOPLE

Kofi is a member of a vibrant church in a city in East Africa where there is both a significant Christian population and a strong Muslim community. A few years ago he met a European believer reaching out to Muslims in his country and training others to do the same. Kofi felt a strong burden for the Muslims in his city and began witnessing. Today there is hardly a Muslim-background believer from that community who has not been helped by Kofi along the way. He disciples and coaches new believers, gives them shelter when they are persecuted, connects underground believers to the local church, and helps the church get a vision for the Muslims around them.

In many African and Asian countries there are strong churches in the midst of Muslim communities. Until recently their members have seldom dared to reach out to their neighbors, but this is changing. The potential of these nearby believers to reach Muslims is great since they don't need visas, they speak the national language, and they often have the same or a similar culture.[1]

Culturally proximate believers often have natural relationships with Muslims in their neighborhood, especially in urban centers where Muslims and Christians are both present. Examples of this can be found in cities like Jakarta, Delhi, Cairo, and the big cities of the Arabian Peninsula where there are significant numbers of Christian and Muslim migrant workers from all over the world. Muslims and Christians live in the same neighborhood, attend the same schools, meet regularly at the workplace or shops, and participate in the same activities in their community. A variety of day-to-day interactions that are natural links for the gospel to flow through are already in place.

BIVOCATIONAL MODELS

In a particular majority Muslim country in Asia, there is an intentional effort to mobilize university students and professionals to reach out. Training programs such as Kairos, Perspectives, and Xplore have been useful in creating awareness and promoting opportunities for students to get involved in going, giving, sending, praying, and mobilizing others.[2] Students who are interested in going long-term are using their professions to find a job in areas with the greatest need. In this country, many of the unengaged live in remote areas in which it is difficult for foreign workers to gain long-term residence. Since few professionals are

---

1 Ben Naja, *Releasing the Workers of the Eleventh Hour: The Global South and the Task Remaining* (Pasadena, CA: William Carey Library, 2007), chapter 4.
2 *Kairos*, www.kairoscourse.org; *Perspectives*, www.perspectives.org; *Xplore*, www.mobilization.org/resources/live-missionally/xplore.

interested in working in these areas, it isn't difficult for national believers to find jobs there, especially if they are doctors, dentists, or teachers. Many young professionals have been deployed to the unengaged through this approach to sending.

Bivocational ministry is a common practice among Global South workers. There are very few salaried pastors or church workers for the thousands of Filipino diaspora churches, especially those in the Middle East. With eternity's values in view, a growing number of Filipino believers recognize that their overseas work is their witness and the workplace is the place for it.[3] Arabic teachers from Egypt, football coaches from South America, English teachers from the Philippines, and entrepreneurs from other parts of the world are examples of ways to place workers from the Global South and to help them overcome financial constraints. But to do this we need to create sending structures that intentionally recruit and care for such bivocational workers.

Bivocational ministry among Muslims is strategic and sustainable. For proximate believers, a job or business represents not only a source of income to sustain the worker's family but also a natural way to meet people. Best of all, they already have the skills necessary for their work. What they need is a paradigm shift—that is, we need to develop sending structures that equip bivocational workers and offer them progressive coaching to effectively integrate witness in their work.

LABOR MIGRATION

Sarah is a follower of Jesus from Southeast Asia who was working in the Middle East. One day she met Abdul, a Muslim businessman who had also relocated for business. Eventually they got married, and soon Abdul accepted the Lord and became an active member of the local fellowship. Less than two years later Sarah and Abdul returned to his home country. Although it is a very restricted location, they are intentionally salt and light. Many members of Abdul's family decided to follow Jesus over the next seven years, with a total of more than three hundred Muslims receiving Christ.

International labor migration is a strategic vehicle to mobilize and send Global South workers. For example, according to Gulf Labour Markets and Migration (GLMM), almost half of the 51.5 million people living in the Gulf Cooperation Countries (GCC)[4] are foreign nationals.[5] The majority of migrant workers in these countries are from India, Egypt, Pakistan, Bangladesh,

---

3 Jojo Manzano and Joy Solina, eds., *Worker to Witness* (Makati, Philippines: Church Strengthening Ministry, 2007).
4 The GCC is a regional political and economic council consisting of all the Arab states of the Persian Gulf except Iraq.
5 GLMM, "Total Population and Percentage of Nationals and Foreign Nationals in GCC Countries, 2010-2016," http://gulfmigration.eu/gcc-total-population-percentage-nationals-foreign-nationals-gcc-countries-national-statistics-2010-2016-numbers/.

Philippines, and Sri Lanka. It is estimated that there are almost three hundred thousand Filipino evangelicals working in the Gulf countries![6] So we can see that workers from the Global South are already positioned strategically in the heart of the Middle East. Many of these believers are there for economic reasons, but they would have significant impact in reaching the GCC if they understood their roles as ambassadors of their Lord.

Furthermore, the same mass migrations are also bringing more and more Muslims to places where they can encounter the gospel, many from villages and towns where there is no witness yet among their people. Imagine if they return home full of faith.

BUSINESS AS MISSION (BAM) AND BUSINESS FOR TRANSFORMATION (B4T)

One of the first questions that foreigners are asked is "Why are you here?" Answering this question with integrity is critical to long-term work. Business models are increasingly being utilized as an answer to this question and to provide entry into otherwise closed communities.

In one South American country, young people began to respond to concerted prayer efforts with a desire to go. Although "Send me" was the cry of their hearts, structures did not exist, unfortunately, to accomplish this. Eventually some visionaries addressed the challenges by creating a traditional mission sending structure, but there were too many candidates and not enough money. Later a model was established that would help individuals raise support and go in faith, while at the same time operating businesses. Now there are multiple teams from South America following this model in North Africa and using those businesses as lighthouses to reach the lost.

While this model is not without difficulties, God's people are finding creative ways to help address them. For example, one organization is starting a business incubator in Asia to help people from all over the world turn their Business for Transformation (B4T) idea into reality.[7] One lesson already learned is that, in most cases, individuals operating in the B4T model still need a certain amount of ongoing support. Otherwise they are forced to spend so much time doing business that they are ineffective at ministry.

FACTORS FOR SUCCESS

Work among Muslims is often lonely and discouraging and at times is even met with hostility. Added to that, research shows that small, young sending agencies

---

6 Commission on Filipinos Overseas, "Yearly Stock Estimation of Overseas Filipinos, 2013," http://www.cfo.gov.ph/program-and-services/yearly-stock-estimation-of-overseas-filipinos.html; Jason Mandryk, Operation World, 7th ed. (Colorado Springs: Biblica, 2010)
7 For more information, contact incubator@rannetwork.com.

have high attrition due to individuals being sent alone or lacking support. Therefore we have to do everything we can to help these workers stay on the field. Research also indicates, however, that partnering with other sending agencies and sending teams increases retention.[8] Thus new sending structures should find ways to partner with the older, more established senders to increase their workers' chances at success.

Ownership of the vision is also essential to success. It is crucial for national leaders to understand that sending harvest workers to the least-reached is a God-given calling and responsibility for the whole church. Hence church and organizational leaders must create opportunities for obedient people to step out in faith. Yet the truth is that creating a sending structure from scratch can be daunting. Mobilizing, training, sending, member care, fund-raising, logistics, and other administrative support are but a few areas to be considered. Rather than being a cause for concern, though, these are examples of places that partnership can be sought out while new national systems are being created.

> About ten years ago Hannah heard the challenge of reaching unengaged Muslim people groups in her Asian country. She had the vision of sending workers but did not know how to go about it, so she started with prayer. She shared the vision with her church leaders and friends; intercessors, campus ministry leaders, students, business people, and others joined her. Seven years ago they started a local organization to facilitate their vision. They partnered with existing campus ministries and other international organizations to mobilize students and professionals for missions.

> Funds were raised as local believers gave generously to support the vision. Local businesspeople helped create opportunities for those who need to relocate to unengaged areas where no employment exists. They also invited experienced workers among Muslims (local and expat) to teach at the pre-field training and have a local member care team that visits their teams regularly.

Hannah's story is an example that can be replicated. It is a story of a big vision with small beginnings. It is also a story of kingdom collaboration. In less than seven years this indigenous sending structure sent several teams to unengaged people groups in their country. They focused on areas that are difficult for foreign workers, but not for nationals, to get long-term residence. They have also started sending teams overseas.

---

8 Robert Hay et al., eds., *Worth Keeping: Global Perspectives on Best Practice in Missionary Retention* (Pasadena, CA: William Carey Library, 2007).

THE GLOBAL CHURCH FOR THE GLOBAL TASK: TOGETHER IN PURSUING MOVEMENTS

Yonas is the leader of a large denomination in sub-Saharan Africa. Thirty years ago he received a vision to send workers from his country into the Muslim world. He waited patiently, prayed, and worked toward that goal. Twenty years later he felt that the time was ripe; he stepped down from his job to focus on sending workers to the least-reached. James, a friend from the Global North who spent many years reaching Muslims in East Africa, came alongside Yonas and his vision. James' mission organization intentionally trains its members to be effective not only in reaching Muslims directly but also in serving alongside proximate believers who share the same vision. Today Yonas' organization trains and sends hundreds of workers into the harvest within their own country as well as into North Africa and the Middle East—places that are virtually closed to Westerners.

WHERE TO BEGIN

Leaders often have difficulty starting a new sending structure due to the numerous barriers they need to overcome, not the least of which is finances. Therefore it is good to remember that many countries which have successfully started sending structures have begun with concentrated prayer for the lost. In South America the church was called to its knees to lift up the Muslim people of the Middle East and North Africa. With prayer came passion; with passion came some people who felt called to go, and others who had a greater willingness to participate financially to send workers.

There are many examples of fully funded Global South workers being sent out locally and beyond—but not enough. The number is still very low compared to the huge numerical sending potential. In order to reach the Vision 5:9 Network goal of effectively engaging all Muslim people groups by 2025, the full potential of churches in Asia and Africa needs to be unleashed.

Local sending to proximate Muslims maximizes the relational, geographical, linguistic, and cultural advantages of millions of nearby believers and offers the highest Global South sending potential. All the local churches in Asia and Africa, including the diaspora churches in the Arabian Peninsula, have the potential to form their own teams to reach their Muslim neighbors. Moving from proximate to the end of the earth is often the pathway of mission participation. Starting and building with partnerships is the key to fulfilling the vision.

CONCLUSION

African, Asian, and Latin American countries have traditionally received missionaries. Now the tide has turned. Although many churches in the Global South have very little experience or financial resources, they are beginning to send workers. At the eleventh hour of missions' history, workers from the Global North and South are working together.[9] It is not about the North or the South, but about the global church working together to finish the global task.

There are local church leaders like Yonas and ordinary believers like Adel, Niveen, Kofi, Sarah, and Hannah who are now actively involved in reaching Muslims because of colaborers from the Global North who came alongside them. The potential of the proximate church in Asia and Africa is still growing; and there is a need for more "alongsiders" who do not seek their own organizational growth but seek to catalyze, assist, facilitate, coach, and multiply indigenous sending.

Every context has its own unique challenges that must be overcome and its own unique strengths upon which to build. The challenges presented to foreign mission agencies, the phenomena of immigration, and the growing strength of the Global South churches requires creativity and experimentation if we are to see the potential of those future (and current) workers realized. Whether proximate, student, B4T, or traditional, the models are endless for seeing the message of Christ taken to every tongue and tribe.

DISCUSS AND APPLY

- What do the current global mission trends mean to you and your organization?

- Which story in this chapter do you like most? Why?

- How will you apply what you learned from this chapter?

BIBLIOGRAPHY

Goldman, Bob. "Saul's Armor and David's Sling: Innovative Sending in the Global South." *Mission Frontiers*, May/June 2007. http://www.missionfrontiers.org/issue/article/sauls-armor-and-davids-sling.

Naja, Ben. *Releasing the Workers of the Eleventh Hour: The Global South and the Task Remaining.* Pasadena, CA: William Carey Library, 2007.

---

9 See Matthew 20:6-7.

24 | MOBILIZING FOR THE UNENGAGED THROUGH DIASPORA MINISTRY

Brian Hébert serves as associate pastor at Wilcrest Baptist Church in Houston, Texas, associate professor of intercultural studies at Fuller Seminary, and lecturer in intercultural studies at Houston Baptist University. For more than ten years he has led a diaspora ministry in Houston.

MAIN POINTS NOT TO MISS:

- Traditional mission mobilization strategies are not adequate for the task of reaching the unreached.
- The significant Muslim diaspora in the West has opened a new kind of mission mobilization.

"What will it take to engage the nearly four hundred unengaged people groups by 2025?" My friend's question distilled the abstract goal and vision of engaging the unengaged into a focused question. The simple answer is that the global mission community would need to engage five people groups every month to reach the goal.

"For the sake of argument," he continued, "let's say that we need a team of three family units to count a people group as engaged and that only one in ten people who apply with an agency will actually arrive on the field. This means that the global mission community will have to mobilize twenty-four thousand people toward the task."[1]

Clearly the need is so great that if the task is to be completed we will need new strategies wherein we find, train, and mobilize the next generations of missionaries. The point of this chapter is to demonstrate two things: first, that mobilizing the church to engage the diaspora is part of the solution to mobilization for the unengaged in their homelands; and second, through diaspora ministry a new kind of missionary training, sending, and partnership is available.

OPPORTUNITY: THE GLOBAL MUSLIM DIASPORA

Contemporary diaspora movements such as the Syrian and Rohingya refugee crisis highlight the push and pull factors leading to an increase in the Muslim diaspora population. These immigrants fit a number of categories: refugees, students, businesspeople, even medical tourists. While diaspora missiology is still emerging, the scale of the Muslim diaspora is already very significant. If all diaspora Muslims were to gather in one location, it would be the sixth-largest Muslim country in the world, ranking just ahead of Turkey and Iran.

Globally, Muslims account for 25 percent of all immigrants.[2] These immigrants span across North Africa all the way to the Pacific Rim and have migrated to most Western countries. These Muslims come from sixty-eight nations.[3] Although Muslims have been in the United States since colonial times, the majority of the population is relatively new. Eighty-four percent of Muslims in the US arrived after 1980. Thus 65 percent of them are first-generation immigrants with strong family ties abroad.[4] Missionaries who become involved with this diaspora have direct access to many Muslims who are first- or second-

---

1 These numbers are purely hypothetical and intended to serve as an illustration. They are not based on information from any agency. If one extends this logic to include all UUPGs, then sixty thousand people would have to be raised.
2 Pew Forum, "Faith on the Move: The Religious Affiliation of the International Migrants", March 2.
3 Ibid.
4 Ibid., 10.

generation immigrants from every corner of the Muslim world and who still have ties to their families, friends, and networks back home. The recent increase and arrival of these diverse groups of Muslims make them great places to begin to love Muslims as neighbors.

DIASPORA MINISTRY AS A BRIDGE TO THE WORLD

Theory

In the preceding chapter, the focus was on the workforce that is present within a (typically) Christian diaspora, such as the Filipinos, Nigerians, or Koreans. This chapter is different. It is focused on the impact that people in the host country can have in reaching the diaspora in their *own country, and the global impact that can result from this.*

Bridgers

The term *bridger missionary* (or *bridger*, for short) is used to signify missionaries who are citizens of the host nation and who intentionally connect with diaspora Muslims.[5] Kinship bridging, then, is the attempt of bridgers to gain access to other countries, families, and social networks based on diaspora mission. Kinship bridging is the practical realization of God's sovereignty in establishing the time and place where people live (Acts 17:26) by engaging the diaspora first and then following family and network connections globally based on invitations received through interactions with diaspora peoples. Simply put, kinship bridging means choosing where one goes in the world by partnering with those God has sent to them. There are numerous ways in which kinship bridging can help people from various backgrounds overcome cultural, linguistic, ethnic, religious, and geographic differences. The accompanying table describes the various ways of connecting to diaspora groups and the kinds of networks to which they will be introduced.

---

5 In the original source where I formulated this idea, I used the term "exogenous" to denote a person who is outside of the group. Brian Hébert, "The 'with' of Diaspora Missiology: The Impact of Kinship, Honor, and Hospitality on the Future of Missionary Training, Sending, and Partnership," in *Diaspora Missiology: Reflections on Reaching the Scattered Peoples of the World*, EMS no. 23 (Pasadena, CA: William Carey Library, 2015).

TYPES OF BRIDGING

Designation	Description of the Bridge	Mission Activity
Bridger-1	A bridger Christian befriends a diaspora Christian who introduces him to his social network of Christians	Partnership with the local church. Discipleship or leadership training. The hosts help the guest acclimate and receive his ministry.
Bridger-2	A bridger Christian befriends a diaspora Christian who introduces him to a social network of Muslims	Partnership with the local church. Evangelism if possible. The hosts help the guest acclimate and connect him with their Muslim friends and neighbors.
Bridger-3	A bridger Christian befriends a diaspora Muslim who introduces him to his own social network of Muslims	Practices missions *to* and then *with*. The hosts help the guest acclimate and provide him with social legitimacy in the Muslim community.

Some concrete examples will help explain the chart. A "Bridger-1" might befriend a Lebanese student. Through their friendship, the Lebanese student invites his friend back to his country to stay with his family and minister with his church. Ministry in this context is partnership with the local body of Christians through discipleship or leadership training. The hosts help the guest acclimate and receive his ministry.

An example of a "Bridger-2" is a Christian who partners with a diaspora Syrian Christian in order to reach the Syrian's home network of Muslim friends and acquaintances. The priority is to reach Muslims through his friend's social network. Ministry in this context is partnership with the local body of Christians through missions to the neighboring Muslim community if possible. The hosts help the guest acclimate and connect him with their Muslim friends, neighbors, and contacts.

And finally, a "Bridger-3" bridges the largest cultural gap. An example would be a Christian who works in an international company and befriends a Muslim. Through that connection he is able to transfer to or visit his home country. The bridger missionary's focus is first on the extended family and then on their network. Ministry in this context is pioneer work within a Muslim network. The hosts help the guest acclimate and provide him with social legitimacy in the Muslim community.

Culture

Kinship bridging is built upon four cultural traits: kinship, networks, hospitality, and reciprocal, obligation-formed relationships. These four traits will look different in every culture, and specific study will be necessary to determine if a given culture is a likely host for kinship bridging.

Kinship

Kinship is often understood only as biological relationships. This definition, however, neglects the reality that kinship is more than "a network of biological relationships, it is also a network of social relationships. It establishes social ties, patterns of behavior, obligations and responsibilities, and patterns of authority. In short, it is a 'road map' or structure of interpersonal relationships."[6] With this broader understanding of kinship, there are three ways that someone might be classified as "kin": through birth, marriage, or honorary status. As outsiders, if we want to become part of the social kinship system, presuming marriage is not an option, then the "honorary" tie is the avenue.

Although many cultures do not have official honorary roles such as Godparent or blood brother, the culturally and relationally savvy outsider can hope to achieve the status of the honored guest, which is often outside the bonds of blood relationship. By achieving this status, the outsider now has an identity through that particular family or clan within the broader community.

Networks

Kinship and networks share similarities; in fact, kinship groups generate their own networks.[7] Networks are "similar to institutionalized social relations, such as tribal affiliations and political dynasties, but also distinct from them, because to be networked entails making a *choice to be connected across recognized boundaries.*"[8] Networks can be focused around areas of mutual interest, social action, political opinion, or religious and moral values. Networks often transcend both geography and family.

Social networks often form around structures such as ethnicity, technology, media, or ideologies. Today people are mobile and often migrate en masse, so these networks function to keep them connected to each other across globalized relationships. For example, Arabs, Egyptians, Lebanese, and Moroccans are no longer found only in the Middle East but are now distributed throughout

---

6 Stephen A. Grunlan and Marvin K. Mayers, *Cultural Anthropology: A Christian Perspective*, 2nd ed. (Grand Rapids: Zondervan, 1988), 162.
7 Harris, *Kinship* (Minneapolis: University of Minnesota Press, 1990), 64.
8 Miriam Cooke and Bruce B. Lawrence, *Muslim Networks from Hajj to Hip Hop* (Chapel Hill, NC: The University of North Carolina Press, 2005), 1.

the world. Due to kinship ties these diaspora groups are still connected, and their ethnic networks have reshaped to reflect that. The rise of technology and its spread across the world enables people to remain connected in ways that weren't previously possible, not only to their own families but with others as well. Technology is enabling new networks and "tribes" to form around ideas, movements, places, and interests.

Hospitality

Eastern and Southern cultures are renowned for their hospitality. Cultural traits such as honor and shame and prioritizing personal relationships over efficiency and goals has cultivated a kind of enforced hospitality in these contexts. Enforced hospitality is a determined focus on the part of a host to meet the needs of the guest, even when the guest refuses, in such a way that brings honor to his own family. To refuse to provide hospitality, in all of its demands, would bring great shame on the family, village, tribe, and broader religious community.

In such a context, the status of honored guest carries social significance that transcends simply being invited over for dinner and entertained. This status carries with it the identity, privilege, and status of the host family within a given context. In a society that is ruled by personal and family relationships, the identity a host family provides may be the most satisfying to locals as a "reason for being." In countries that do not provide missionary visas, the identity of being a humanitarian worker may not carry as much weight as the simple, relational answer: "He is a friend of our overseas relatives."

Obligation and Reciprocity

Mutual obligation and reciprocity are the rules through which relationships are built, maintained, and optimized. In this context, friendship is a significant relationship that mandates mutual help and support. Friends are obliged to help each other out. To refuse to help is to refuse the relationship. In these cultural contexts people are known for their creative and diverse ways of saying no and still preserving the relationship. Through the course of asking for and receiving help, the relationship is strengthened through reciprocity. The two parties build trust as they invest energy and resources, knowing that the other party is going to act with the same self-interest. Therefore diaspora ministry should be holistic because this forms the relational "down payment" toward future hospitality and reciprocal obligation with an individual and his or her family—regionally or internationally.

CONCLUSION: DIASPORA MOBILIZATION

Over the past decade I have had the privilege of leading a team of "bridger missionaries" like I described at the beginning of this chapter. The original goal was to train and mobilize people who would be willing to adopt a "field" mind-set and strategy while they deliberately focused on diaspora Muslims, with the intent of planting indigenous, language-based churches. The challenges of transience, politics, economics, and persecution have proven to be formidable barriers. However, in the midst of focusing on that goal, we have not only catalyzed a local team but have just sent our thirty-sixth bridger missionary overseas for long-term work. Many of these people who have moved overseas started in that direction when they heard one of our trainers present on our strategies for reaching Muslims locally. This led them through several years of practice and training wherein they gained experience working on a team and building relationships with Muslims from many countries and walks of life. They also learned to share the gospel in ways that are culturally and relationally relevant.

Though not all of these bridger missionaries followed the pattern I have presented here, we are seeing more and more interest in this model. A new group of trainees are intentionally partnered with teams that have diaspora connections to particular countries. These relationships have led to several invitations from Muslim family members in the home country to come live and work there.[9] God is using the bridge of diaspora missions to Muslims not only to engage the world's "sixth-largest Muslim country," but also to strategically, and relationally, place kingdom workers throughout the world. Kinship bridging might just be the link that joins churches and agencies in partnership, not only through sending and funding but also through training and connecting.

DISCUSS AND APPLY

- How might I learn about the diaspora Muslims who live in my city?
- How could I begin to engage with them to reach their kinspeople in their home countries?

---

9 For security reasons, I cannot go into detail on the specifics of country and people group.

BIBLIOGRAPHY

Abu Toameh, Khaled. "Why Arab Leaders Do Not Care About Medical Services in Their Countries." Gaston Institute International Policy Council. http://www.gatestoneinstitute. org/1741/arab-countries-medical-services.

Bagby, Ihsan. *The American Mosque 2011: The Basic Characteristics of the American Mosque.* Report no. 1. Council on American-Islamic Relations. Washington, DC: CAIR, 2011.

Boyd, David. *You Don't Have to Cross the Ocean to Reach the World: The Power of Local Cross-Cultural Ministry.* Grand Rapids: Chosen Books, 2008.

Braziel, Jana Evans, and Anita Mannur, eds. *Theorizing Diaspora: A Reader.* Malden, MA: Blackwell Publishing, 2003.

Cooke, Miriam, and Bruce B. Lawrence. *Muslim Networks from Hajj to Hip Hop.* Chapel Hill: The University of North Carolina Press, 2005.

Green, Stephen T., Daniel Horsfall, and Russell Mannion. *Medical Tourism: Treatment, Markets and Health System Implications: A Scoping Review.* 2011, 14. Report available at http:// www.oecd.org/els/health-systems/48723982.pdf.

Grunlan, Stephen A., and Marvin K Mayers. *Cultural Anthropology: A Christian Perspective.* 2nd ed. Grand Rapids: Zondervan, 1988.

Harris, C. C. *Kinship.* Minneapolis: University of Minnesota Press, 1990.

Hébert, Brian. "The 'with' of Diaspora Missiology: The Impact of Kinship, Honor, and Hospitality on the Future of Missionary Training, Sending, and Partnership." In *Diaspora Missiology: Reflections on Reaching the Scattered Peoples of the World.* EMS no. 23. Pasadena, CA: William Carey Library, 2015.

Hiebert, Paul G. *Cultural Anthropology.* 2nd ed. Grand Rapids: Baker, 1983.

McGavran, Donald. *The Bridges of God.* Rev. ed. New York: Friendship Press, 1981.

Pew Forum. "Faith on the Move: The Religious Affiliation of the International Migrants." March 2012.

Pew Research Center. "Muslim Americans: Middle Class and Mostly Mainstream." May 22, 2007. http://www.pewresearch.org/2007/05/22/muslim-americans-middle-class-and-mostly-mainstream/.

Van Dusen, Allison. "U.S. Hospitals Worth the Trip." *Forbes,* May 29, 2008. http://www.forbes.com/2008/05/25/health-hospitals-care-forbeslife-cx_avd_outsourcing08_0529healthoutsourcing.html.

Woo, Rodney. *The Color of Church: A Biblical and Practical Paradigm for Multiracial Churches.* Nashville: B&H, 2009.

25 | EXTREME THREATS REQUIRE GOOD PREPARATION

Brian Eckheart served in Cairo, Egypt, for three years, where his team had the privilege of inviting Muslims to follow Jesus. In 1993 he was arrested for proselytizing and jailed for three months. He is now the field security and crisis manager for Frontiers.

MAIN POINTS NOT TO MISS:

- Risk is an unavoidable part of ministry in the Muslim world.
- Good preparation for facing these risks has both spiritual and practical dimensions.
- Teams and organizations have an obligation to be proactive, not reactive, about the threats their members face.

> We can be risk-aware without being risk-averse.

It was 4:30 a.m. on the second day of Ramadan in 1993. A pair of handcuffs designed for a smaller man bit into my wrists. I sat on a hard bench in the headquarters of the secret police. I watched bloodied men shuffle past in the corridor. My heart raced as a policeman rained a barrage of questions at me: "What are you doing in this country?" "What church sent you here?" "Who have you been talking to?"

For ninety days I was held in a three-meter square prison cell with three of my teammates before being deported from the country.

That was my first major encounter with the challenge of ministry in the Muslim world. Since then I have helped members of my organization cope with a litany of adversities—visa denials, expulsions, imprisonments, murder by fundamentalists, kidnapping, etc.

While these threats are not the norm, they are an undeniable facet of doing ministry in many Muslim-majority countries. If you seek to invite Muslims to follow Jesus, you cannot afford to ignore these threats or pretend they could never happen to you. Instead, all involved need to prepare to face the threats. If you are a field worker, you need to prepare yourself. If you are a leader, you need to prepare your organization.

PREPARE YOURSELF

If you labor for very long in the harvest field of the Muslim world, it is almost inevitable that you will face some kind of threatening challenge—such as the sudden withdrawal of a visa, a serious injury in a traffic accident, or something more rare, like a kidnapping. Preparing for those potential challenges can lessen their impact and reduce your fear. You can start your preparation by grappling with your biblical theology of risk and suffering. Developing local relationships and clarifying your identity will lessen your risk factors. And practical planning can help you be ready to react wisely and quickly if an urgent crisis erupts.

Develop a Theology of Risk and Suffering

Many of the still-unengaged places of the Muslim world are like a "perfect storm" for the missionary: spiritually dark, physically difficult, and politically dangerous. However, the darkness, difficulty, and dangers do not change our calling. As we take the gospel to Muslims we must be prepared to take certain risks for the sake of those who do not yet have access to the good news, but we must not pretend the risks don't exist. We can be risk-aware without being risk-averse.

Before moving to a country for service, field workers will benefit by carefully developing a theology of risk and suffering. Then, when the inevitable difficult situations emerge, they will have principles at hand to help them respond.

Build God's Truth as Your Foundation

In the organization I work for we have developed a list of ten Bible-based truths that serve as a foundation for risk-taking and suffering. By internalizing the truths of God's Word, workers strengthen the convictions that will provide them with a solid foundation of support when they face difficult, painful, or seemingly hopeless situations.

- As a child of God, nothing can separate me from his love. (Rom 8:15, 38–39)

- God governs all situations. And he will not expect more of me than what he gives me strength for. (Jas 4:15; 1 Cor 10:13; Phil 4:13)

- Through the Holy Spirit, God will work for my good and will glorify himself even through the difficulties I am in. (Rom 8:28; Eph 1:13–14; 1 Cor 10:31)

- Notwithstanding my current circumstances, I live victorious through the promise of Jesus and his coming kingdom. (James 5:8; Rom 8:37)

- Every new day I shall live in the comfort and the joy of knowing Jesus to be with me. (2 Cor 1:5; Acts 4:13; 16:25)

- What I cannot control, I let go of. And I contend to align my thoughts and actions with Jesus and his purpose for me. (1 Pet 5:6–7; 2 Cor 10:5; Heb 12:1)

- My fellow human beings I will love. But I will fight against all God-opposing spirits. (Matt 5:44; 1 Pet 5:9; Eph 6:12)

- Through wise words and actions, I seek to cause good. (Matt 10:16; Rom 12:18, 21)

- Living or dying, I wholly belong to Jesus and will bear witness to him. (Rom 14:8; Rev 12:11)

- Knowing that my brothers and sisters in the Lord stand behind me, I will also protect them. (Eph 4:3; Rom 16:3–4)

TAKE RISKS, BUT DON'T PUT GOD TO THE TEST

Jesus was the ultimate risk-taker. Our Lord left the presence of the Father to come to earth where he would be ridiculed, spat on, betrayed, beaten, crucified in a terrible death, and even ultimately abandoned by God the Father.

So yes, Jesus took risks, but he also had a ministry to attend to and followers to train. In other words, he had a purpose to fulfill. Therefore Jesus, in the riskiness of his calling, drew a line for himself. He would not bring himself into a situation that would force God to act in a certain way, because he did not need his Father to prove either his power or his faithfulness.

> Then the devil took him to the holy city and had him stand on the highest point of the temple. "If you are the Son of God," he said, "throw yourself down. For it is written: "'He will command his angels concerning you, and they will lift you up in their hands, so that you will not strike your foot against a stone.'"
>
> Jesus answered him, "It is also written: 'Do not put the Lord your God to the test.'" (Matt 4:5–7)

We sometimes face the same temptation: we may want God to prove himself by demonstrating his love or his power in situations where there is danger. Yet the greatest demonstrations of God's love and power are the Cross and the empty tomb. If we remember this we will not tempt God by putting him to the test, placing ourselves into risky situations for egocentric reasons.

Jesus lived out this principle of not putting God to the test. In fact, sometimes he even actively averted risk.

> After this, Jesus went around in Galilee. He did not want to go about in Judea because the Jewish leaders there were looking for a way to kill him. (John 7:1)
>
> "Very truly I tell you," Jesus answered, "before Abraham was born, I am!" At this, they picked up stones to stone him, but Jesus hid himself, slipping away from the temple grounds. (John 8:58–59)

At the same time, Jesus made it clear that discipleship is costly.

> Then Jesus said to his disciples, "Whoever wants to be my disciple must deny themselves and take up their cross and follow me. For whoever wants to save their life will lose it, but whoever loses their life for me will find it. What good will it be for someone to gain the whole world, yet forfeit their soul? Or what can anyone give in exchange for their soul?" (Matt 16:24–26)

This calling is echoed in the letters of Paul and in the lives of disciples across the centuries, including the multitudes of Christians who have died as martyrs. But the call to lay down your life encompasses more than physical life.

The German pastor and martyr, Dietrich Bonhoeffer, put it this way, "The call to discipleship, the baptism in the name of Jesus Christ means both death and life (Bonhoffer, 2001, 44).[1]

We need encouragement, motivation, and strength to hold firm these kinds of convictions. There is constant tension between the call to pour out our lives for the kingdom and the responsibility to steward that same life as a gift.

BUILD HONEST RELATIONSHIPS

> We encourage people to work out a summary of their core identity in one or two sentences. Such a phrase has come to be known as a "short and legitimate statement."

Since many threats on the field cannot be completely avoided, perhaps the best way to deal with them is to develop honest, close relationships with honorable people in your community. Hospitality and honor are cultural norms in most Muslim environments, so if you develop close, trusting relationships in your community, they will be more likely to look after you. They will also be more likely to let you know when they think they can't help or protect you, so that you can look elsewhere to find the help or protection you need.

It's also wise to develop at least a few significant relationships with other expatriates in your area—either with Christian colleagues or secular expatriates. There will obviously be differences in the way secular people think about risk and suffering, but generally speaking the more information the better; and a clear, real identity allays suspicion.

Cross-cultural gospel workers need a clear identity that makes sense to others. No matter whether a neighbor questions you over a cup of tea or a government official questions you during an interrogation, they need a wise and reasonable answer to questions like "Why are you here?" and "What are you doing?"

In our organization, we encourage people to work out a summary of their core identity in one or two sentences. Such a phrase has come to be known as a "short and legitimate statement," or SLS. Such a statement needs to make sense to people legitimately. What you say about yourself must match what you do and how you are perceived.

What you say about yourself must be true, but you need not say everything that is true. If possible, express how your presence is meant to benefit people in your host country and build bridges to people's hearts.

---

1 *Dietrich Bonhoeffer, The Cost of Discipleship* (London: SCM Press, 2001).

In conversations, you can start by introducing yourself with your SLS. If appropriate, you can expand on it as the relationship grows. However, there must be limits to what you will speak about. Imagine the safe ground of any particular conversation as a box. Inside the box you have stored innocuous topics you desire to talk about. These may include your family, hobbies, or sports news, as well as accomplishments for the good of your host country. In a serious interrogation, you may pull out from your "box" your humanity, including your basic needs.

Controversial and provocative topics are outside this box. So is information that will jeopardize others, such as names and phone numbers of colleagues. Since a refusal to answer is often culturally unacceptable, it is better to transition and respectfully redirect the conversation.

Question that leads outside the box: *"How do you like our president?"*

Answer that transitions back inside the box: *"I don't know much about him, or about politics at all. We have come here because we love the people. My family and I are concerned for your well-being. That's why we work for an NGO that teaches hygiene to women."*

If you are under pressure in any situation, fall back on your "safe and legitimate statement." Offer less, not more. And be sure to never change your SLS under pressure.

TAKE PRACTICAL STEPS

It is also important to develop a contingency plan so that your family and colleagues know what to do, where to go, and whom to call in emergency situations. My organization provides a contingency plan template, and each team is supposed to create their contingency plan using it. Such a plan can include:

- Names, addresses, and other contact information for team members and relatives
- Names and contact information of the team's overseer/manager
- Which member of the team will be the main point person to communicate with your organization's leaders and others in a crisis?
- If the team is working with other organizations, who is the lead agency in a crisis?
- Does the team have a spokesperson in your sending country?
- In the event of a crisis that requires immediate evacuation, what are your team's designated meeting places inside your country of service and outside it?

- What are the communication and response plans for each of the main threats your team will likely face?

- Given very short notice, what do you need to take with you? (Have a bag packed with travel documents, medications, and other items important to you in case you need to leave quickly.)

DEVELOP EVACUATION PRINCIPLES

There may be times when you will need to decide whether to leave your city/country or to stay. It is very helpful to develop principles and questions to help you make this decision in advance so you are not struggling with this under the pressure of the moment.

- How does your theology of risk and suffering inform this decision?

- On a family level, are you operating in faith—either in faith to stay or faith to leave? Decisions made from a place of fear won't be good decisions.

- How will your team communicate about this decision? What if not everyone agrees?

- What impact will leaving or staying have on your ministry?

- What will you do if it is dangerous to get to the airport or to fly?

- What weight should you give to advice from embassies or other news sources? Embassy information is usually generic—intended to address the needs of the widest constituency. Therefore, evaluate your own situation by considering whether you have good friends nearby, live in a safe part of the city, or can get to a safe haven. What weight should you give to your gut instinct about whether or not you are safe?

PREPARE IN ADVANCE FOR A CHAOTIC TIME

Certain procedures are helpful to have in place before a situation spirals out of control. Here are a few hard lessons my organization has learned.

- Save your organization's emergency contact number in your phone.

- Keep your organization's crisis manager and your overseer in the communications loop.

- Network! The sharing of information is vital.

- Keep a good stock of food, water, petrol, bottled gas, and SIM cards that work on hand.

- Keep some cash on hand—a combination of local currency, international hard currency, and perhaps some from a neighboring country where you might need to evacuate.

- Don't assume you'll always have access to the Internet or mobile phone coverage.
- Things can change faster than you think.
- Know your exit routes, including flying, driving, taking a ferry, etc.
- Make sure you're on your embassy's contact list.
- Identify at least one local friend who is willing to shelter you if necessary.
- In some situations, getting out of the city and going to a village can provide more safety.
- Review your contingency plans regularly.
- Make sure that your main home office has a copy.

PREPARE YOUR ORGANIZATION

As important as it is for individuals to be prepared to face extreme threats, it's equally important for organizations to prepare in advance. Leaders need to be clear about the ultimate goal, balanced with an understanding of their moral and legal obligations toward their members. They should offer appropriate security training and supporting resources to members. And when the worst kinds of things happen, organizational leaders need to be ready to provide after-crisis care.

Clarify the Ultimate Goal: God's Glory

If God's glory among Muslim peoples is the goal of your organization, the leaders will need to grapple with how that goal affects their perspective on what is most important. How can they keep God's glory in focus?

Do truckers have safety as their goal? No. Although safety is important, in reality a trucker's ultimate goal is to deliver goods. Our ultimate goal is God's glory among unreached Muslim peoples. That goal may override safety and security at times. Considering this, organizations need to think through a corporate theology of suffering and risk, wrestling with the same tension as individual field missionaries. Leaders and decision makers need to talk honestly and openly about the levels of risk they are comfortable to sustain to pursue the goal of God's glory.

Fulfill Your Duty of Care

"Duty of care" is a term that encompasses an organization's obligation to ensure the safety and well-being of others. You may have legal obligations in this regard, and failure to meet that duty of care can result in legal and civil penalties in some countries. But at the very least it carries moral obligations to those we serve.

While your duty of care is not to be taken lightly, that doesn't mean you must stop all ministry in dangerous environments. It does mean you should provide your personnel with tools, resources, information, and security training to cope with their environment.

Offer Appropriate Security Training

In today's world, duty of care requires ministries to provide their members with security training that is appropriate to their location. People who work in a relatively low-risk environment can receive adequate training through a variety of online resources and training courses. However, people who live and work in high-risk environments may need to go through a more rigorous, live training course.[2]

Provide Supportive Resources

Another part of your duty of care is to provide appropriate resources, such as security briefings for specific areas or templates for developing local contingency plans. You will also want to ensure that your organizational leaders have access to appropriate and up-to-date personal information on each member of each family, so that you will be prepared to assist in an emergency.

Another key resource is a team of appropriately trained security and crisis management specialists. These specialists can help prepare your members to minister in threatening environments, and they can fulfill a vital role during a crisis. Working in the Muslim world, we cannot escape all risks. But through theological, practical, and organizational preparation we can handle them better.

DISCUSS AND APPLY

- What is the practical difference between being "risk-aversive" and "risk-aware"?

- Do you, and those in ministry with you, have a "short and legitimate statement" to explain who you are?

- What practical steps should you, your team, or your organization take after reading this chapter?

---

2 In the training industry, such courses are known as "hostile environment awareness training" (HEAT), or sometimes simply "hostile environment training" and are offered by many different organizations.

26 | THE GIFT OF PRESENCE

Shodankeh Johnson is a husband and the father of seven children. He is leader of New Harvest Ministries in Sierra Leone. NHM has sent long-term workers to fourteen countries and seen hundreds of churches planted among fifteen Muslim people groups.

John Becker is the director of ministries of AIM International and formerly the international coordinator of the Vision 5:9 Network. He has been serving unreached peoples in Africa, Europe, and North America for the past twenty-two years.

MAIN POINTS NOT TO MISS:

- Prayer is a critical part of being incarnationally present to a people.
- Really listening to people is often the first step toward building the local capacity.
- Treating the host people as partners encourages active participation, which leads to transformation.

Over ten years ago the Vision 5:9 community set out with ambitious goals of effectively engaging every Muslim unreached people group. But it is not enough to simply place a certain number of missionaries among a people—because mission engagement is incarnational. *Effective* engagement is an intentional, long-term presence, with relevant cultural expression of the gospel, in order to see movements to Christ.[1] This approach to ministry is something we would like to call the "gift of presence." The power of this gift is played out through prayer, coming as learners, meeting felt needs, and kingdom collaboration.

PRAYER AS PRESENCE

> Through persistent prayer we have seen very hostile communities opened.

Prayer is the greatest spiritual resource God has provided to accomplish the work of multiplying disciples and churches. It opens the way for the gospel and continues to fuel its impact—like oxygen and wind fueling a wild fire.

Jesus, as the incarnate Word in the flesh (John 1:14), demonstrated prayer. The first thing he did before he began his public ministry was to go out to pray. Now that he was "infleshed," he needed to take the posture of prayer. He was dealing with the reality on this earth. The disciples noticed this, and so they asked Jesus to teach them how to pray (Luke 11:1). Prayer was built into their ministry because of his example. Following Jesus' example, prayer is the foundation and on-ramp to everything leading from engagement of Muslim unreached people groups (MUPGs) to kingdom movements. Prayer is the most powerful and effective access ministry and has caused a cascading effect throughout movements.

There are many ways to act out this commitment to prayer. For example, research clearly shows that fruitful workers mobilize extensive, intentional, and focused prayer. They invite others to join them through committed intercession for themselves and the people they are engaging. They recognize that this can be as important as inviting people to join the team that lives in the host culture.[2] They ensure that the network of prayer groups are informed about the specific communities being served so that they fast and pray for each of them. The result is that God answers by opening the right doors at the right time with the right provision.

---

1 Vision 5:9 Global Trends definitions (a pioneer church-planting effort resident; a commitment to work in the local language and culture; a commitment to long-term ministry; a commitment to sow and train in a manner consistent with the goal of seeing multiplication of disciples or a church-planting movement).
2 Don Allen, et al. "Fruitful Practices: A Descriptive List." *International Journal of Frontier Missiology*, 26:3, Fall 2009, 111-22.

We have found it most fruitful to start each engagement with intercession for the following five things:

1. Open doors, open hearts, and open hands
2. The selection of project leaders
3. A supernatural move of God
4. The leading of the Spirit
5. God's provision of needed resources

Another prayer dimension is to recognize that the workers who are fruitful often are those who pray for God's supernatural intervention as a sign that confirms the gospel.[3] Beyond any doubt, we are convinced that strategic fasting and prayer consistently leads to the undoing of dark powers. Sometimes praying for the sick is a wonderful accelerator of access itself. Through persistent prayer we have seen very hostile communities opened, unlikely persons of peace identified, and whole families saved. All the glory goes to the Father who hears and answers prayers.

We believe that much of the fruit currently being harvested in North Africa is the answer to a year of prayer for one of the North African countries in 2001. One long-term worker was privileged to meet the king, and this bold servant expressed that he regularly prayed for the country. The king, pleasantly surprised, stated that he welcomed Christian prayers for his kingdom. Taking a courageous step, the worker went on to ask if the king would welcome Christians to pray across the country. The king agreed!

This resulted in a year of prayer known as "Arise and Shine," culminating with an unprecedented prayer and worship celebration in which hundreds of intercessors gathered on Palm Sunday after prayer-trekking around the country. Testimonies were shared of how God had miraculously answered prayers and opened doors for the transforming power of the gospel across mountainous villages and ancient walled medinas. In one situation, some of the locals asked for prayer for rain as they were experiencing a multiyear drought. The team went up on a mountainside to pray and persevered in the spirit of Elijah—who, after praying seven times, was told by his servant, "A cloud as small as a man's hand is rising from the sea." (1 Kings 18:44. Rain suddenly came in abundance, and the local villagers celebrated and praised the God of their praying visitors.

---

3 Ibid.

A demonstration of God's power has been a key factor for many Muslims who have come to faith in Jesus Christ. Aware of this, many fruitful workers live out the gift of presence by praying specifically for God to intervene through dreams, healing, deliverance from evil spirits, and other signs to confirm the truth of the gospel. They display empathy for their friends by boldly praying for them in their presence. No matter how God answers, the worker who openly prays illustrates that God is concerned for daily needs and that he is the source of blessing and wholeness.[4]

Prayer as incarnational presence also proved true among the Koti people of Northern Mozambique. This movement originated on a small, insignificant, and notoriously dark island called Buzu. The gospel first arrived through an "Acts-like" shipwreck on Buzu of a survey team to the Koti Islands. The islanders were eager receivers of Jesus, believing that God had brought the messengers to them. However, when the gospel came, the physical island of Buzu began to suffer. Fierce north winds and waves picked up their pace, hitting the island with a relentless persistence. The islanders were distressed—where would they live if the waves fully covered their island?

When new church planters took up residence, they decided to call for a special time of prayer and fasting. Inspired, the local elders sent word throughout the island. For many days, men, women, and children prayed and fasted as they marched around the island in a procession, pleading with the Lord to display his power. To their amazement, the north wind stopped. As a result, the movement has spread from the island of Buzu to all the other islands and to neighboring tribes as well.[5]

LEARNING THROUGH LISTENING

> But compassion alone is not enough because it can be misguided. Our compassion must be the product of being "present" to a people so that it is shaped in partnership with them.

Another way that we offer people the gift of presence is through showing real compassion for them, something that is an essential value found in every kingdom movement. But compassion alone is not enough because it can be misguided. Our compassion must be the product of being "present" to a people so that it is shaped in partnership with them. The first step is active listening to understand felt needs. Workers who are fruitful in this way

4 Ibid
5 James Nelson, "The Forgotten Island," chap. 4 of *Where There Is Now a Church: Dispatches from Workers in the Muslim World* (Colorado Springs: Global Mapping International, 2014).

build positive relationships with local leaders to gain access through ministries that make the love of Christ visible and leave an indelible mark in hearts.

By sensitively and carefully relating to local authorities, including non-Christian religious figures, workers develop respect and good standing in their host community. Those who are intentional about choosing their relationships with local leaders are more likely to be fruitful.[6]

A proven approach is to do a needs assessment in partnership with the local community. Depending on the locals to provide leadership, labor, and materials is an empowering discovery and builds their sense of capacity.

This form of presence becomes an important way to develop mutual respect and trust. In turn, the relationship eventually leads to story-telling and Discovery Bible Studies (DBS). We have found that a variety of these access ministries can play a role in helping advance the kingdom of God among the unreached.

In one area of Sierra Leone where education was an obvious need, intercessors took that need to God in prayer. While strategic prayer was taking place, the community was engaged to discover what resources were available and what the community was ready to provide to meet their own need. The community decided to supply land and construction materials for the development of a temporary school structure, and to pay for a portion of a teacher's salary. The ministry team provided the teacher, who was fully certified, and also a veteran worker who was disciple maker and church planter.

This is one example of a strategy, driven by presence, that has launched more than one hundred primary schools, most of which are now owned by the community. From this simple program God has also raised up twelve secondary schools, two trade technical schools, and Every Nation College, which has accredited schools of business and theology. A simple act of compassion, done in partnership with the local community, is bringing about a community transformation, which in turn is making God famous![7]

SALVATION THROUGH SERVICE

Another expression of being truly present to a people is when laborers in the harvest take a posture of service in a Christlike manner as a visible manifestation of the kingdom of God. "For what we preach is not ourselves, but Jesus Christ as Lord, and ourselves as your servants for Jesus' sake" (2 Cor 4:5).

6 Don Allen, et al. "Fruitful Practices: A Descriptive List." *International Journal of Frontier Missiology*, 26:3, Fall 2009, 111-22.
7 Shodankeh Johnson, "Passion for God–Compassion for People," *Mission Frontiers*, November/December 2017.

A large Muslim community in the southern part of Sierra Leone had been very difficult to engage. It was difficult for people who identified as Christians to even enter that place. Many were praying for that town, but time passed and none of the usual strategies worked. Then suddenly something happened!

The national news began to report that there was an unusual health problem: young men were becoming ill and dying due to deadly HIV infections related to the fact that the village never circumcised their boys. Through prayer and reflection, the Lord confirmed that this was finally the opportunity to serve this town. A volunteer medical team was organized and went to the community with the proper equipment and medications and asked if they would be allowed to help. The town leaders quickly agreed, and on the first day they circumcised more than three hundred young men.

Over the next days as the men were healing, there was opportunity to begin Discovery Bible Studies (DBS). The response was remarkable. Soon kingdom multiplication began happening with churches being planted. The place where Christians could not even enter was transformed in just a few short years.[8]

The presence of compassionate service mixed with courageous witness bears much fruit among Muslims. Some take great risk simply to live in dangerous environments. Others require courage to speak openly about Jesus in hostile settings. The fruitfulness of these workers does not come from recklessness, but their boldness reflects the power of the Holy Spirit and points to Jesus Christ, in word and deed, even in the face of opposition.[9]

Heroic service became a trademark of several workers in West Africa when Ebola struck in 2014. These servants decided they could not stay in safe places while disaster was all around them. The Ebola outbreak was especially pronounced in Muslim communities where burial rites were causing the epidemic to explode in many villages. People could not even touch dying parents or children. It was in this context that several of God's servants volunteered in the most hazardous places. Though some survived, many lost their lives serving these Muslim communities.

The Muslim chief of one area was discouraged by his own people trying to escape the quarantined village and amazed at seeing Christians coming to serve. He privately prayed, "God, if you save me from this, if you save my family, I want us all to be like these people who are showing us love and bringing us food."

8 Ibid.
9 Don Allen, et al. "Fruitful Practices: A Descriptive List." *International Journal of Frontier Missiology*, 26:3, Fall 2009 111-22.

The chief and his family did survive, and he kept his promise. Memorizing passages from the Bible, he began to share in the mosque where he had been an elder. A church was birthed in that village, and the chief continues going village to village sharing the good news of God's love.[10] This is a beautiful case of history repeating itself. In the first century, many Romans converted to Christ after watching Christians risk their lives to care for the sick during a series of plagues.[11]

PARADIGM OF PARTNERSHIP

As we have shown, when workers are truly present with a people, it opens many ways of partnering with them. And we believe that many of the remaining unengaged people groups of the Muslim world are only accessible through this kind of kingdom collaboration. We must lay aside organization importance, placing "bride before brand,"[12] and enter into divine partnerships. Rick Wood writes, "The global mission community is increasingly coming together in networks and partnerships. There is the growing realization that the task is too big for any one organization to tackle and so much more can be accomplished by working together than can be done separately."[13]

A powerful example of this has been developing through the Greater Nuba *Actsion Coalition, or GNAC.*[14] In this partnership are some forty ministries, varying in scope from Bible translation, humanitarian relief and development, medical services, disciple making, and church planting. The Nuba Mountains of Sudan, home to over ninety-six ethno-linguistic people groups, over fifty of which are unengaged MUPGs, have been the victim of genocidal abuse by the Sudanese government.[15] The death toll is unknown, but the indiscriminate bombing of hundreds of villages has displaced an estimated 3.7 million people.[16] Basic necessities such as food, shelter, medicine, and education have been disrupted. GNAC was founded to address this. Mostly led by displaced Nuba leaders, these kingdom-minded servants are crossing traditional tribal boundaries to bring the hope of the gospel. They are utilizing collaboration to summit mountains that would be insurmountable by any single organization.

10 Johnson, "Passion for God–Compassion for People."
11 Rodney Stark, The Rise of Christianity (San Francisco: HarperSanFrancisco, 1997), 73-94.
12 A term expressed by Thomas Hieber, Diaspora Peoples of Europe Consultation Amsterdam, 2014.
13 Rick Wood, "Coming Together Around a Common Biblical Vision," *Mission Frontiers*, March/April 2017.
14 www.gnac4nuba.com.
15 https://www.nubareports.org/.
16 Kimberly Curtis. "A Massive New Estimate of South Sudan's Death Toll Is Released as the Country Takes Steps Toward Peace." UN Dispatch, Sept 28, 2018. https://www.undispatch.com/a-massive-new-estimate-of-south-sudans-death-toll-is-released-as-the-country-takes-steps-toward-peace/

One GNAC field leader recently stated,

> God is opening amazing doors for outreach in this place and it is a historic
> moment, because this is the first time in Nuba Mountian's history where
> we see all tribes gathered in one place. Also, Muslims are so open to the
> good news and many are coming to the Lord. He reported that in one new
> camp a great revival is taking place and many Muslims are coming to faith.
> Signs and miracles are being manifest with many people receiving healings.
> That has become an open[ing] for many Muslims to invite us to their homes
> to pray for them. Four new home groups have started from the visitations and
> [are] now under our local discipleship team.[17]

This is just one example of many in which on-the-ground partnerships offer
a form of what we are calling "the gift of presence." Beyond regional networks
such as GNAC, there is positive growth of global networks like Vision 5:9 and
others who are collaborating for engagement of every people group and region.

Kärin Butler Primuth expresses this well:

> Through these networks, ministries around the world are meeting, sharing
> information and resources, and collectively working together to respond
> to some of the greatest challenges and opportunities of our day... . At a
> deeper level, these multicultural networks are one of the most visible and
> functional demonstrations of unity in the Body of Christ. In a world that is
> increasingly divided by race, culture, and religious identity, networks create
> a means for the global Church to demonstrate a powerful witness through
> unity, love, and partnership.[18]

When networks produce on-the-ground partnerships, this form of presence is
a profound and tangible demonstration of the unity of Christ's body—the church.

CONCLUSION

The "gift of presence" is a way of making Christ known that happens across
many dimensions of engagement with a people group. We read in John 1:14,
"The Word became flesh and made his dwelling among us. We have seen his
glory, the glory of the one and only Son, who came from the Father, full of
grace and truth." But in order for the still unengaged people groups of the
world to know about the gift of Christ's presence, we must first become present
ourselves. Billy Graham said it this way:

---

17 Unpublished Field Report for GNAC, April 2018.
18 Kärin Butler Primuth, "How Networks Are Shaping the Future of World Mission," *Mission Frontiers*,
    March/April 2017.

Christ's coming in the flesh—His invading the world, His identifying Himself with sinful men and women—is the most significant fact of history. All of humanity's puny accomplishments pale into nothingness when compared to it... . The distant heavens and the remote earth, the elusive God and the wayward human, were brought close to each other. The fact runs throughout the whole Bible: "God was in Christ reconciling the world to Himself, not imputing their trespasses to them, and has committed to us the word of reconciliation" (2 Cor 5:19).[19]

Our work is never about us. It is about him. The gift of presence begins with prayer. It develops relationships of trust through listening and learning. It continues in incarnational service. It demonstrates the power of transformation even at personal risk. It goes together as we live out being the body of Christ. As we give the gift of presence, Christ will be glorified among all peoples.

DISCUSS AND APPLY

- How is the "gift of presence" different from the usual way we do Christian aid in poor communities?

- What organizations or networks might you partner with?

- What practical things could you do to better listen to what your host people are saying?

BIBLIOGRAPHY

Allen, Don et al. "Fruitful Practices: A Descriptive List." *International Journal of Frontier Missiology,* 26:3, Fall 2009, 111-22.

Curtis, Kimberly. "A Massive New Estimate of South Sudan's Death Toll Is Released as the Country Takes Steps Toward Peace." *UN Dispatch,* Sept 28, 2018. https://www.undispatch.com/a-massive-new-estimate-of-south-sudans-death-toll-is-released-as-the-country-takes-steps-toward-peace/.

Graham, Billy. "The Mystery of the Incarnation," *Decision Magazine,* November 22, 2006, https://billygraham.org/decision-magazine/november-2006/the-mystery-of-the-incarnation/.

Johnson, Shodankeh. "Passion for God—Compassion for People," *Mission Frontiers,* November/December 2017.

Nelson, James. "The Forgotten Island," chap. 4 of *Where There Is Now a Church: Dispatches from Workers in the Muslim World.* Colorado Springs: Global Mapping International, 2014.

Primuth, Kärin Butler. "How Networks Are Shaping the Future of World Mission," *Mission Frontiers,* March/April 2017.

Stark, Rodney. *The Rise of Christianity.* San Francisco: HarperSanFrancisco, 1997, 73–94.

Wood, Rick. "Coming Together Around a Common Biblical Vision," *Mission Frontiers,* March/April 2017.

---

19 Billy Graham, "The Mystery of the Incarnation," *Decision Magazine,* November 22, 2006, https://billygraham.org/decision-magazine/november-2006/the-mystery-of-the-incarnation/.

27 FACTORS THAT MULTIPLY MOVEMENTS

Shalom (pseudonym) is a movement leader in Africa, involved in cross-cultural ministry for the past twenty-three years. His passion is to see disciple-making movements ignited, accelerated, and sustained among unreached groups in Africa and beyond.

Trevor (pseudonym) is a teacher, coach, and researcher. He finds joy in finding apostolic agents God has chosen and helping them maximize their fruit through sharing fruitful practices in bands of brother-leaders. He has partnered with Asian apostolic agents for twenty years, resulting in multiple movements in unreached people groups.

This chapter was written by Shalom with added commentary by Trevor, a movement catalyst. His commentaries are highlighted in gray boxes.

MAIN POINTS NOT TO MISS:

- A healthy dissatisfaction can push us to seriously reevaluate our ministry methods.
- New believers must stay connected to their existing social networks for there to be any possibility of a movement.
- Workers need to focus beyond their own ministry and on the second and third generation of disciples, churches, and their leaders.

For six years I (Shalom) was involved in engaging one of the hardest people groups in our region of Africa. Then the Lord spoke to me that we needed to focus on a greater vision for *all the unreached people groups* in our region. We realized that we needed to do something differently in order to achieve the Great Commission among these people groups. We had zeal and commitment, but we didn't know how to engage them effectively. Our results from traditional methods had been good, but compared to what needed to be done, they were inadequate.

> We've learned that multiplication happens if new believers stay close to their social group and their context, so that multiplication can happen and happen quickly.

As we began applying the principles of disciple-making movements (DMMs) listed below, we began to see God moving us into a true multiplication paradigm: multiplication of disciples, leaders, and churches. In just three years (2015–17) our movement saw over 13,500 baptisms and over 3,950 churches started. On average, 3.6 churches are being planted every day and forty-five new disciples come to the Lord. Also, more than twenty new local, indigenous partners are being developed every year. The principles we have been applying can be summarized in the following ways.

1. The first factor that ignited this movement was that God created a healthy dissatisfaction among us. He convicted us that good is not the best and led us to stop being content with a small amount of fruit. While I was wrestling with this healthy dissatisfaction, an international church-planting coach approached me and stirred up that conviction with DMM principles.

2. We looked at Scripture and recognized a simple, powerful pattern in Luke 10 and Matthew 10. Jesus clearly said to go and do a specific thing: Look for the person whom God has prepared ahead of time—a *person of peace*. That person will not only welcome you and your message but will also pass it on to family members and/or neighbors.

> TREVOR (movement catalyst): We call these people *key persons*. A key person may be the first person who believes the gospel and passes it on. Or they may legitimize or finance those who share the gospel, or share "gossip" about miracles. Whether or not they personally come to faith, key persons open the door for the gospel into their social group.

3. Another key factor is the importance of *aiming for multiplication* rather than addition. Although it's good to add new people to an existing church, addition tends to pull people away from their social context. We've learned that multiplication happens if new believers stay close to their social group and their context, so that multiplication can happen and happen quickly. I saw that in chapter after chapter of Acts God gave the early church rapid multiplication. And we have seen a similar dynamic as we shifted our aim to rapid multiplication rather than addition.

> **TREVOR:** Focusing on multiplication makes us rethink all we do. It requires that we harness the power of preexisting social bonds between local people. The gospel is added into preexisting social groups.

4. Another factor that contributed to the movement was our shift from knowledge-based discipleship to *obedience-based discipleship*. When we looked at the Great Commission, we saw that the heart of Jesus' command was "Make disciples," which means we must teach them to obey all the Lord's commands. That truth impacted us deeply. Knowledge is useless without obedience. So we integrate obedience into everything we do.

> **TREVOR:** Movements multiply quickly when God's Word is immediately applied. We shorten the pathway to maturity in Christ by immediately applying the Word, because believers become doers of the Word.

5. We focus on reaching families—the *oikos*. If we focus on reaching individuals, they end up disconnected from their family and their natural network of relationships. That makes it hard for the gospel to spread. The book of Acts very rarely recounted an individual coming to faith alone. The overwhelming majority came as households and groups. Over and over we see the *oikos* as a basic unit of God's kingdom: Lydia and her household, the Philippian jailer and his household, Cornelius and "his relatives and close friends." Individuals are not an end in themselves. They are a doorway to the family. That has made a big difference. We always ask our people: "With whom are you going to share? With family? With friends? With extended family?" The family focus is very integrated into the fabric of our movement.

> **TREVOR:** "Family" boundaries are flexibly negotiated between people in many contexts where we focus. Besides the nuclear family, other relatives, friends, and coworkers mutually "act like brothers" to each other, cooperating with each other to accomplish their shared goals. The gospel spreads through these "constructed families."

We aim for indigenous incarnation of the gospel, so that the churches we plant "smell" like the community. It's not like one tribe is giving *their* Jesus to another tribe. We want people to think and feel, "This is *my* Jesus. He speaks my language. He talks like me." That kind of incarnational ministry has contributed a lot. As much as possible, we try to reduce cultural barriers. We try to give people nothing but the gospel and allow the indigenous people to contextualize to whatever fits in their community, without compromising the full truth of the Word of God. That way they are not robbed of their culture and the gospel is not foreign to them.

TREVOR: In our country, the gospel must be fitted for each context in 130 different unreached people groups, with many religious variants. Our near-culture workers do cultural research to discover dialogue themes that local people prioritize. They use these themes in *transformational dialogues* with local people in their social groups. Local believers then imitate this pattern of cultural research to develop transformational dialogues of their own. This pattern of research to fit transformational dialogues to context has enabled group multiplication to bridge over to forty-seven unreached people groups (UPGs) in twelve countries. By the third generation of group multiplication, discipleship has become very strongly fitted to each context.

6. Another very important factor for us is access ministry. This is genuine ministry that serves a need of the community and creates a bridge between disciple makers and the community. We say, "Access ministry is answering the prayer of the lost." Access ministry shares the love of Christ not only with our mouths but also through our deeds, bringing a holistic gospel message. We see our Lord Jesus serving the needs of the community as well as sharing the message of the kingdom. He asked us to do the same. We seek to discover unique access for each place, focusing on whatever the Lord brings into our hearts.

TREVOR: We integrate need-based ministries with multiplication of believer groups. Need-based ministries give access to new communities. They also solidify a movement's social role in the wider community. Local leaders empower other believers to meet the needs of their neighbors. This increases both the quality of their shared life in Christ and their social legitimacy, reducing security risks. Need-based ministries also develop bonds between local leaders as they work together to serve others.

7. We intentionally develop indigenous leaders from within the harvest. Without indigenous leaders, it's very difficult for the gospel to spread. So we intentionally focus on grassroots leadership development. The leaders emerge from the community and are identified by the community. Most of our leadership training happens on the job in short segments.

We call it a movement if it is at least 4 generations of churches, with 100 churches in a social segment or people group in less than 4 years.

TREVOR: We begin developing indigenous leaders by entrusting first-generation groups to local facilitators by the fifth week. Leaders' groups equip these new leaders and keep them growing. We knit together bands of brothers/sisters. These brotherhood bands cement relational bonds between local leaders. These bands oversee believer groups in each region.

8. Another multiplication factor is our generational focus. We measure everything in terms of generations—whether disciples, churches, or leaders from the harvest. We call it a movement if it is at least four generations of churches, with one hundred churches in a social segment or people group in less than four years. We have seen fourteen movements in this region. Some of the movements have churches of up to nineteen generations.

> TREVOR: Our slogan, "Third generation, not first generation," changes an activist's paradigm from focusing on their own ministry to empowering their spiritual children, grandchildren, and great-grandchildren. Once their people get to multiple groups in the third generation, a "cluster" of about ten believer groups is linked and chooses elders. When small believer groups multiply into a linked cluster of groups, it is healthy enough to keep multiplying.

9. We as an organization are not working alone. There's no ego or logo in this movement. This is God's movement; God the Holy Spirit is initiating and doing this. Nobody should take credit for it. We are a kingdom-centered network working together to get to movements. We come together from many denominations, churches, and indigenous organizations. The goal is not to make our ministry bigger but to make the kingdom bigger, because God's kingdom is much bigger than our denomination or our ministry. The Great Commission is too big to do alone. We need each other. We don't compromise critical elements, but we share a voluntary commitment to work together in focusing on kingdom movements.

10. Our organization has a responsibility as catalysts. We are like hot coals burning; and we pass the hot coal to start the fire elsewhere, with a high focus on certain unreached people groups (UPGs) and unengaged UPGs (UUPGs). Then those communities become another movement, which becomes another hot coal that can jump over to another UUPG. We're moving from being a harvest field to a harvest force—sending out the hot coals. We're now sending workers not only within our region but also beyond our region. This hot-coal strategy has worked so effectively here that we're planning for it to go further.

> TREVOR: Poor local laborers and university students are two types of people who most often become "hot coals." These new believers adopt our fruitful practices, move for work, then multiply groups in new areas and people groups. This "jump-over fruit" multiplies clusters and then movements. These movements are empowered by mentors who do follow-the-fruit trips to equip local leaders.

11. Local ministries regularly sharefruitful practices and best practices with each other. Strategy coordinators, movement leaders, and grassroots leaders discuss what is working. They are iron sharpening iron. We examine honestly, "What things do we need to start doing? What things do we need to continue doing? And what things do we need to stop doing?"

> TREVOR: Our focus on fruit encourages us to discover and share fruitful practices. This involves: a) seeing "God as the fruit lover, we as his coworkers"; b) prioritizing fruit rather than activity; c) experimenting to discover fruitful practices; d) leaders sharing fruitful practices in learning communities; and e) Bible study on how Christ reinterpreted honor through humility, which makes leaders' learning communities possible.

12. We intentionally focus just on the Word of God, using a simple discussion model that leads people to obedience and transformation. We call it Discovery Bible Study (DBS)—a simple tool that enables groups of lost people to discover for themselves God's will for their lives. Through the help of the Holy Spirit, we take them on a journey from lostness to falling in love with Jesus. This enables them to come to the Lord with their family and get baptized and form a faith community. This simple DBS approach has a powerful transformational impact. It's also a great way for believers to grow in maturity and obedience toChrist. They continue to discover what the Scripture says, how to say it in their own words, and what God wants them to obey.

> TREVOR: Our principle of "Groups, not individuals" means we always work in groups, from pre-evangelism through leader development. Our DBS model of facilitating groups uses seven questions to turn social groups into greenhouses that provide good conditions for spiritual growth.

13. We don't focus on religion; we focus on spirituality. If we try to give people our religion, they miss the bigger message. Jesus told us to pass on a life, having himself as the model. Our goal is not transferring our religion but sharing Jesus. That's the message. That's where the life transformation happens.

14. Prayer has been a major backbone of the work. Actually it should be the factor listed first. Without prayer we cannot do anything. Trying to experience a disciple-making movement without prayer is like trying to fly without wings. We prioritize informed intercessory prayer. Each of the movement leaders engages in serious prayer—for the harvest field as well as the harvest force. In movements, spiritual warfare is very real. Therefore we have to mobilize intercessors who will stand with us.

15. Connected with prayer is God confirming his Word through signs, miracles, healings, deliverance, and visions, especially among the UPGs on whom we focus. God confirms his message by revealing himself to people in very unique

ways, in relation to their situation. He shows his power in their lives and in their families' lives. Showing God's care for people in need is a key factor in the growth of this movement.

16. Every believer has a part in implementing the Great Commission. Obeying the Great Commission doesn't require a special calling. We believe the Matthew 28 calling to make disciples is different than the Acts 13 calling to apostolic work (see factor 20 below). Every believer has a part to play in making disciples—from the new believer to the person who has followed Christ for a long time. In fact, those who have been believers for two years or less are the most effective disciple makers and church planters. They have a passion, a commitment, and a boldness to share with their families the sweetness of Jesus.

> **Trevor:** A key multiplication factor in our model is *apostolic agents.* This works with Shalom's point above: a movement grows based on active disciple making by every believer, so apostolic agents need to catalyze believers to actively make disciples. This is how movements occur. Finding these specially gifted apostolic agents and helping them maximize their catalytic service helps initiate movements. Movements then need a multiplication pattern that grows beyond the first apostolic agents. Training of leaders must multiply to generations of leaders who do not know the first leader. A model in which first- to fourth-generation leaders equip fifth- through eighth-generation leaders is a pattern that keeps on multiplying.

17. We have redefined church according to the model we see in the New Testament. The church is not a building. The church is a group of baptized believers who gather to worship the Lord as a community and then go out to implement the Great Commission. It's a very reproducible and organic community of faith. They meet and reproduce. We always ask, "Is this reproducible? Will they be able to do this without us?" We call it a rabbit strategy rather than an elephant strategy. As much as possible, we try to minimize the number of believers in each group: on average, twenty-five people, or two families. We don't mean just two or three people. That's the seed that grows to become a church. These churches meet in different kinds of places. Some meet at different times, like Friday evening or Saturday morning. Some even meet every day. It depends on the situation and their availability, but it's not just a Bible study.

> **Trevor:** An organic, biblical model of a community of believers is vital for multiplication. We must recapture the biblical ideas that 1) healthy communities of believers naturally multiply; and 2) healthy communities of believers are linked in a network system—they are not independent groups. The church didn't have buildings or organizational structure in New Testament times, so we know these elements are not essential. Believer groups existed in three sizes in the New Testament: small home groups, citywide networks, and regional networks. These

believer communities of different sizes and ethnicities linked into a brotherhood. Organic *ekklesia* has two wings: local churches, plus missional bands that give birth to the churches and link them.

18. We use an equipping strategy appropriate for the context. The majority of our contexts are in oral cultures. People learn a lot by *doing*. So we show one thing, teach one thing, and do one thing. It's very simple and reproducible.

19. The movement leaders have conviction to focus on movements. They, as catalysts, *own* this vision. This model has not been imposed on them. They eat, breathe, and speak disciple-making movements. They see everything through the glasses of movements. The Lord has used these key leaders and their conviction to transform their denominational circles as well as local churches.

Seven-Question Model (Discovery Bible Study):

1. What are you thankful for?

2. What challenges are you facing? (Read the text. Have someone retell the story.)

3. What do you learn about God from this passage?

4. What do you learn about Isa Al Masih (Jesus) from this passage?

5. What do you learn about people from this passage?

6. What will YOU do/apply this week after reading this passage? What will WE do this week?

7. With whom will you share what you learned from this passage?

CONCLUSION

These are some of the factors the Lord has used to facilitate rapidly multiplying disciple-making movements in our African and Asian contexts. We believe these things could be useful and used by God in any context. So we challenge you to open your heart to the leading of the Holy Spirit. Maintain intentional obedience to God's Word. Stay committed to communicate the gospel of the kingdom—without adding to or subtracting from the truth. And when God starts moving, remember to give him all the glory, because without him we can do nothing. In all things and at all times God's glory must increase and we must decrease. To him be the glory for ever and ever.

DISCUSS AND APPLY

- How might you harness the power of pre-existing social bonds for church planting in your context?

- What would a "focus on movements" look like in your ministry?

BIBLIOGRAPHY

Butler, Robby. "Indigenous Movements: How Peoples Are Reached." *Mission Frontiers*, March/April 2018. http://www.missionfrontiers.org/issue/article/indigenous-movements.

McGavran, Donald. *The Bridges of God: A Study in the Strategy of Missions*. Eugene, Oregon: Wipf & Stock Publishers, 2005.

28

INDIGENOUS MEDIA CAN SPARK DISCIPLEMAKING MOVEMENTS TO CHRIST

Calvin and Carol Conkey live in Chiang Mai, Thailand, where they direct Create International, a global ministry focused on producing effective media resources for unreached people groups. They also serve as the Vision 5:9 media resources task force facilitators. Calvin and Carol have earned master's degrees in intercultural development and intercultural communication, respectively.

MAIN POINTS NOT TO MISS:

- Indigenous people play an important role in developing and delivering media that can help foster a movement.
- New technology is facilitating a move away from "mass media" to contextually targeted media.
- The best media strategies have several integrated components working together.

While attending "Abide, Bear Fruit" in Thailand, we recognized, amid a sea of precious people focused on loving Muslims, one of our Indonesian cultural advisors from a film our team produced over fifteen years ago. Although his hair was now graying, his smile and contagious love of Jesus were still memorable. We had prayed to make contact with him again during this busy week. The next day God answered that prayer. Ahmed and his team member came by our resource table glowing with a recent report of how our film continues to impact his people group. He asked if we could remind him how to find the film on the Internet, as most young people want to watch it on their mobile phones.

As we watched the film together, Ahmed reminisced about various actors. "When your team was producing this film, only two of the cast of twelve were believers. But they are all now believers in Isa al Masih. They are now the grandparents of a large movement to Jesus that *your movie sparked among my people!*"

How can field workers better utilize media to spark movements among Muslim people groups?

IGNITE THE POWER OF INDIGENOUS MEDIA

The majority of the remaining Muslim unreached people groups prefer "oral-visual" means of communication. The Spirit-led use of media to impact individuals and nations represents an enormous factor in the effectiveness of fulfilling Jesus' mandate to share his gospel with all peoples. Ideally this should comprise an effective combination of orality and indigenous media, which together help Muslims truly *hear* and *see* the gospel through indigenous ways of thinking developed into various media formats.

Many times, it is not the gospel message that our audience rejects, but rather the way the message is presented. Therefore, as media communicators we must present the good news in a way that a particular people group can hear with understanding and then pass on with accuracy. Culture is the ever-changing context in which we proclaim a biblically faithful, never-changing gospel. (Stetzer 2014).[1] As media producers and cross-cultural workers, we need to discern several things in order to develop this kind of contextually appropriate media. These three stand out:

1. the people's true and perceived needs
2. the most effective kind of media to use
3. the message's cultural context in order to develop a strategy that best communicates to the people

---

1   Ed Stetzer, "Engaging an Ever-Changing Culture with a Never-Changing Gospel." *Christianity Today*, August 21, 2014. https://www.christianitytoday.com/edstetzer/2014/june/avoidingchurch-culture-pendulum-swings-engaging-ever-chang.html.

A CASE STUDY: GOD PROVIDES THE RIGHT PARTICIPANTS

Three months prior to coming to the field our team had been praying for God to provide the right lead actor. When we met Hassan we realized that the Lord had answered our prayers. Jesus had visited him in a dream and said "Follow me!" Thus Hassan said, "Isa must desire me to be in your film!"

Not only did Hassan perform excellently, but he also offered wonderful "redemptive" analogies that helped us communicate with his people.

Scripting Insights

Once the team had arrived on the field, they promptly started refining their initial script with advice from both local people and experienced foreign workers. Roy, a foreign worker who knew the context well, stressed the importance of honor and shame in that culture, then offered the following story:

"I just attended a wedding where every guest was expected to present a gift for the bride's family. But at this wedding the father did something unthinkable: he called out a guest by name. The father complained that when he had attended the wedding of this man's daughter he brought twenty kilograms of rice for the family. But today this same man reciprocated with a mere five kilos of the same." This kind of public shaming was extremely unusual, and would result in significant consequences.

"The humiliated guest ran out of the room, and everyone assumed that he was returning home for his knife to gain revenge for this public shaming. Sure enough, minutes later he returned with a knife. However, the blade was wrapped in a white cloth and carried on two flat palms. The man fell to his knees in front of the father, raising the knife above his head. After a long moment, the father of the bride reached over, grasped the knife, and embraced the man. The gathering erupted into cheers and the party went on." Roy then explained, "This man was poor and powerless, so by his act of humility he sought and received forgiveness from the bride's father."

Our team realized this was a powerful redemptive analogy and worked hard to integrate it into the script with the help of a local cultural consultant named Ahmad. The actors were visibly touched as they played out this redemptive analogy of forgiveness through humility, which brought honor to both parties. Later this also produced an incredible impact on the audience, because the contextually rooted imagery helped the film convey a clear understanding of the gospel message.

A Gathering Sparks an Idea

One day during the filming our team observed several Muslim men sitting in a circle inside a village home praying dua[2] and discussing the Qur'an together. We asked Hassan if we could utilize a similar form somewhere in our film to show this as an appropriate way for new believers and seekers learn about the teaching of Isa al Masih.

Prevalent stereotypes of what it meant to be a believer were dismantled when curious Muslims watched these culturally appropriate worship groupings. They realized for the first time that they could fully please God while still studying the *Injil* and worshiping in a style familiar to them. We discovered many were ready to follow Isa al Masih. When they received this increased understanding, the impact was like removing a levee and allowing the water to flow.

Holy Spirit Pirating

In the months after we completed this film, the whole cast of twelve became followers of Isa al Masih! The actors and other new believers began distributing hundreds of copies of the film to their friends and family. Because this film was produced in the local language and culture, it became extremely popular, and pirated versions started showing up in everywhere.

A few years later we uploaded the film to YouTube. Soon there was a big spike of people watching and downloading the film, with more than one hundred thousand views in a few days. We later found out this happened because some local imams heard of the film and asked the largest Muslim organization in the world to help stop it. They put a YouTube link on their website, warning people not to watch this film. Naturally, that caused the opposite effect! Later, Islamic scholars saved face by declaring that the film was not offensive to Islam nor did it speak against the prophet Muhammad.

Eventually viewings went back down, but not before nearly a half a million people had seen the film. With over a million known viewers, the film has clearly been a factor in this movement growing beyond the cast and their families to more than 2,500 Muslim-background believers—expressed in hundreds of multiplying fellowships, reaching to at least three generations of multiplication. Meeting Ahmad once again more than ten years after making the film brought tears to our eyes, especially as he thanked us for all our hard work to see this film continue to reach his people.

---

2 *Dua* is a term for informal Islamic prayers.

CULTURAL KEYS OF IGNITING INDIGENOUS MEDIA MOVEMENTS

The story above unfolded over more than a decade, with successive waves of a breakthrough and illumination. Brothers and sisters in this growing movement testified that our film encouraged the new believers to live as followers of Isa Al Masih in the midst of a devout Islamic culture. Their people felt empowered by visualizing how they could fully follow Christ yet preserve their cultural identity.

Our films show people from that culture coming to a crisis through a current issue in their community. Through a series of events, they are exposed to Christ responding to those needs. They may encounter a believer, have a dream, or find Scriptures that speak to their problem. An invitation is frequently given within the context of the story, actually demonstrating the lead character coming to Christ within a group context. The film continues with the actor then sharing their new faith with family and friends and entering into fellowship. Community-oriented cultures shy away from individual conversion, as it can mean complete isolation. Seeing families open to the gospel and believers from their own culture in contextualized fellowship is very reassuring and gives viewers the courage to step out in faith.

When developing a communication strategy toward these collectivist, community-oriented cultures, we must be aware that members of these groups are convinced that

- Your choices affect your community.
- Honor and shame is the "operating system" of the community-oriented culture.
- Honor is the social currency of these communities.
- Shame is far more potent in these cultures than the idea of sin; there is greater fear related to violating social norms than to transgressing God's rules.
- The fear of bringing shame upon one's family is worse in many cases than death.

Incorporating these principles in films shows our audience that to follow Isa al Masih is a community experience, not simply an individual one. This is crucial for today's collectivistic (community-oriented) societies found in the remaining unreached peoples. In this way we're effective to sow the seed that personal transformation should lead to social transformation (Matt 28:19–20). Rather than further explain these principles, it is better to illustrate them through a series of brief case studies of media use in the Muslim world.

SEEING IS BELIEVING—VISUALIZING COMMUNITY IDENTITY IN AFRICA

For an evangelistic film in Africa, a Wolof believer named Jacob was cast as the leader of a new house church. After filming the scenes of a truly indigenous fellowship using his cultural forms, he told us "We need to spread this type of fellowship all across the Wolof people."

A veteran cross-cultural worker in the room said with frustration, "Ah, I have been trying to tell you this for over seven years!"

Jacob replied, "Yes, I know, but I needed to *see* and experience this type of gathering. Now I can embrace and reproduce these groups."

Media fulfills a crucial role by visually *modeling* how a community could come to faith in Christ and then form a contextually appropriate fellowship. It is absolutely vital for them to see the church in action within that cultural context. Viewers are encouraged that there are other kingdom believers participating in life together. They love seeing the "ummah of Christ" in our films' ending global montages. Muslim-background believers have advised us, "We need more media resources to illustrate how to live our faith in Isa al Masih within our community."

FACE-TO-FACE AND CYBERSPACE

Previously, mass media strategies required expensive technologies like television, cinema, and satellite in order to reach a broad audience. By necessity, the content needed to be "broadened" in its meaning and focus, often using a "trade language." Unfortunately, as the content was consumed by a broad culture and linguistically diverse audience, much of the message's meaning and impact was lost in the generalization. Thankfully, great strides are being made in tailoring communication for the audience.

The rapidly increasing use of mobile devices and social networking across the unreached world is providing an ideal platform for transmitting tailor-made, tightly focused, contextually indigenous audio-visual media to communicate the gospel. Through these inexpensive, dynamic distribution channels, mass media communications are no longer limited to traditional "broad-cast" strategies. We live in a new age of "narrow-cast" media that can be transmitted to specific cultures and language groups with a "tailor-made" message.

Because of the incredible reach of companies like YouTube and Facebook, the simplest of evangelistic websites currently provide the potential impact of an international streaming ministry. Believers can spread the gospel to the ends of the earth with what is even now in their hands—mobile phones. In 2019 the number of mobile phone users is forecast to reach more than four and a half billion. We can impact the nations by turning those mobile devices into powerful tools for gospel films and other discipleship training—all in the heart language.

In many countries Internet access may not available to the average person, even though that individual may own a mobile device (mobile phone or tablet) that has Wi-Fi and Bluetooth connectivity. This has created a vacuum of desire and a need to discover and join free Wi-Fi networks that are linked to the Internet. Enter the portable Wi-Fi network server: a small battery-powered device with the ability to broadcast its own open Wi-Fi network! The DoveStream is one such device created to both host and broadcast gospel media to a nearby audience. It is not only portable, but completely independent of the Internet. It has its own rechargeable battery and comes with a special setup USB stick. Once you turn it on its password-free Wi-Fi network appears on your Wi-Fi–enabled mobile devices, and upon joining this network one is able to access all of the films streaming from the unit, www.equip2go.org/dovestream.

Media and technology saturation are globally approaching 100 percent through mobile devices. The opportunities to use the mobile platform are expanding and must be leveraged for the Great Commission. Many in restricted access nations often need to interact online in the privacy and security of their home and a personal computer or mobile phone. Think of all the church could do if we did not compartmentalize, limit, and isolate ourselves by thinking of ourselves as a place—but as people.[3] While building relationships, media can be viewed together or given to individuals to watch later. Gospel media can be shared on mobile phones to enhance personal interaction. Learn what people want to talk about, and engage with them.

Despite these amazing opportunities, however, no technology can completely replace real-world, life-on-life relationships. If people enjoy the content of the film or media piece, they may want to interact—sometimes by meeting face-to-face and other times by dialoguing online. No matter what the media strategy, these need to be cultivated as part of an integrated media strategy.

---

3 Carl Jones, "When We Think of the Church as a Building," *Relevant*, August 23, 2013, https://relevantmagazine.com/god/church/when-we-think-church-building.

AN INTEGRATED MEDIA STRATEGY

Media can optimize every level of church growth and discipling nations with various media forms complementing personal interaction and aiding indigenous movements to Christ. Also, depending on security concerns, some of these media forms can be preformed more discreetly.

A possible scenario: Radio spots, flyer distribution, and social media posts could together spark community interest for attending a large public sharing time with a movie or short video, or even a private small group meeting in a home. In higher security situations, seekers who are engaged through social media could later meet at a coffee shop to learn more. At the presentation, tracts, DVDs, or SD cards could be distributed, giving people something to take home and reflect on privately. The social media posts, literature, or verbal request could extend an invitation to a home gathering. Believers could then develop relationships with seekers and continue follow-up meetings, clarifying the message. When seekers commit to following Jesus, a workbook and video for new believers could be used to enhance the Bible study during the week. Radio and Internet YouTube videos could help the new believer grow in faith. A multimedia kit including things like DVDs, SD cards, Internet links, workbooks, and webinars could be given to the leaders providing discipleship tools. A short film depicting an indigenous home group studying the Bible can be shown or produced. Individuals could learn many other things—intercession, evangelism, or cross-cultural ministry—through video profiles and prayer booklets.

> Media can optimize every level of church growth and discipling nations with various media forms complementing personal interaction.

CONCLUSION

In over thirty years of media ministry, we have seen that indigenous, contextually shaped media *is* sparking movements. We believe that God is inviting audio-visual storytellers and media producers to carry out his dreams and passions, to tell this generation the greatest story humankind has ever heard. Missionaries, nationals, and other partners can contribute by sharing insight and knowledge of effective ways to communicate in their cultural context as we see resources produced, believers equipped, nations transformed, and the kingdom of God advanced.

DISCUSS AND APPLY

- How can you best incorporate indigenous media and appropriate technology into your present and future ministry?

- Download a film in the language of your people group through indigitube. tv. Show this film on your mobile phone or laptop, or send the link to a seeker. Engage in the content with them; ask questions to see if they understood the message. Continue to follow up with them using other culturally relevant media resources, such as films, stories from the Bible, contextual Internet resources, and more.

If you would like assistance in developing a media strategy or information about media production or resources for your people group, please contact us at creategcrc@gmail.com.

SUGGESTED RESOURCES

- Media2Movements.org has some amazing resources utilizing social media and Facebook ads to reach out to many Muslims nations.

- Indigitube.tv is a gospel media viewing and sharing website with more than six hundred films and animations in over 150 different languages. All of these films are downloadable for free and are linguistically and culturally adapted to impact specific unreached people groups.

- The Create International App is jam-packed with over two hundred gospel films, in hundreds of different languages, specifically for evangelizing unreached people groups. Simply download the app to your mobile device, select "Gospel Films," and do a search for the language or people group you are reaching. The films will play at the resolution that is best for your mobile device and Internet speed, and Create International will allow you to download them for free at http://www.oikosapp.com/indigitube/.

BIBLIOGRAPHY

Baig, Sufyan. "The *Ummah* and Christian Community." In *Longing for Community: Church, Ummah, or Somewhere in Between?* edited by David Greenlee, 70–78. Pasadena, CA: William Carey Library, 2013.

B., John. "The Story-Teller." *Mission Frontiers,* May/June 2014, 16. http://www.missionfrontiers.org/issue/article/the-story-teller-the-dhow-and-the-fishers-of-men.

Jones, Carl. "When We Think of the Church as a Building." *Relevant,* August 23, 2013. https://relevantmagazine.com/god/church/when-we-think-church-building.

Klem, Herbert. *Oral Communication of the Scripture.* Pasadena, CA: William Carey Library, 1982.

Palusky, David. "Opportunity to Reach the Least of These." *Mission Frontiers,* May/June 2014, 30–31. http://www.missionfrontiers.org/issue/article/opportunity-to-reach-the-least-of-these.

Stetzer, Ed. "Engaging an Ever-Changing Culture with a Never-Changing Gospel." *Christianity Today,* August 21, 2014. https://www.christianitytoday.com/edstetzer/2014/june/avoiding-church-culture-pendulum-swings-engaging-ever-chang.html.

Wu, Jackson. "Does the 'Plan of Salvation' Make Disciples? Why Honor and Shame Are Essential for Christian Ministry." In *Leadership Development for the 21st Century Asian Mission,* edited by Hoyt Lovelace. Seoul: East-West Center, 2017.

29 | PEACEMAKING IN ALBANIA AND KOSOVO

David Shenk has been involved in peacemaking within the world of Islam for many years. He bases his ministry on the following three principles: Be committed to Jesus as Savior and Lord. Be an emissary of Christ. And be a witness to the gospel among all who inquire.

MAIN POINTS NOT TO MISS:

- Fair and friendly dialogue between Muslims and Christians removes barriers to the gospel.
- Christian peacemaking is an important part of healing the wounds of a people who have been at war.
- Biblical peacemaking is not about politics, but about applying the Word of God to a difficult situation.

"We will never consider a dialogue with evangelicals," the prestigious university professors exclaimed! Several evangelical peacemakers were meeting with these Muslim professors at a university in Kosovo to explore the possibility of a public dialogue on peacemaking. Yet the professors were not impressed. This was back in 2000, and Kosovo was still smoldering from the ruin of its civil war. To many, a Christian/Muslim public dialogue on peacemaking within the wounds of Kosovo's recent wars seemed to be nonsense. Orthodox Christians and Muslims nurtured deep resentments and anger toward one another. The religious situation was further complicated by the legacy of the Communist era. For half a century, during the Communist era, Albania was an atheist state and reflected some of the harsh extremes of Marxism—for example, a mother could be imprisoned for praying with her child. All in all, it was a confusing time, with refugees crisscrossing the land.

Although Kosovo and Albania are different countries, they are ethnically and in language very similar. Then the war brought other forms of interreligious confusion. In regard to the different religions, different evangelical groups had extended ministries of compassion into both Albania and Kosovo during the war. The refugees were grateful for the help of the evangelical churches. But there was much confusion concerning religious and ethnic identity.

Wherever groups of traditional evangelicals ministered, they also invited both Muslims and Orthodox Christians into the fold of evangelical faith. A public dialogue would likely further encourage youthful spiritual adventurers into a more exuberant Protestant faith. Traditional religious leaders, such as Sunni Muslims, were concerned about the growth of these newly arrived churches. Consequently, both Muslims and Orthodox Christians believed there was no need for the existing thirty Protestant congregations in Kosovo to seek for other spiritual pastures.

For these reasons the majority Muslim community and minority Orthodox community would not consider the possibility of a public dialogue on peacemaking. However, as the leaders of the evangelical alliance left the university, they left several copies of a book for them to read on the table. The name of the book was *A Muslim and a Christian in Dialogue*.

DIALOGUE FOR PEACE

Badru D. Kateregga, a Musim, and I wrote this book together in 1997. We have been friends since the 1970s when we were both teaching on world religions at the University of Nairobi, Kenyatta campus. Kateregga was from

Uganda and I was from the United States. It was in that context that we decided to write *Dialogue*.

We wrote so that teachers and students could understand both Islam and the Christian faith better. The *Dialogue* is written in twelve chapters for the Muslim faith and twelve for the Christian faith. Each chapter includes a response from the Christian side and a response from the Muslim side. If one of us believed the Christian or Muslim response had not been accurately presented, then there was opportunity to write a clarification. Recent editions include discussion questions at the end of each chapter. Muslims appreciate *Dialogue* because they believe the Sunni Muslim faith has been represented well. Christians appreciate *Dialogue* because they believe it represents the Christian faith well. Since the book has been well received in many lands, it is now available in twelve languages and has even been endorsed by Al-Azhar University in Egypt.

As described above, the Islamic professors said they would not support an opportunity to have a public dialogue on peacemaking. There was keen disappointment on the Protestant side. But the church in Kosovo united in prayer and asked God for a change of heart. We were astonished when one of the professors later said, "I have read your book. It is a dialogue that is seeking truth; it is not about destroying Muslims or Christians. So I am eager for a dialogue that seeks the way of peace in a way that does not attack Muslims." That professor was eager for the very trust-building conversations the *Dialogue* sought to encourage!

A date was set for use of the largest hall in Kosovo, which accommodated about seven hundred people. When the night arrived, the auditorium was packed out. I was informed that every key leader in the region came, as well as from across the country. Some drove considerable distances. There were representatives from Orthodox and a kaleidoscope of Protestant backgrounds. On the other side, both Sunni and Shia leaders not only came, but came eager for a conversation. It was set to be a night to remember.

This dialogue within the centers of authority in Kosovo was in the process of developing for some time. I felt this reality in my first visit to Kosovo in 1979. As far as I know, at that time there was only one evangelical couple in Kosovo. They were in prayer that doors would open that had been shut for many years. To help equip the church, a writer developed a Bible study for evangelicals in Kosovo and surrounding areas that could provide study helps for those seeking ways to reach their neighbors.

It was remarkable. The materials to equip evangelicals were becoming available for distribution in the churches. The reason these Bible study materials for Muslims were so appreciated was because the materials were based especially on biblical accounts that are acknowledged in the Qur'an. So seekers felt at home as they read the biblical accounts of narratives with which they were familiar. The consequence was remarkable acceptance. These materials also gave Christians a spirit of confidence as they shared with Muslims. There was little or no negativity; and rather than rejection, the doors of contextual ministry in Sarajevo opened.

In peacemaking we have found that it is critically important to aim not only for personal change but for transformation of society as a whole. That means we must give special attention to grassroots empowerment that will work toward the healthy development of civil society; this is part of the social transformation which is so essential.

Christians usually speak of these transformations only at the individual level, as the new birth, whereas we believe that Christ meets a person in order to have transformational impact on an entire society. That is what was happening in the Kosovo revolution. This dramatic change was in the exhilarating process of radical transformation. That was why they asked me to meet with the political and religious leaders. They knew they needed change, and they wanted a man of God to be the catalyst.

However, developing trusting peacemaking relations requires more than a hearty handshake or even the development of study materials. The urgency of the conversation impressed me when meeting with key Muslim and Christian leaders, all of whom said that it had been rare indeed for religious leaders to enter into conversations about faith. Nevertheless, that is precisely the kind of conversation that is beginning to unfold in Bosnia, Sarajevo, and Kosovo. We anticipate that in the near future there will be several interfaith forums that will focus on cultivating trusting relations among the various religious communities.

HEALING THE WOUNDS OF WAR

The complex and awful results of an ethnic war was the context that this dialogue in Kosovo unfolded. This once-in-a-lifetime experience began with the simple theme of peacemaking. I shared the accounts of Jesus our peacemaker. Here indeed Islam and the gospel diverge—for in Islam there is no message of reconciling love, for there is no cross. I pled for participants to open their lives to the reconciling love of Jesus Christ. My Muslim dialogue associate was encouraging an alternative message. In Islam there is no cross. Muslims believe Jesus was all-powerful; therefore, God would never let the Messiah be crucified.

The Muslim presenter stressed the need for justice in order for Kosovo to move forward. I spoke on the call of God to forgive. I pled, "Unless this nation forgives, the cycle of retribution will never cease." I spoke about Jesus on the Cross, who is our atoning sacrifice for sin. In his sacrificial death Jesus breaks the cycles of retribution so that we are forgiven and transformed to offer forgiveness for those who have done us wrong. On the Cross Jesus cries out in suffering, reconciling love. In the Cross we also meet the justice of God. In Jesus crucified and risen we meet both the justice and the forgiveness of God. As the Christian presenter, I drew from themes within the New Testament, such as 1 Peter 3:8–12:

> Finally, all of you, be like-minded, be sympathetic, love one another, be compassionate and humble. Do not repay evil with evil or insult with insult. On the contrary, repay evil with blessing, because to this you were called so that you may inherit a blessing. For, "Whoever would love life and see good days must keep their tongue from evil and their lips from deceitful speech. They must turn from evil and do good; they must seek peace and pursue it. For the eyes of the Lord are on the righteous and his ears are attentive to their prayer, but the face of the Lord is against those who do evil."

Both of us were committed to presenting a scripturally based foundation for our presentation on peacemaking. For example, the Muslim presenter reminded us that in Islam every sura, except one, refers to God as the merciful and compassionate One. We were further reminded that when Cain was coming to kill Abel, Abel called out to God, saying that he would rather die than take weapons against his brother. And God said that Abel had chosen the better way. My Muslim colleague spoke of Islam as the religion that requires justice. He insisted that forgiveness cannot happen unless there is justice. He reminded us of the necessary requirement of justice in order for peace to prevail.

For two hours the dialogue continued. Jesus and forgiveness were the prevailing concerns. I pressed the mostly Muslim audience to consider the remarkable restoration that God in Jesus Christ offers to all those who yearn for forgiveness. This event gave time for everyone to ponder the meaning of Jesus the Messiah as the Lamb of God in whom we are forgiven.

THE SOLEMN DEBATE

A year later Kosovo was again on the brink of conflict. The dialogue just over a year earlier was in reality a preparation for the next dialogue. The first dialogue was about peacemaking and forgiveness. The next event was related to civil society in a pluralist world. The central issue was how people of differing faiths can live in peace in one society.

At the heart of the debate was the question concerning the shape Kosovo would take politically as it moved toward independence. Would Kosovo become a Muslim state or a secular state with space for a variety of religious expressions? The Islamic university invited me to speak at a student/faculty assembly. My assigned topic was "Truth and Freedom."

I knew that this assignment most likely was about the creation of a constitution. There were strong voices calling for Kosovo to become a secular state. I suppose all faculty and students were present in the university assembly. Some were theologians who had been commissioned to write the new constitution for the newly independent Kosovo. One cannot exaggerate the significance of what was happening. Here was an American Protestant theologian meeting with the top Muslim clerics. These clerics had been commissioned to write the constitution.

> The entire dialogue was grounded in Scripture. In such discussions it might be helpful sometimes to reference authorities such as the United Nations, but essentially Muslims will want to hear what Christians believe about their Scriptures, not the secular sources of authority.

Protestants probably had the most to lose if the decisions moved away from assurance of religious freedom. The key leaders of Kosovo were present in the university that day. The issues were not trivial.

The greatest authority in that forum was Scripture. I could have relied upon other sources of authority, of course. For starters, I could have quoted from the United States Declaration of Independence as an example of a preamble to a statement of rights. That text, however, would not have impressed our Muslim hosts. The Declaration of Independence is not a scripturally grounded theology. When Muslims are engaged in dialogue, they mostly rely upon the Qur'an.

When Christians engage in dialogue, the Muslim expectation is that the Christians will base their witness on the Bible. In fact, the Qur'an commands Christians to ground their witness in the Bible (Ali Imran 3:187), so that is what I did. The entire dialogue was grounded in Scripture. In such discussions it might be helpful sometimes to reference authorities such as the United Nations, but essentially Muslims will want to hear what Christians believe about their Scriptures, not the secular sources of authority.

Here is a summary of what I said: "All the Abrahamic faiths are grounded in Scripture. Therefore, this assembly is gathered around the conviction that God has revealed truth through Scripture. I will ground my presentation on the Torah and the Psalms, and I will also refer to the gospels (*Injil*). Any references to the Qur'an I will defer to the Muslim theologians among us."

With humility, I confess that I am a "Person of the Book." What do these Scriptures say that is relevant to our discussions on truth and freedom?

First, in the opening paragraphs of the Torah, we read, "God created humankind in his own image, in the image of God he created them; male and female he created them" (Gen 1:27).

Then, in a second paragraph of the Torah, we read, "God blessed them and said to them, 'Be fruitful and increase in number; fill the earth and subdue it'" (Gen 1:28).

In a third paragraph of the Torah, we read that Adam and Eve abused the freedom God had given them (Gen 3:1–10).

In a fourth key revelation, we read that God promises to redeem Adam and Eve from the calamity of their disobedience (Gen 3:15).

These four key verses in the Torah are most significant. The first human couple are created in God's image and are to cultivate and care for the good earth. They fail in this responsibility by misusing their freedom. But God does not abandon them. In fact, God promises to send a redeemer.

PRINCIPLES OF CIVIL SOCIETY

These four themes are very important when we are considering a healthy political system, something we usually refer to as "civil society." We have considered briefly the four threads that civil society needs to weave together as we develop the political requirements of such a healthy society. The church carries special responsibility, for Christians are called to live according to the principles of Jesus' teachings as revealed in the Sermon on the Mount (Matt 5:1–7). What are these characteristics of a healthy society?

1) To believe that every person is equally created in God's image, and therefore every person is to be respected.

2) To respect the truth that each person is given freedom from God to decide to obey God or to reject God.

3) To cultivate integrity in all relationships. Ultimately this means to honor God.

4) To seek to care for the oppressed. This means to be compassionate toward those who have fallen.

When I served as academic dean for a university in Lithuania, we often considered that these same four principles applied to developing a healthy university. These are the principles—the "tools"—needed for a healthy institution to thrive or for a healthy society to develop. Applying these principles to the values of society helps to encourage the development of vibrant civil societies. A significant function of the church is creating this kind of healthy society. It is a good thing when both the church and the ummah can work together to develop a healthy society. When we do so, we bear witness to the One who made peace between God and man on the Cross.

Also, in all our political discussions and conversations, let us never forget that Jesus was a refugee, Muhammad was an orphan, and Moses was a castaway. Each of them suffered as an outcast in one way or another. Thus we need to care for the suffering in ways that honor God. For example, if God gave Adam the freedom to choose, how can we today develop a political system that practices freedom of religion?

CONCLUSION

Also, in all our political discussions and conversations, let us never forget that Jesus was a refugee, Muhammad was an orphan, and Moses was a castaway.

A few weeks after the lecture at the university in Kosovo, leadership of the evangelical alliance and the university met to discuss religious freedom in the country. Furthermore, the constitution was in fact developed so that it affirmed freedom of religion for all citizens of Kosovo! By affirming religious freedom for Kosovo, the tool box for developing civil society was significantly expanded. That decision by the civil and political authorities opened the door significantly for the growth of a variety of religious communities in Kosovo. That decision is one way that the citizens of Kosovo can open doors for the growth of healthy civil society.

This is one of the ways that we can fulfill what Jesus commanded his disciples—to be the light of the world and the salt of the earth. There are many other places in the Muslim world where this kind of healthy dialogue could prove not only to bless society at large but also to open doors to proclaiming the gospel of Jesus Christ, which is the "gospel of peace" (Eph 6:15).

DISCUSS AND APPLY

- How might this kind of dialogue apply to your context? Between people groups? Between families or clans? Or maybe on a personal level with your people?

- Is there anything in your ministry that brings an unbiblical division to society? How could you change that?

BIBLIOGRAPHY

Ali, Haile Ahmed. *Teatime in Mogadishu: My Journey as a Peace Ambassador in the World of Islam.* Harrisonburg, VA: Herald Press, 2011.

Shenk, David. *Christian. Muslim. Friend.: Twelve Paths to Real Relationship.* Harrisonburg, VA: Herald Press, 2014.

30 | FRUITFUL PRACTICES LEARNING COMMUNITIES

Nate Scholtz served for seven years as a reproducing disciple of Jesus and English teacher among a previously unengaged Muslim people group in the Middle East. Today, he networks grassroots communities of normal Christians befriending the Muslim diaspora in North America.

Larry Burke has worked in the African Sahel for over twenty-five years, being involved in Bible translation and exploring creative ways of engaging the unreached with God's Word. Since 2007 he has been part of the Fruitful Practice Research team, focusing on the ways in which language issues affect fruitfulness in ministry.

MAIN POINTS NOT TO MISS:

- The best place to learn and advance ministry skills is in a committed community of like-minded gospel workers.

- Such communities need champions to start and nurture them.

- A network of "trusted brokers," sharing information from different organizations, can bring huge benefits to everyone involved.

WELCOME TO THE COMMUNITY OF THE CALLED

On the final evening of the "Abide, Bear Fruit" consultation in October of 2017, Dudley Woodberry offered this exhortation, "God's plan is that there be a chain of witnesses from the apostles until the day when Christ comes again." He went on to share the story of how he was called into missions under the preaching of Samuel Zwemer. He recollected that before Zwemer was able to finish his sermon that night, he collapsed and had to be carried out of the church. Dr. Woodberry said, "We have the opportunity to make the next link in the chain ... to finish the message that Samuel Zwemer was not able to that day."

Then all the elder statesmen and stateswomen among us lined up along the front of the vast banquet hall to anoint and pray over anyone who wanted to come forward and commit to that calling. These elders proceeded to pray for a seemingly never-ending line of people from many nations and tribes. Many wore the traditional garments of their home cultures. Many who came were from Muslim backgrounds, but now follow Jesus.

Woodberry distributed the oil generously on our community, with all four fingers dripping as he raised his hand to their foreheads. My hands were coated as he brushed against them. The holy weight of the moment was etched into my life's story as I (Nate) too was anointed and received prayer.

We felt a great sense of community that day. I find, however, that workers among Muslims often feel isolated. Yet we don't have to. We can strive to bring together those who share our vision and passion wherever we are working in the harvest. One structure for doing this is by intentionally creating "learning communities" that implement the fruitful practices that were previously discovered by the host of witnesses who have gone before.

In this chapter we want to tell the stories of several learning communities. We'll include small-scale groups involving only a handful of people as well as large-scale initiatives involving many organizations and people working toward common goals. Along the way we'll draw out some reproducible principles for how to create similar communities.

LIZ'S STORY: BUILDING A COMMUNITY IN SEATTLE

The "Hub Community" in Spokane Washington buzzed with conversation in the middle of its third weekly meeting. Liz realized she was elated to finally work with a group of like-minded people. All those in attendance had Muslim friends and shared Liz's passion to bring Jesus into their lives.

After the meeting she reflected on how it had all come about, starting with when she met Fatima about a year earlier. This Muslim student from Iraq had moved into Liz's neighborhood near the college. They struck up a conversation, and Liz was surprised at how easily they became friends. From the beginning she planned to share her faith, but she was nervous about saying something dumb that would drive her new friend away.

> Her problem was that she didn't know of anyone else who had a Muslim friend, and her friends at church weren't exactly enthusiastic about the topic.

Liz had some general background knowledge about Islam, but she really wanted to talk to people who had personal experience. Her problem was that she didn't know of anyone else who had a Muslim friend, and her friends at church weren't exactly enthusiastic about the topic. So she decided to attend a missions conference, scouring the exhibition booths and asking everyone she met for advice.

One of the presenters at the conference suggested that Liz email me (Nate). I wrote back and asked her to help me test a theory: *Within driving distance of Muslim communities of any density, there are at least one hundred Christians who have befriended a Muslim with a desire to invite them into the kingdom.* In my experience I have found that the real barrier is that these believers are often unaware of one another. I explained that rather than focusing on trying to get her church friends to care about Muslims, she should begin by developing a strategy for finding those people in her vicinity who already did.

Liz took on the challenge. She actively looked for those who shared her passion like it was a treasure hunt. She collected new contacts one by one, finding many others like her. When she had a list of fifteen interested people, she organized a meeting at her house.

After sharing a meal at the first "Hub Community" meeting, each told a little about themselves and their Muslim friends. Before they were even halfway through the group, it became clear to everyone that they had been missing out on the support they could have been giving each other all along. They all had similar experiences, and in some cases they had even befriended the same people. Of equal importance, they were all within easy driving distance of one other. They quickly and intuitively realized the benefits of learning together. Over the months to come, they continued to encourage one another, pray, and share ideas.

As Liz reflected on the unfolding events, she offered a prayer of thanksgiving for the community that God had provided to meet her need for encouragement. He had certainly built her confidence in him through the process of faithfully leading her in finding each one of them.

Liz's story illustrates several of the key components of a practitioner community:

- Champions are desperate for the fellowship of a group of like-minded others. They have capacity and incentive to gather their own support group, who will also benefit each other.

- The kind of people who will gather tend to already be active and eager to respond to the champions' efforts. They have the necessary context of a Muslim friend to frame a shared learning experience.

- When they meet together, they tell stories about their interaction with Muslim friends. They actively seek out ways to live out their faith more effectively. They pray for one another and hold one another accountable. In general, they practice peer discipleship with a specific goal in mind.

This model is not uniquely suited to the North American continent. In fact, a community-oriented approach is even more natural in many other parts of the world.

IZZAKA'S STORY: AN AFRICAN COMMUNITY OF PRACTICE

Skepticism ruled the day. Izzaka was far from convinced that these people could help him. For many years his passion had been to communicate the gospel to his own Muslim people who are spread across a large swath of Africa. Izzaka had come to know Christ while at university in a neighboring country, then returned to his own country to share his faith. Years had since passed and Izzaka had seen some fruit, but progress was painfully slow; and he often felt isolated and alone.

Izzaka had heard of a training program geared specifically to help MBBs effectively share their faith. He agreed to participate, but he started with a negative attitude. What could these people tell him that he didn't already know? Would it really make a difference in his ministry?

Two years later Izzaka's perspective was very different. He *had* seen the fruit— with his own eyes. At that initial training he had met a small group of people who had similar backgrounds and who shared his passion. After spending time together during the training they covenanted together to continue to meet on a regular basis.

They agreed to certain parameters on how they would cooperate, committing themselves to a common framework of ministry. Although they worked in scattered locations and with different people groups, there were many similarities between their ministries. When they met together, they focused on the following key activities.

Concerted Prayer

One of the core principles adopted by the members of the original training group was the importance of prayer, something they took seriously. They prayed for specific needs, for key contacts in each area (a person of peace), and for each of their contacts as the work developed.

Commitment to Hear God Speak through His Word

Traditional forms of Christianity heavily influenced the members of the group. They were determined, however, to keep the Bible itself as the ultimate authority. Central to their work was a commitment to the model of inductive Bible study, designed to help seekers first to identify key biblical principles and then to immediately put them into practice.

Meeting Practical Needs

There were many desperate needs in the community the network was serving. They were constantly discussing ways to minister meaningfully, as a group, to the physical needs that surrounded them. They shared their experiences and contacts with outside organizations that could also contribute to solutions.

Preparing to Meet Opposition

Given the context in which they worked, persecution and intense spiritual warfare was a big part of their daily lives. Being part of this group gave them unified strength to stand and face the difficulties that came.

Although Izzaka and his friends had never heard of the terms "fruitful practice learning community" and "community of practice," their group had effectively functioned in this way from its inception. Izzaka had started out skeptical, but it didn't take long for him to discover the value of working in community.

JIM'S STORY: THE TRUSTED BROKER NETWORK MODEL

Practitioner communities are not always grassroots-level endeavors. Some form as cooperative structures at the top levels of organizational influence. This model is something we are calling a "trusted broker network." *At the core of this idea is the* "trusted broker," a key people-networker who has earned relational connections within a specialized sphere of influence related to a particular focus of ministry. These connections provide unique access to a large amount of valuable and potentially sensitive information pertaining to that group's activities. "Trusted" implies strong relationships, and "broker" implies they have something significant to trade.

A trusted broker network is a relatively small group of trusted brokers from different organizations who have margin and desire to interact on an ongoing basis, to advance a specific cause. They confidently pool their knowledge as a result of the trusted relationships they have built, while simultaneously guarding the security concerns of their constituents.

> A trusted broker network is a relatively small group of trusted brokers from different organizations who have margin and desire to interact on an ongoing basis, to advance a specific cause.

As the research director of the International Mission Board (IMB), Jim Haney maintained a massive database of the world's people groups. This database was fed updated information from many global organizations. Though the database was not limited to Muslims, Jim's affiliation with the Vision 5:9 Network accentuated his specific interest in those Muslim people groups that qualified for the classification of "unengaged." Thousands of man-hours went into updating and maintaining the accuracy of this list. Countless decisions for allocating field workers and financial resources are made each year based on it.

Despite having created a useful tool, Jim was troubled. Other networks had similar lists, and there were discrepancies between them. He was concerned that the lack of information unity was undermining the confidence of the missions community. He thought, "None of us can accurately track the world's people groups by ourselves. We can only do this if we work together and share information."

There were only a few key records-keepers, and Jim knew all of them. He understood why each list categorized groups differently, since each represented different organizational visions, with varied frames of reference. Jim realized, however, that if organizations continued to work in isolation from each other it would appear as if one was "right" and the others were "wrong."

Jim began to bring together the information brokers who shared three criteria:

- A vision of seeing unengaged people groups engaged.
- Recognition of the problem of tracking engagements effectively and accurately.
- Possession of significant assets to contribute toward a solution.

These powerful information specialists are now calling their group "Engaging Together." They meet quarterly by Internet to confer with each other. Each session they discuss a different region of the world, inviting regional subject matter experts to guide their thinking. They coordinate their decisions about people group engagements and try to negotiate consensus. This experiment shows promise for standardization that will provide consistency in recording and reporting for everyone.

Unlike the example from Liz's "Hub Community" story, Jim started by gathering known specialists who had already created the value that he asked them to contribute. Building trust wasn't easy. There were obstacles such as organizational politics, security issues, and personal suspicions. According to Jim, this part was hard work. He summarized, "For collective impact to work, trusted brokers must submit their knowledge and insights to each other so that all may know what is known to each individually."

These same struggles are replayed in cross-cultural collaborations among leaders in Africa.

LARRY'S STORY: THE SAHEL INITIATIVE

Partnership guru Phil Butler once said, "If you can't do it yourself, you need a partnership." In the Sahel region of Africa, it was pretty clear that we had reached that point. The Wycliffe Global Alliance had set a goal of beginning a Bible translation in every language by 2025, but it was looking like something we would never achieve.

The Sahel region refers to the last stretch of inhabitable land at the edge of the Sahara Desert. There are many challenges in this part of the world, including an inconsistent supply of food, scarcity of water, and constant political conflicts. The practical challenges are enormous, but the spiritual challenges to church planters and Bible translators are even greater in this predominantly Muslim culture.

Bible translation work in the Sahel has been ongoing for many years, but obstacles abound. The Sahel Initiative formed to specifically address the translation problems in this region. It is a higher-level fruitful practice learning community, similar to Jim Haney's "Engaging Together" group mentioned earlier. The Sahel Initiative sought to bring together four focus groups from different disciplines:

- Church planting
- Bible translation
- Development
- Media

Representatives from sending organizations, churches, and other networks with these foci joined forces to explore fruitful practices leading to kingdom movements. In beginning the Sahel Initiative, they took at least four key steps that others could repeat to launch other such initiatives.

Identifying an Initial Champion Empowered by Their Organization

The initial vision for the Sahel Initiative came from a person in leadership of a large organization. Although he didn't personally have enough time to pursue the vision, he was able to identify someone who had greater availability and was motivated by a study program focused on the question at hand. When this champion emerged, the initiative began to take shape.

Assembling a Like-Minded Group

The next challenge is gathering a key group of people who are well situated to flesh out the vision. The composition of this group is critical. For the Sahel Initiative, getting key people together around a table at one place and time was an enormous challenge, but when it happened it was an early sign of God's blessing.

Developing a Shared Vision and Purpose

The founding committee for the Sahel Initiative found agreement around a shared vision statement, objectives, and a basic structure for the new network. This took a while, but it was time well spent. By the end of the first meeting, the purpose of the initiative was clear.

Getting an Early Win

There are undoubtedly many new networks and partnerships that die on the drawing table. So in order to gain momentum, people need to see something positive happening. An early victory or success story can go a long way to solidifying the initial commitments. This occurred at the first Sahel Initiative conference in 2014, when delegates gathered from across the region for the first time. People and organizations were clearly ready to move in cooperation with each other.

In early 2018 the *third* Sahel Initiative conference took place, this time in Addis Ababa, Ethiopia, with two hundred representatives from the four focus disciplines we had adopted (church planting, Bible translation, development, and media). As we discussed our common vision and reflected on what God was doing, the momentum of collaborative excitement continued to build.

THE WEDDING FEAST AND A PREPARED BRIDE

The formation of a fruitful practice learning community could be compared to the preparation of a banquet. The starting point, of course, is knowing that people are hungry. They need to eat! *We* need to feed them. Everything begins with the identification of this hunger and a deep desire to address the need.

The Banquet Preparations Start with a Chef

In the context in which we work, preparing a meal that really meets the needs of those who are hungry is a significant challenge. It's a bigger job than one person or organization can handle. We are going to need the help of like-minded people who share our vision and can help us find the resources we will need to move forward.

As a first step in forming a fruitful practice learning community, someone has to step forward who will bring the key people together. This person is the champion who catalyzes the formation of the learning community. He or she needs to be able to clearly communicate the driving vision and connect with others to spread the word.

Who Are the Wait Staff?

We need to attract the right people who are equipped with vision, who recognize the common barriers to progress, and who each have some assets to bring to the table that will comprise a well-rounded, tasty meal.

What's on the Menu?

Once the right people are present, it is time to start clarifying and finalizing the vision. All of those around the table have responded to the call. The goal at this point is to craft a unified vision and core objectives that capture the passion of all those involved and can provide the motivation needed to advance. Given the needs and those around the table, what can be done? It may be as simple as the example of our grassroots practitioner communities, or it may be elaborate and global in focus. The principles, however, remain the same.

Let's Eat!

Once it is clear what is on the menu, it's time to make it happen. Unfortunately, that is often easier said than done. Fruitful practice learning communities learn from their mistakes, continue to seek how God is leading, and try again. Doing this in community provides support and encouragement along the way.

Hear the challenge of Samuel Zwemer, echoed by Dudley Woodberry. The chain of witnesses from the apostles until the day when Jesus comes again is a connected community stretching across the history of God's family. The culmination of God's plan is the wedding feast of the Lamb! We chart the pathway for the church becoming his prepared bride through a unified approach in hastening his kingdom among all peoples.

DISCUSS AND APPLY

- In what aspects of your ministry could you benefit from closer collaboration with other workers?

- Are you part of any field networks, formal or informal, that could provide a platform for sharing practical knowledge about your common calling?

- Can you name two or three people whom you would like to interactively learn from, and share with, on your field?

SERMON № 5

ALLAN MATAMOROS

Scripture Reading: Romans 15:14-24

Our biblical passage refers to a time when Paul the apostle was intending to visit Rome. He had been busy preaching the gospel in the eastern part of the empire. Then he began to understand that his time was coming to an end there, and he started to see the western part of the Roman dominions as his new mission field. Therefore, in this letter Paul is not only addressing issues related to the church, but also presenting his plans to go to Spain.

At that moment, Paul was in Corinth raising funds to help the poor in Jerusalem. Because the apostle had to take the contributions to people in need in Jerusalem, he is determining when would be the best time to visit Rome. Basically he writes as he was still making plans for his next trip.

Paul makes very clear that he was planning to involve the church in Rome in his new missionary journey. When he said that he wanted to pass through Rome to let the church assist him, he was expecting that the church would get involved in his mission. The whole idea was not just mobilizing the church to participate with prayers and financial contribution. I believe that Paul had in mind the desire to involve the church in a broader way. He intended to establish significant partnerships in the work about to be started in the western part of the empire, in his attempt to reach Spain. In this passage, I believe we see Paul's concerns about a few key things.

Legacy

In the first few verses, Paul is introducing himself as a priest who was committed to presenting the Gentiles as an offering to God. In fulfillment of his ministry, he had fully proclaimed the gospel from Jerusalem to Illyricum. Thus Paul is writing to report information about his ministry and to share his legacy with the church in Rome. Paul knew that he was leaving a legacy because of the manifestation of the Holy Spirit empowering his thoughts, words, and actions.

As we look back into history, we must praise God for the legacy of our predecessors in the missionary work among Muslims. Fortunately, today we can join hands with brothers and sisters from the four corners of the world. We have Africans and Americans, we have Asians and Europeans, all working together for the sake of the gospel.

Ambition

Paul highlights his ambition to preach the gospel where Christ was not known. He did not want to build on someone else's foundation, but to proclaim the good news to people who had never heard. Paul was able to present a tremendous legacy because he was driven by a holy ambition. He had a fire in his heart, and it was the ambition to make the gospel known that led his destiny among the nations.

As a missionary movement, we have been dreaming of reaching the unreached, the unengaged, the under-engaged. We have before us an ambition to reach 1.8 billion Muslims living in different contexts and circumstances: big urban cities, poverty, violence, terrorism, and war. God is calling us to leave our comfort zones and minister to them. It is not going to be easy. We have to be prepared to pay the price to follow this holy ambition.

Collaboration

Paul had built a legacy of sacrifice among the unreached, and at this stage in his life he had fully proclaimed the gospel in large areas. Paul's ambition led him toward the unreached and allowed him to access the most difficult corners of the Roman Empire. The apostle was always finding new doors and moving forward to see the impossible happening.

Since Paul was always working in collaboration with brothers and sisters in the ministry, he was able to go back to Antioch often and receive assistance from the Macedonian churches in Thessalonica and Philippi. All of this was accomplished because he had people joining hands with him. This explains how he was able to build a legacy.

We are a network with more than 180 mission organizations working together in order to reach the Muslim world. But we need more collaboration like this within the body of Christ. We are only going to reach the 1.8 billion Muslims with the gospel if we stand on the legacy of our brothers and sisters who came before us, keeping the holy ambition to fulfill the Great Commission and working in collaboration as one body.

We need to realize that we have a huge task before us, and we are not going to fulfill it if we decide to work alone. I desire to see a wave of collaboration on a global level. I envision the day that Christians from every nation will be working together with the common passion of preaching the gospel to every Muslim people group. Amen.

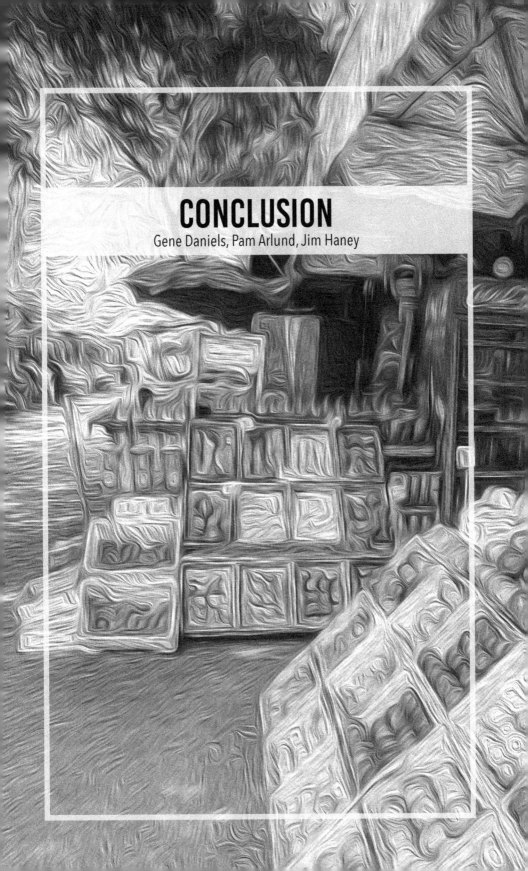

CONCLUSION

Gene Daniels, Pam Arlund, Jim Haney

There are many ways to conclude a book like this. We could summarize all the great ideas into themes, or we could review and highlight some of the ones we think are most important. However, the goal of this project from the beginning has been to see Jesus worshiped by all the peoples of the earth, and particularly by Muslim peoples. And that goal is not reached by knowledge, but by obedience. Of course, we have to "know something" to obey, but the authors who have contributed to this volume have already given you much to think about. Now the challenge comes to doing something with it.

This challenge begins not in the head but in the heart, and so we began where all of the Christian life begins, by abiding in Jesus: "Yes, I am the vine; you are the branches. Those who remain in me, and I in them, will produce much fruit. For apart from me you can do nothing (John 15:5 NLT). In this same teaching, Jesus says: "When you produce much fruit, you are my true disciples. This brings great glory to my Father" (John 15:8 NLT).

Jesus makes it clear that if we abide in him, we will produce much fruit. The hard thing is figuring out what abiding in Jesus practically looks like in the rough and tumble of ministry in the Muslim world. This volume is offered to help give you food for thought on tshat topic.

Also, our hope is that this book will help tell of the great works that God is doing in the Muslim world—through young and old, male and female, Christians from all backgrounds. But again, if it only becomes knowledge without obedience that leads to fruit, then we have missed the mark.

We know this much is true for *all* of Christ's followers: "You didn't choose me. I chose you. I appointed you to go and produce lasting fruit, so that the Father will give you whatever you ask for, using my name" (John 15:16 NLT). You have been chosen to produce lasting fruit. The only question is where that fruit is.

We believe that hearing from such a wide diversity of fellow workers will also inspire you to take the knowledge gained here and ask the Lord of the harvest how he would like you to be involved in his great harvest in the Muslim world. For each reader of this book the answer to that question will be different, for the Lord is unique and so are each of his followers.

Some places to start your conversation with the Lord might be:

- As a result of what I have read here, how will my life be different?

- How will my relationship with Jesus and my world be different?

- Will I pray differently?

- Will I interact with my own community in new and different ways?

- Will I help send more workers into the harvest?

- With whom will I share what I have learned here?

May you be blessed with the joy of walking alongside Jesus as he calls Muslims, through you, to become his disciples.

–The editors

CPSIA information can be obtained
at www.ICGtesting.com
Printed in the USA
BVHW081058120919
558275BV00011B/

3 4711 00232 0994